THE COSMIC MIRROR

Beyond Illusion,
Discover Your True Self

Compiled, Crafted, and Curated by

DR. HARI CHINTHAKUNTA

With Divine Grace and Blessings from His Holiness
Sri Vidyanarayana Thirtha

INDIA • SINGAPORE • MALAYSIA

THE COSMIC MIRROR
Beyond Illusion, Discover Your True Self

Sri Sri Sri Vidya Narayana Thirtha Swamyji
Dwaraka Badirikashram, Bengaluru

Interpretation of the Messages of **His Holiness Sri Vidya Narayana Theertha**

Sri Jagadguru Shankaracharya Samsthanam,
Dwaraka Badarikashram, and Sri Vidya Narayana Foundation,
Bangalore

Compiled, Crafted, and Curated by

Dr. Hari Chinthakunta

With Divine Grace and Blessings from His Holiness Sri Vidyanarayana Thirtha

At the Lotus Feet of the Eternal Guide: A Humble Dedication to the Mystic Circle of Divinity.

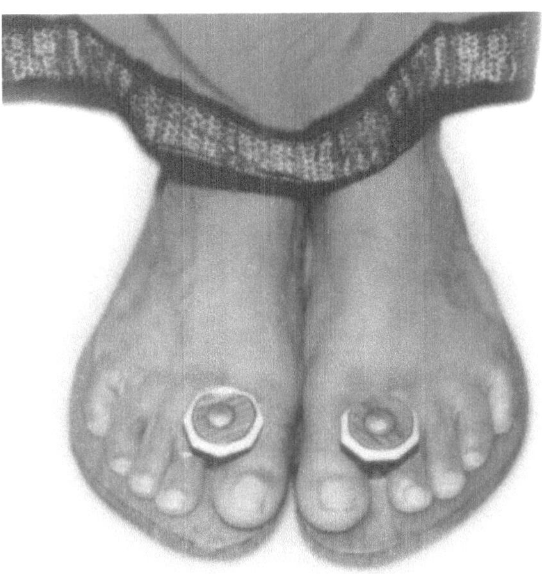

His Holiness sri vidyanarayana theetha

Sri Jagadguru Shankaracharya Samsthanam,
Dwaraka Badarikashram, and Sri Vidya Narayana Foundation,
Bangalore

CONTENTS

PREFACE

The Cosmic Mirror: Revealing Your True Self is not just a book; it is a spiritual odyssey that transcends the boundaries of time, culture, and personal identity. This profound work invites readers from all walks of life—whether youth, corporate executives, or seekers from different walks of life—to embark on a transformative journey toward self-realization. This book is not confined to any particular group but serves as a universal guide to those seeking deeper purpose and a harmonious existence.

In a world dominated by the rush of modernity, where the search for success and material accomplishments often eclipses the quest for inner peace, **The Cosmic Mirror** calls upon us to rediscover the most fundamental truth of our existence: that true fulfilment lies within. This book draws upon the timeless teachings and divine wisdom of **His Holiness Sri Vidyanarayana Theertha,** the revered spiritual leader from **Sri Jagadguru Shankaracharya Samsthanam, Dwaraka Badarikashram, Bangalore**, guiding us through the depths of our own consciousness.

The wisdom contained within this book has the potential to inspire individuals across all sections of society—from the vibrant energy of youth, eager to explore their potential, to the corporate executives, often caught in the web of external success and seeking deeper meaning, to spiritual seekers, longing for truth. **The Cosmic Mirror** offers a pathway that nurtures a balanced life, grounded in spiritual awareness and purpose.

This work brings together the wisdom of spirituality, science, and energy, showing that the universe itself reflects our innermost thoughts, emotions, and actions. Through this lens, the book serves not just as a guide to individual peace but also as a call for global harmony and understanding. As each individual comes to terms with their true self, the ripple effect can bring about collective healing and progress for the world.

In India, the land of countless sages, saints, and seers, the concept of self-realization and divine wisdom has been passed down through millennia. Our great sages, like **Adi Shankaracharya, Sri Ramakrishna Paramahamsa**, and **Swami Vivekananda**, have shown us the way to transcend the material realm and connect with our higher selves. **The Cosmic Mirror** continues this legacy, offering a modern bridge between ancient spiritual truths and contemporary life.

Through the sacred words of the Bhagavad Gita, the Upanishads, and the teachings of great masters, this book helps us remember that we are not limited to our physical bodies but are eternal souls, each part of a larger divine tapestry. As the **Bhagavad Gita** reminds us, "You are not the body; you are the eternal soul" (Gita 2.30). And as the **Chandogya Upanishad** affirms, "The Atman (Self) is Brahman, the ultimate reality" (6.8.7). These ancient truths reveal the unity of all beings and the deep connection between the individual self and the Supreme.

The book is structured around twelve thematic areas, each designed to explore a unique aspect of the transformative journey toward self-awareness and divine realization. Each chapter builds upon the previous one, creating a path from recognizing inner abundance to awakening universal truths. From learning to cultivate inner peace to the embodiment of spiritual dharma in daily life, **The Cosmic Mirror** offers practical and profound wisdom for every individual. It emphasizes how the pursuit of selfless service, duty, and detachment can lead us toward a more harmonious existence.

At its core, **The Cosmic Mirror** is an invitation to rediscover the eternal self beyond the transient nature of the material world. As **Sri Ramakrishna Paramahamsa** beautifully stated, "The divine is within you; you must realize it," the book serves as a guide to unlocking the divine potential within each of us. With the blessings and grace of **His Holiness Sri Vidyanarayana Theertha**, the author humbly offers this work, recognizing that the true wisdom contained within these pages is not of the author alone, but a reflection of the divine guidance received throughout the journey.

The mystic energy and divine grace of **Sri Vidyanarayana Theertha** illuminated the path for the completion of this task, and for this, the author is eternally grateful. "Pen is mine, but the thoughts are His." It is with deep humility that this book is presented as a beacon of light, a mirror that reveals the true essence of our being and guides us toward the ultimate goal of spiritual liberation.

May this book serve as an inspiration, encouraging readers to explore the vastness within, transcend the limitations of the ego, and contribute to the collective peace and harmony of our world. As the **Upanishads** declare: "That which is the Supreme is both within and beyond you" (Isa Upanishad 1). This journey of self-discovery is not only a path to personal enlightenment but also a vital contribution to the creation of a peaceful and unified world.

– **Dr. Hari Chinthakunta**

EXPRESSIONS OF GRATITUDE

With profound humility and deep gratitude, I bow before the Divine, seeking the blessings of Lord Vinayaka, the remover of obstacles. May His divine grace illuminate the path before me, removing every hindrance on my spiritual journey. To Lord Subramanyeswara, I offer my heartfelt prayers for strength, courage, and wisdom to face every challenge. May His divine protection shield me from all negative influences, guiding me toward the truth.

I humbly offer my reverence to Goddess Bala Tripura Sundari, whose grace purifies my heart and mind. Her love and wisdom lead me toward the highest spiritual fulfilment. I also bow before Lord Venkateshwara, the Lord of Seven Hills, whose eternal protection fills me with unwavering devotion and wisdom, helping me navigate the complexities of life with grace.

I humbly respect Sai Baba of Shirdi, whose universal love and compassion transcend all boundaries. His teachings of selfless service, humility, and devotion are the very foundation of this work. Through His blessings, I have found strength and clarity on this journey. May His grace guide me and all those seeking the truth.

With reverence, I also bow before the revered Kanchi Paramacharya, whose spiritual wisdom and insights have inspired generations. His teachings on devotion, discipline, and simplicity are the cornerstones of a

life dedicated to the Divine. May His blessings continue to illuminate the hearts of all who follow the spiritual path.

My gratitude extends to the Saints, Sages, and Seers of the traditional spiritual lineage, whose wisdom and guidance have illuminated the paths of countless seekers. Their teachings continue to inspire and uplift me, and I express my deepest appreciation for their enduring contributions to the world.

I offer my deepest gratitude to my divine parents, Avadootha Nanna and Karunamayi Amma, whose unconditional love and nurturing have shaped my soul's journey. Their constant support has been a beacon of light in my life. To my divine sister, Sai Niveditha, and my brothers, Naga Yogiraj and Balayogi Ganesh, I express my heartfelt thanks for

their unwavering love and strength, which have sustained me through every challenge.

Most of all, I extend my boundless gratitude to my revered Gurudev,

His Holiness Sri Vidyanarayana Theertha Swamy. It is through His divine grace that this book has come into being. I am merely an instrument of His will, and His wisdom, guidance, and blessings have led me to pen this work. I acknowledge that the true author of this book is not me but the divine energies that flow through Him. Through His grace, I have come to realize the profound truth that we are not separate from the Divine but are one with it.

The book *The Cosmic Mirror: Revealing Your True Self* is a reflection of His teachings. It is through His grace that I have come to understand the importance of looking inward, recognizing the true self, and realizing that the essence of the Divine resides within each of us. This book is not merely a collection of words but a spiritual offering meant to guide and awaken the soul to its true nature.

This work marks my fourth book, following *The Hidden Radiance*, *The Whispers of Divine Light*, and *Zero to Zero: The Mystic Circle*. Each of these books carries its own message, and I encourage readers, especially spiritual aspirants, to explore them. They each offer unique insights and tools for those on the path of self-realization and spiritual awakening. May they help you in your journey toward the divine and in recognizing the limitless potential within.

I also extend my heartfelt thanks to Sree Lekha and Sai Leela for their moral support throughout this journey and to Mrs Konanki Lakshmi Kala for her meticulous proofreading, which has greatly improved the clarity and flow of this work. Without their dedication and help, this journey would not have been as fulfilling.

Bhagwan Sri Ram SIR, whose guidance has been an unwavering source of inspiration, deserves special mention. His wisdom, though subtle, has profoundly shaped my life and this book. Through His mentorship, I have found the strength to explore and write about the deeper truths of existence. His presence, though invisible, continues to guide me, and His teachings are a constant reminder of the divine light within each of us.

This book would not have been possible without the grace of these divine beings, whose blessings have illuminated my path and made this work a reality. I humbly offer it to all who seek to realize their true self and awaken the divine light within.

Lastly, I offer my deepest gratitude to the Cosmic Mother, the divine energy that pervades the universe and guides all souls toward self-realization. Her blessings have been the guiding force behind this work, and I offer this book as a humble tribute to Her infinite wisdom and grace.

May this book serve as a beacon of light for all those who seek truth, peace, and harmony. May it inspire each reader to look within, to recognize their true self, and to realize that they are one with the Divine, ever connected to the source of all creation.

With boundless love and deepest gratitude,
 – **Dr. Hari Chinthakunta**

INVOCATION

"The universe does not conceal the truth—it reflects it. To see clearly, one must first awaken the vision within."

True self-discovery is not a privilege reserved for a select few—it is the essence of human existence. The journey inward is not about renouncing the world but about recognizing that beneath all its transience lies an unshakable reality. His Holiness **Sri Vidyanarayana Theertha**, a living embodiment of divine wisdom, has illuminated this path for countless seekers. His teachings are not bound by sect or tradition; they transcend time 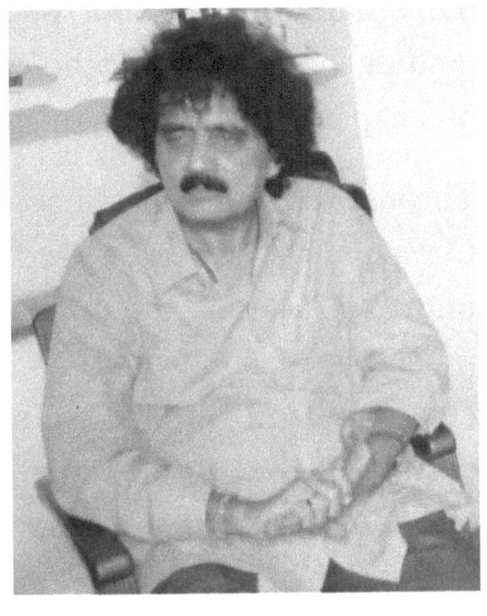 and space, guiding all those who long to rediscover their true nature.

With the blessings of this revered master, **Dr. Hari, a devotee of truth and selfless service**, has woven together *The Cosmic Mirror: Beyond Illusion, Discover Your True Self*—a book that is not merely to be read, but to be experienced. It is a gentle yet profound reminder that beyond the external pursuits of life, there exists a boundless treasure within each of us, waiting to be unveiled.

This work speaks to the **aspiring youth**, the **leaders navigating a complex world**, the **seeker longing for meaning**, and the **traveler searching for the essence of existence**. It is for anyone who has ever questioned, *Who am I? What is my purpose? What lies beyond the veil of this material world?* The answers do not come from outside; they arise from the depths of our being. *The Cosmic Mirror* is an invitation to pause, reflect, and rediscover the light that has always been present within.

At a time when the world is driven by ambition, distraction, and fleeting pursuits, this book brings us back to the eternal truth: the real journey is within. Drawing upon the divine wisdom of **Sri Vidyanarayana Theertha**, the revered Peetadhipathi of **Sri Jagadguru Shankaracharya Samsthanam, Dwaraka Badarikashram, Bangalore**, it serves as a guiding force for those who wish to rise above the illusions of the world and experience the bliss of true awareness.

Through the lens of **spirituality, science, and cosmic energy**, *The Cosmic Mirror* reveals a truth known to sages and mystics since time immemorial—that the universe does not exist apart from us, but as a reflection of our own consciousness. By transforming our thoughts, emotions, and actions, we shape not only our destiny but also the destiny of the world. **Individual transformation leads to collective harmony**, and in that harmony, we rediscover our divine nature.

India, the sacred land of enlightened beings, has nurtured the wisdom of self-realization for millennia. The timeless voices of **Maharishi Vasishtha, Mahavatar Babaji, Sant Kabir, Jnaneshwar, Mata Anandamayi, and Swami Abhedananda** have all pointed toward the same eternal truth: *Beyond the changing waves of life, there is a stillness where the self and the divine are one.*

The great sage **Ashtavakra** declared, *"You are not bound. You are pure awareness itself. The knot of illusion is only in the mind."* The enlightened poet **Tukaram** expressed, *"Why do you wander outside in search of truth, when within you shines the eternal sun?"* Such wisdom reminds us that our identity is not confined to the body, nor to the fleeting experiences of the world—we are infinite, beyond birth and death, beyond all limitations.

This book is designed as a journey through **twelve interconnected themes**, each revealing a new dimension of self-discovery. It offers both profound wisdom and practical insights, enabling us to cultivate inner balance, live with clarity, and embrace the highest truths in our everyday lives. Through the practice of **selfless service, detachment, and unwavering awareness**, one begins to walk the path toward liberation.

At its heart, *The Cosmic Mirror* is an offering of divine grace—a call to awaken, to recognize the vastness of our being, and to dissolve the illusions that keep us bound. As **Lalleshwari, the Kashmiri mystic,** once said, *"Awaken to the presence within, and the world will shine with a new light."* This book does not impose beliefs; it gently guides the reader toward realization, toward the truth that has always existed within.

"The hand may hold the pen, but the wisdom flows from the divine." It is in this spirit of humility that this book is presented—not as an intellectual pursuit, but as a mirror reflecting the infinite possibilities of the soul.

May this work serve as a **source of inspiration, a light for those seeking clarity,** and **a bridge between the known and the unknowable**. May it awaken the fearless spirit within, dissolve the shadows of doubt, and lead all who read it toward the profound stillness where true joy resides. As the **Avadhuta Gita** declares, *"The self is beyond all form, beyond all name—pure existence, infinite and free."*

The journey of self-discovery is not merely personal; it is a contribution to the harmony of the world. Let the realization of one become the liberation of many.

– **Naga Yogiraj, Monk, Himalayas**

PRELUDE

The quest for self-discovery is not an exclusive privilege—it is the foundation of human existence. Looking inward does not mean turning away from the world; rather, it is the recognition that beyond the surface of change lies an enduring truth. His Holiness Sri Vidyanarayana Theertha has illuminated this inner path, offering guidance that surpasses traditions and time.

Inspired by his wisdom, Dr. Hari presents *The Cosmic Mirror: Beyond Illusion, Discover Your True Self*—a book that is more than a mere collection of words; it is an experience. It calls upon seekers to transcend fleeting distractions and recognize the boundless essence within. This work speaks to every individual—the restless youth, the burdened leader, the reflective thinker, and the spiritual traveler—who has ever questioned existence. The answers do not lie in the external world but within the depths of one's own being. *The Cosmic Mirror* serves as a gateway to inner clarity, urging us to embrace our true nature.

In a world consumed by ceaseless pursuits, this book redirects attention to the one journey that truly matters—the journey inward. Drawing from the insights of Sri Vidyanarayana Theertha, the revered Peetadhipathi of Sri Jagadguru Shankaracharya Samsthanam, Dwaraka Badarikashram, Bangalore, it offers a roadmap for those seeking to go beyond illusion and experience the essence of existence. Blending spirituality, consciousness, and universal principles, *The Cosmic Mirror* reveals that reality is not something separate from us but a reflection of our own awareness. By refining our thoughts and actions, we not only transform ourselves but also contribute to the greater harmony of the world.

For millennia, India has been a crucible of self-realization, nurturing sages who have illuminated the truth of existence. From Adi Shankaracharya to Ramana Maharshi, from Mirabai to Sri Aurobindo, their voices echo the same wisdom: the world is transient, but the self is eternal. The great sage Dattatreya proclaimed, "Freedom lies in seeing the self beyond all limitations." Mystic poet Lalla declared, "The ocean of truth is within—dive deep, and you will find it." Their words remind us that the divine is not distant; it resides in the core of our being.

Structured around twelve transformative themes, this book weaves together profound wisdom and practical guidance, enabling the reader to cultivate balance, clarity, and purpose. Through selfless service, inner detachment, and unwavering mindfulness, one gradually treads the path toward liberation.

At its essence, *The Cosmic Mirror* is a gift of spiritual awakening—an invitation to transcend illusion and embrace the infinite within. As Hazrat Inayat Khan beautifully put it, "The soul's light is veiled only by the clouds of our own making." This book does not dictate doctrines; it gently reveals the truths that already exist within every seeker.

"The mind may seek knowledge, but true wisdom arises from silence." In that spirit, this book is not merely a discourse but a reflection of the limitless potential within the human soul. May it guide those who yearn for clarity, dissolve the veils of doubt, and open the path to an awareness that is beyond words. As the *Yoga Vasistha* affirms, "The universe is but a thought in the infinite mind—know this, and be free."

Self-discovery is not a solitary endeavour; it is the awakening of a collective consciousness. Let each realization become a ripple that spreads harmony across the world.

– Yogini Sai Niveditha

Soulful Foreword

Self-discovery is not a privilege—it is the essence of human life. Looking within does not mean disconnecting from the world; it means recognizing a deeper truth beyond constant change. His Holiness Sri Vidyanarayana Theertha has illuminated this inner journey, offering wisdom that transcends time and tradition.

Inspired by his teachings, Dr. Hari presents The Cosmic Mirror: Beyond Illusion, Discover Your True Self. This book is more than words on a page—it is an invitation to explore the vastness within. In a world filled with distractions, it reminds us that clarity, peace, and purpose are not found outside but within our own being. Whether one is searching for meaning, burdened by responsibilities, or simply curious about life, this book offers a guiding light.

At its core, The Cosmic Mirror is about seeing reality as a reflection of our awareness. Through the insights of Sri Vidyanarayana Theertha, it provides a path to inner freedom, helping us refine our thoughts and actions. When we transform ourselves, we contribute to a more harmonious world. True wisdom does not come from seeking more—it comes from understanding what already exists within. This book gently reveals that truth, urging us to move beyond illusion and embrace the limitless self.

– Balayogi Gasha

Spiritual Overture

Life is not merely a passage of time; it is a sacred journey of transformation—a sacred unfolding that calls us to transcend the ordinary and embrace the extraordinary. It is a quest not just for survival, but for the realization of our deepest truth, the discovery of the divine essence that resides within us, and the awakening to the higher purpose that connects us to the cosmic expanse. *The Cosmic Mirror* serves as a doorway, inviting all seekers to embark on a profound inward journey, where the soul aligns with the eternal truth, the mind becomes one with wisdom, and the heart beats in harmony with divine love.

As I often express, *"You are not a mere fragment of this universe; you are the entire universe manifested in a single being."* Life's journey is the realization of this fundamental truth—that every individual is a reflection of the divine, an embodiment of the cosmos itself. The purpose of life, therefore, is not found in external achievements or fleeting desires, but in awakening to the timeless wisdom that lies at the core of our being. *"You are that"*—the divine, the eternal, and the boundless energy that governs all existence. This realization is the foundation upon which the journey of life is built.

In this book, we explore themes such as *Inner Abundance, Self-Transformation,* and *Spiritual Clarity.* True fulfillment is not derived from material wealth but from the deep understanding that we are inherently abundant, that the very essence of life flows within us. As I always remind my disciples, *"The wealth you seek outside is already within you; all you must do is recognize it.*" This journey is not one of external acquisition, but of internal realization, where the truth of who we are becomes clear.

Truth and Science are not separate, but complementary paths that lead to the same ultimate realization. The material world reveals its mysteries through science, while the spiritual realm opens its doors through inner wisdom. As I often share, *"Science explores the surface of reality, but spirituality uncovers its very core."* Together, they provide a holistic understanding that unites the rational and the mystical, bridging the gap between the material and the divine.

Life's flow is an intricate dance of energies. *Energy and Flow* teaches us to harmonize with the cosmic currents, to move with grace and purpose through the unfolding of life. Every action is guided by an unseen force, a divine hand that leads us toward higher consciousness. As I often say, *"Like a river flowing to the sea, your soul is drawn toward the eternal truth, guided by the unseen hand of divine grace."* We are not meant to struggle against the flow of life, but to surrender to its direction, trusting that it will lead us to the ocean of enlightenment.

No path of spiritual evolution is complete without the wisdom of the Guru. *The Guru's Light* illuminates our way, dispelling the darkness of ignorance and guiding us toward divine realization. *Dharma in Action* emphasizes the importance of selfless service in this journey, for it is through serving others that we realize our highest potential. As I have often said, *"The Guru is not just a teacher; the Guru is the flame that lights the path of every seeker."* True strength lies in surrendering to the wisdom of the Guru, for it is through this surrender that we receive the divine guidance that leads us to the ultimate truth.

Mystic Evolution reveals the higher dimensions of consciousness, transcending the ego and unveiling deeper truths. As I frequently remind my disciples, *"The change you seek in the world begins within. When you transform yourself, you contribute to the transformation of all."*

Through self-realization, we uplift ourselves and, in doing so, uplift those around us. The journey of inner transformation is not only personal but collective, for the evolution of one is the evolution of all.

In navigating *Life's Dualities*, we learn to embrace both joy and sorrow, knowing that true peace lies in the acceptance of life's ever-changing nature. *"The sage does not cling to joy or sorrow, but remains centered in the eternal truth,"* I often teach. By transcending the extremes of life, we find the stillness that allows us to experience the divine presence in all things.

The Power of Discipline is the foundation that allows us to master our thoughts, emotions, and actions. Without discipline, the mind remains chaotic and unfocused. Through disciplined practice, we unlock higher realms of consciousness and align with the divine. As I frequently remind my disciples, *"Discipline is the key that opens the door to the divine within."*

Finally, *Sacred Convergence* speaks to the integration of spirituality, science, and society. The path of self-realization is not a solitary journey; it is one that contributes to the collective awakening of humanity. *"When you awaken within, you awaken the world around you,"* I often say. The light you find within yourself radiates outward, creating a ripple effect that awakens the divine in others. This collective awakening is the true purpose of the spiritual journey.

This book is not just a collection of teachings, but a map—a guide for seekers on the path to self-realization. It is an invitation to walk the inward path that leads to boundless wisdom, infinite grace, and the ultimate realization of the self. As I always say, *"The journey inward is the only journey that leads to the eternal truth. In the silence of your being, you will find all that you seek."*

Dr. Hari, the author of three exceptional masterpieces, has meticulously compiled, curated, and crafted the discourses I have shared on various occasions. His devotion, intellect, and unwavering commitment to preserving and presenting these teachings in their purest form deserve recognition. His work is not just a reflection of his expertise, but of his deep inner calling to serve and uplift humanity. Through his efforts, these sacred teachings will reach and transform countless seekers, lighting the way for them on their own journeys of divine realization. It is with great respect and appreciation that I extend my cosmic blessings to him, for his dedication will continue to inspire generations to come.

– His Holiness Sri Vidyanarayana Theertha

INNER ABUNDANCE

Inner abundance is not in what we hold but in what we realize.
It is the silence that speaks, the stillness that moves, the wisdom that
awakens.
Beyond gain and loss, the soul remains full—untouched, unshaken, ever
radiant.
True wealth is in surrender, in seeing
without seeking, in giving without grasping.
The one who knows the Self lacks nothing—for the infinite resides within."

– His Holiness Sri Vidyanarayana Theertha

CHAPTER-1

WEALTH BEYOND POSSESSIONS

Introduction

In the teachings of His Holiness Sri Vidyanarayana Theertha, goodness is celebrated as the highest form of wealth—a treasure that cannot be measured or diminished. Swamy reminds us that life becomes a blessing when the heart is pure. He shares, "Our true wealth is goodness, which will never be lost. It is also power. When the heart remains pure, life will be pure, and  all actions will be blessed." These words challenge us to redefine our priorities and embrace virtues like love, compassion, and patience as the foundation of a fulfilling life.

According to Swamy, goodness is not confined to extraordinary acts but shines in the simplicity of everyday moments. It is found in a kind word, a selfless gesture, or the strength to forgive. By choosing goodness in thought, word, and deed, we radiate positivity and inspire transformation—not just in ourselves but in the world around us. Swamy's teachings encourage us to approach life with courage and clarity, allowing virtues to guide our actions, even when faced with challenges.

To walk the path of goodness is to live in harmony with the divine essence within us. It is an invitation to rise above materialism, ego, and fear and instead align with the purity of spirit. Through goodness, we discover the true power of a life lived selflessly—one that touches hearts, uplifts souls, and brings us closer to spiritual fulfilment. Swamy's profound message is a timeless reminder: goodness is the eternal wealth that leads the way to peace and divine realization.

Q&A: Exploring the Teachings of Swamy

Q1: What is the true meaning of wealth according to Swamy?

A1: Swamy explains that real wealth is goodness. Material wealth can be lost or taken away, but goodness is eternal. For example, when we help someone without expecting anything in return, the satisfaction and joy we feel is a form of lasting wealth. Swamy emphasizes that goodness strengthens our character and creates positive energy wherever we go.

Q2: How does purity of heart affect our life?

A2: A pure heart leads to a pure life. When we cleanse our hearts from anger, jealousy, or bitterness, we experience peace. For instance, when we forgive someone who has wronged us, we feel lighter and happier, freeing ourselves from negative emotions. This purity attracts more positivity and spiritual growth in our lives.

Q3: What is the role of patience in personal growth?

A3: Patience is key to spiritual and personal growth. It helps us endure challenges and make thoughtful decisions. Consider a plant: it takes time to grow, but with patience, it eventually flourishes. Similarly, in our lives, patience helps us face hardships without giving up, allowing us to grow stronger and wiser with time.

Q4: How can forgiveness liberate us?

A4: Forgiveness frees us from the grip of anger and resentment. Swamy explains that holding onto grudges only harms us, while forgiveness brings peace. For example, if a friend betrays you, forgiving them helps you move on with your life. This act of liberation heals the heart and restores harmony.

Q5: What is the importance of selflessness and sacrifice?

A5: Selflessness and sacrifice strengthen relationships and foster love and unity. Swamy teaches that true happiness comes when we prioritize others' well-being. For example, when a parent sacrifices their time to care for their child, it creates a priceless bond of trust and love. Sacrifice doesn't mean giving up everything; it's about making space for others in our lives.

Insights from Swamy's Teachings

1. **Goodness is Eternal**
   Goodness never fades; it's the greatest treasure we can possess. It builds trust, creates peace, and strengthens relationships.

2. **Purity Brings Clarity**
   A pure heart enables us to see the world clearly, respond with kindness, and make decisions aligned with wisdom.

3. **Patience is Power**
   Patience helps us endure difficulties and grow stronger. Like a seed waiting to sprout, patience nurtures our inner strength.

4. **Forgiveness Heals**
   Forgiveness is a powerful tool for peace. It frees us from the chains of negative emotions and allows us to live in harmony.

5. **Selflessness Builds Unity**
   When we serve others selflessly, we strengthen bonds and create a sense of community. Sacrifice for others is the essence of love and unity.

Challenges on the Path

1. **Staying Committed to Goodness**
   It's hard to always act with goodness in a world full of distractions. We need to consistently remind ourselves of the value of kindness.

2. **Purifying Our Hearts Daily**
   Negative emotions are natural, but it's challenging to let them go. It requires daily practice of mindfulness and emotional control.

3. **Practicing Patience in a Fast-Paced World#**
   With everything happening so quickly, patience can feel like a distant concept. But taking time to pause and reflect is crucial for growth.

4. **Forgiving Others and Ourselves**
   Forgiveness is difficult, especially when we've been hurt deeply. Yet, it's essential for our own peace and emotional well-being.

5. **Balancing Material and Spiritual Life**
   In a world dominated by material pursuits, it's hard to prioritize spirituality. The challenge is to find time for spiritual practice amid the busyness of life.

Conclusion: Embracing the Journey of Transformation

Swamy's teachings illuminate a transformative journey towards spiritual enlightenment and personal growth. We harmonise our lives with divine wisdom by nurturing virtues like goodness, patience, forgiveness, and selflessness. Though challenges will inevitably arise, each step we take on this path strengthens our connection to peace, clarity, and inner light.

Swamy's words ignite the flame of love and wisdom within us:

"In every act of goodness, purity, and sacrifice, you draw closer to the divine. Each small step you take leads you further into the light of wisdom and grace."

By wholeheartedly embracing these timeless teachings, we unlock a life filled with profound meaning, unwavering purpose, and a deeper connection to the divine. Through these simple yet powerful acts, we transform ourselves and the world around us, creating a lasting legacy of love, peace, and spiritual fulfilment.

CHAPTER-2

FROM RESTLESSNESS TO PEACE

<u>The Spiritual Journey: Embracing Patience and Persistence</u>

In his enlightening discourse, His Holiness Sri Vidyanarayana Theertha unveils the true essence of the spiritual journey, emphasizing that it transcends rituals and external practices. It is a path of self-discovery, requiring an intimate connection with our inner selves and the divine. Along this journey, we inevitably face doubts, distractions, and frustrations, which can obscure our progress and test our resolve. Yet, Swamy assures us that these challenges are not obstacles but opportunities to deepen our understanding and strengthen our commitment.

His Holiness offers profound insights into navigating these trials with patience, clarity, and unwavering dedication. He reminds us that the spiritual path is not linear but an evolving process that demands faith and self-awareness. Swamy illuminates a way forward by addressing key questions that often arise—such as the purpose of the journey, the nature of the divine connection, and the significance of perseverance. His teachings inspire us to embrace each step with humility and trust, knowing that every experience brings us closer to spiritual fulfilment.

Ultimately, the journey is not about reaching a destination but about cultivating a life of meaning, virtue, and harmony with the divine. His

Holiness's wisdom encourages us to move forward with courage and grace, allowing the light of self-realization to guide us through every moment of our lives.

Question 1: Why does the mind wander during spiritual practices?

Answer: The mind is naturally restless and filled with countless thoughts. It's common for the mind to wander during meditation or other spiritual practices, especially in the beginning. This is not a sign of failure but rather a part of the process. As His Holiness Sri Vidyanarayana Theertha explains, "The mind is like a wild horse, but with the reins of patience and perseverance, you can tame it." Over time, with consistent effort, the mind will gradually learn to focus and find stillness.

Question 2: How can we overcome distractions in the busy world around us?

Answer: In today's fast-paced world, distractions are everywhere—work, social media, personal commitments, and more. These external stimuli often pull us away from our spiritual focus. However, taking moments of stillness throughout the day can help us reconnect. As His Holiness suggests, "In the midst of noise, find the silence within. That is where the divine resides." Even a few minutes of mindful breathing or meditation can create space for the divine to enter our lives, no matter how busy we are.

Question 3: Why is patience so important on the spiritual journey?

Answer: Spiritual growth is not a quick fix. It is a gradual process, like a tree growing from a small seed. The slow but steady progress requires dedication, consistency, and patience to bear fruit over time. As His Holiness wisely puts it, "Patience is the soil where the seeds of transformation are sown. Without it, no tree of wisdom can grow." The deeper we cultivate patience, the more our spiritual wisdom matures.

Question 4: How do we handle frustration when progress seems slow? Answer: Frustration is common when spiritual practices don't seem to yield immediate results. We may feel disheartened or question the effectiveness of our efforts. However, every small step contributes to our inner transformation, even if it's not immediately visible. His Holiness encourages us, "Frustration is the temporary storm that clears the path for inner clarity." Rather than seeing frustration as a setback, we can understand it as a clearing force that brings us closer to spiritual clarity.

Insights

- **Restlessness:** The mind is naturally active and wandering. With persistent practice, it can be trained to focus, allowing the spiritual essence to emerge.
- **Distractions:** In a chaotic world, moments of stillness are essential. Creating small pauses for mindfulness can help us reconnect with the divine.
- **Patience:** Spiritual growth requires time. Like nurturing a garden, each effort—no matter how small—nurtures our wisdom and inner peace.
- **Frustration:** Feeling stuck is part of the process. It signals growth. Even when progress seems slow, every step contributes to our spiritual journey.

Challenges on the Path

- **Restlessness:** The mind's constant activity can make spiritual practices challenging. Overcoming this requires patience and persistence.
- **Impatience:** The world rewards quick results, but spiritual growth is long-term. Patience and commitment are essential for progress.

- **Frustration:** When we don't see immediate results, we can become frustrated. However, this frustration is a sign of growth, signalling the clearing of old mental patterns.

Conclusion: Moving Forward with Patience and Faith

The spiritual journey is not always straightforward but is transformative and worth every step. Distractions, impatience, and frustration are part of the path, each playing a role in our evolution. The key is persistence, patience, and the understanding that growth happens in its own time. As His Holiness Sri Vidyanarayana Theertha beautifully explains, every effort contributes to the unfolding of our true self, no matter how small.

His Holiness reminds us, "When you walk the path with sincerity, the divine will walk with you, step by step." By staying committed and trusting the process, we will eventually experience the divine presence within us.

Therefore, start today—take that small step, whether it's a few minutes of quiet meditation, a short prayer, or simply pausing to breathe deeply. Over time, these small actions will accumulate and lead to significant spiritual growth, bringing you closer to your divine essence.

CHAPTER-3

FLOWING WITH LIFE: THE FREEDOM OF LETTING GO

Introduction

There was once a traveller who wandered across lands and seas in search of peace, yearning for a calm that no place or person seemed to provide. He sought answers from wise men and philosophers, but none could offer the solace he craved. One day, disheartened and weary, he sat by a river and murmured, "I want peace." Nearby, an old sage overheard him and gently  replied, "Remove the 'I' and the 'want,' and you will find peace." In that simple statement, the traveller discovered a profound truth: peace arises not from external pursuits or desires but from within when the ego and attachments are surrendered.

This timeless wisdom is beautifully reflected in the teachings of His Holiness Sri Vidyanarayana Theertha. He emphasizes that true peace is a state of being achieved through inner purity and self-awareness. Swamy reminds us that by letting go of our ego and desires, we can transcend the turmoil of worldly life and connect with the divine essence within. His guidance inspires us to move from ignorance to self-realization, showing that peace is not something we seek but uncover when we relinquish all that binds us.

Through His Holiness's teachings, we are reminded that the journey to peace begins with a quiet mind and a humble heart. It is a path of surrender and self-discovery, where freedom is found not in holding on but in letting go. Peace is not a distant destination; it is the natural state of our soul when we release the illusions of 'I' and 'want.'

Question and Answers

Question 1: How do good thoughts and virtuous actions affect one's life?

Answer: His Holiness often says, "Your actions reflect your thoughts, and your thoughts shape your destiny." When we act with kindness and integrity, we draw positivity into our lives, just as darkness disappears when we bring in light. Even if the world doesn't always recognize it, goodness creates harmony, not only in society but in the heart.

Question 2: What is the role of the inner self in our actions?

Answer: The inner self, or Atma, is our guiding compass. It whispers to us even in the noise of daily life. Think of the story of the thief who felt a pang of conscience before committing a wrong act—this was the inner self-calling. Transformation begins when we listen to this voice and act with moral clarity.

Question 3: How can we find joy and fulfilment in life?

Answer: Real joy is not found in material wealth or fleeting pleasures but in cultivating inner peace. As His Holiness says, "True contentment is the peace that resides within, not the things you accumulate." Life may bring us challenges, but when we face them with patience, they become stepping stones to fulfilment.

Question 4: What is the importance of surrender in the spiritual path?

Answer: Surrendering to the divine is not about giving up but letting go of attachment and ego. When we surrender, we stop fighting life and begin to flow with it, trusting that the divine has a greater plan for us. Through this surrender, we find peace and clarity, paving the way for spiritual growth.

Insights

- **Virtue is the Key:** The purity of our thoughts and actions is the mirror of our soul. By practising integrity, we not only elevate ourselves but also influence those around us.
- **The Inner Guide:** Our inner self is always speaking, but it's up to us to listen. We find guidance and clarity when we tune in, leading us toward moral decisions and spiritual growth.
- **True Fulfilment is Internal:** The pursuit of external success and wealth often leaves us empty. Fulfilment comes from inner peace, connection with the divine, and self-realization.
- **Surrender Leads to Growth:** True surrender is not about giving up on life but embracing it as it is, trusting the divine will. This opens the door to wisdom and transformation.

Challenges

- **The Ego:** The ego is the greatest obstacle to spiritual growth. It clouds our judgment and hinders our ability to grow. Overcoming the ego requires consistent self-reflection and humility.
- **Material Distractions:** In today's fast-paced world, we often chase external rewards, which can pull us away from our spiritual path. Balancing material pursuits with inner growth is an ongoing challenge.
- **Patience:** Transformation doesn't happen overnight. It requires persistence and patience. There will be setbacks, but

each challenge is an opportunity for growth. The key is not to rush but to trust the process.

Conclusion

The teachings of His Holiness Sri Vidyanarayana Theertha are a timeless treasure, offering us the tools to navigate the complexities of life with grace and wisdom. By aligning our thoughts and actions with virtue, listening to the quiet voice of our inner self, and surrendering to the divine will, we can transform our lives. The path may not always be easy, but it is the path that leads to lasting peace and fulfilment. With each step, we shed the old and embrace the new, slowly but surely becoming the best version of ourselves.

As the sage told the traveller, 'Let go of the 'I' and the 'want,' and peace will follow.' The peace we long for is not something to be found outside—it is already within us, waiting to be uncovered when we stop seeking and simply allow it to be."

CHAPTER-4

Nurturing Peace: Transforming the Mind and Heart

Introduction

In today's fast-paced world, stress and overwhelm have become constant companions. We tirelessly chase happiness in material possessions, achievements, or fleeting moments of joy, only to find it slipping through our fingers. But what if the peace and happiness we seek aren't external treasures to be found but inner truths waiting to be realized? His Holiness Sri Vidyanarayana Theertha reminds us that true peace begins within, rooted in the purity of our thoughts, the simplicity of our hearts, and the stillness of our minds.

Swamy's teachings resonate deeply with people from all walks of life, offering timeless wisdom to navigate the chaos of modern living. He encourages us to pause and reflect, to shift our focus from external distractions to the wealth of peace already within us. By practising self-awareness, cultivating patience, and surrendering our restless desires, we can transform stress into serenity and fleeting joy into lasting fulfilment. His message is simple yet profound: happiness is not something to pursue but something to uncover in the depths of our own being.

Through small, intentional changes—moments of mindfulness, acts of kindness, and the courage to let go of what no longer serves us—we can align our lives with His Holiness's teachings. Peace is not a distant dream but a reality we can live daily, no matter our circumstances. As Swamy gently guides us, the path to happiness begins when we turn inward and embrace the truth of who we are.

Questions and Answers

In his talks, His Holiness answers many important questions that can help us find peace and happiness. Below are some of his answers to questions that people often ask.

Q1: How can we find peace in a busy world?

A1: His Holiness says that true peace starts with controlling our thoughts. Even when there's a lot of noise and distractions around us, we can focus on good, positive thoughts. By doing this, we connect with our true selves, and peace naturally comes from within. He advises us to practice being mindful and present, which means paying attention to the moment and not worrying about the past or future.

Q2: How can we change negative thoughts?

A2: Everyone has negative thoughts from time to time, but these thoughts don't define us. His Holiness teaches us to notice negative thoughts without getting attached to them. We can then replace these thoughts with positive and uplifting ones. By doing this every day, we can train our minds to think more positively, bringing us more peace and happiness.

Q3: How important is devotion in spiritual growth?

A3: Devotion isn't just about following rituals; it's about living a life full of love, humility, and kindness. His Holiness teaches that true devotion means connecting with the divine in everything we do. When we live with devotion, we grow spiritually and find peace in our hearts. It helps us see the bigger purpose in life and brings us closer to inner joy.

Key Takeaways

His Holiness teachings offer valuable lessons that anyone can use in their daily life. Here are some of the most important points to remember:

- **Pure Thoughts:** The journey to peace starts with having pure and positive thoughts. When we remove negativity from our minds, we align our actions with our true selves, bringing peace and wisdom.

- **Living with Devotion**: Devotion is about more than prayer or rituals. It's about being kind, loving, and humble in everything we do. When we dedicate ourselves to good actions, even the smallest tasks become meaningful and bring us joy.
- **Awakening the Divine Inside**: We all have a spark of divinity inside us. The key to spiritual growth is realizing this truth and letting go of our ego. By opening ourselves to divine guidance, we can uncover our true potential.

Challenges to Overcome

While His teachings can help us grow, they also come with challenges. Here are some common problems we face and simple ways to overcome them:

1. Dealing with Distractions

In today's world, distractions are everywhere. Whether it's school, social media, or other things, forgetting our spiritual path is easy. His Holiness suggests that we take time each day to be quiet and focus on our inner self. Meditation or just sitting quietly for a few minutes can help us stay calm and centred.

2. Overcoming the Temptation of Material Things

Many people believe that happiness comes from having more things or being popular. His Holiness reminds us that real happiness comes from within, not from what we own or what others think of us. By being grateful for what we already have, we can find peace and contentment in the present moment.

3. Staying Consistent in Our Spiritual Practices

Spiritual growth takes time, and it's important to stay consistent. His Holiness encourages us to keep practising good habits like meditation, kindness, and gratitude every day. Even small actions, like helping others or being thankful, make a big difference over time. The key is to never give up.

Conclusion

The teachings of His Holiness Sri Vidyanarayana Theertha are simple but powerful. They offer a clear path to finding peace, happiness, and a deeper connection with ourselves and the world around us. By focusing on positive thoughts, living with devotion, and awakening the divine within, we can live a fulfilling and meaningful life.

Remember, the journey to peace doesn't have to be complicated. It starts with small steps—being kind to others, practising gratitude, and listening to our inner voice. If we follow these steps, we can transform our lives and make the world a better place.

Let His Holiness' wisdom inspire us to walk this path with sincerity and devotion. When we trust in the guidance within, we can unlock our true potential and live a life full of peace and joy.

CHAPTER-5

INNER RADIANCE

Introduction

In a world dominated by distractions and fleeting pleasures, many young people find themselves trapped in a relentless pursuit of material success, only to feel an unshakable sense of emptiness. What if the path to true fulfilment lies not in what we achieve outwardly, but in what we discover within? His Holiness Sri Vidyanarayana Theertha offers a transformative vision, urging us to look beyond the superficial and reconnect with our inner selves. His teachings of simplicity, purity, and devotion illuminate a timeless path to spiritual awakening, even amidst the noise of modern life.

During an inspiring session, His Holiness addressed themes that resonate deeply with today's youth—friendship, the influence of our thoughts, and the power of listening to our inner voice. He emphasized that our thoughts shape our reality, and by nurturing positive, selfless intentions, we can create a life of purpose and joy. True friendship, he explained, is rooted in mutual growth and understanding, while inner listening allows us to align with the divine essence within, guiding us toward peace and clarity.

His Holiness's wisdom acts as a guiding light, helping seekers transcend the cycle of temporary satisfaction and embrace the deeper truths of life. By following his teachings, young people can discover a sense of direction and fulfilment that is both profound and lasting. It is a reminder that in the stillness of self-awareness and the simplicity of devotion lies the key to enduring happiness and spiritual realization.

Question and Answer Session

Q1: What is the true essence of friendship?

A1: Friendship is not about convenience or mutual benefits. A true friend is someone who supports you unconditionally—through thick and thin—without expecting anything in return. At the highest level, the divine serves as the ultimate friend, guiding and protecting you on every step of your journey. Imagine a friend who always has your back, no matter what. That's the kind of friendship the divine offers. It is a bond rooted in selfless love and unwavering support.

Q2: How can one differentiate between good and bad thoughts?

A2: Think of your mind as a garden. Good thoughts are like seeds that grow into flowers—positive, uplifting, and peaceful. Bad thoughts, on the other hand, are like weeds—they spread negativity, stress, and confusion. When your thoughts are pure, you feel a deep sense of calm and clarity. If your thoughts are clouded with doubt or anger, take a moment to pause, breathe, and reset. Aligning with truth and love is the key to cultivating good thoughts that support your growth.

Q3: How important is the inner voice in spiritual growth?

A3: "Your inner voice is like a GPS, guiding you toward your highest potential. It's the quiet whisper of your conscience, always nudging you toward what is right. Ignoring it can lead to confusion or regret, but when you listen closely, it becomes your compass, pointing you toward choices that resonate with your true purpose. By trusting and acting on this divine guidance, you move ever closer to self-realization, inner peace, and fulfilment.

Insights

1. Purity of Thought: Spiritual growth begins with a clear, positive mind. Purify your thoughts, and divine energy will flow, guiding you toward self-realization.

2. Devotion as a Lifestyle: Devotion isn't just rituals—it's living with humility and love. Embrace it fully, and your heart will radiate peace and compassion.

3. Unveiling Your Divine Nature: We're all born with divine potential. Self-realization is about shedding the ego and uncovering the truth within, guided by inner wisdom.

Challenges to Overcome

1. Negative Thoughts: The mind gravitates toward negativity. Shift your focus to positivity or simply observe without attachment. Your actions define you, not your thoughts.

2. Escaping Materialism: True fulfilment lies within, not in external success. Cultivate gratitude, seek inner peace, and move beyond the chase for material validation.

3. Consistency: Spiritual progress requires daily practice. Small, consistent efforts—whether through meditation or reflection— bring about the greatest transformation.

Conclusion

His Holiness Sri Vidyanarayana Theertha's teachings illuminate the path to spiritual fulfilment, offering simple yet powerful tools for navigating life with purpose and grace. By embracing purity of thought, devotion, and self-awareness, we can transform our lives and experience true happiness. The journey to divine realization is not always easy, but it is deeply rewarding. With patience, sincerity, and a commitment to the truth, we can awaken to the peace and joy that lie within us.

The ultimate message is clear: True fulfilment comes from aligning your actions with your higher self, listening to the voice of your conscience, and dedicating your life to love service, and devotion. This is the path that leads to lasting peace and divine realization.

THE PATH OF TRANSFORMATION

*"The path of transformation begins where
the mind surrenders and the soul awakens.
It is not change but realization—seeing beyond illusion, beyond the self.
True transformation is not in doing, but in being—silent, aware, boundless.
When the ego dissolves, the eternal shines—unmoved, untouched, ever
present.
To walk this path is not to reach somewhere, but to become what you
already are."*

– His Holiness Sri Vidyanarayana Theertha

CHAPTER-6

TRANSFORMING THE SELF: JOURNEY FROM EGO TO DIVINE REALIZATION

Introduction

In the blessed presence of His Holiness Sri Vidyanarayana Theertha, seekers of truth have the rare opportunity to receive profound wisdom that speaks directly to the heart. In one of His enlightening discourses, He reflects on the true nature of human life and the purpose of our existence. Unlike animals, which come and go with little attachment, humans are endowed with the capacity for spiritual growth and transformation. While animals move freely in this world, humans are often shackled by desires, attachments, and ego. His Holiness emphasizes that our true purpose is to transcend these limitations, elevate our humanity into divinity, and live a life of divine realization.

The wisdom imparted by His Holiness calls us to awaken our inner potential, purify our mind and heart, and strive towards a higher goal of self-realization. His words inspire us to embark on a journey of transformation—starting from the mundane to the divine. He invites us to move beyond worldly distractions and embrace a life of purpose, clarity, and spiritual fulfilment.

The Gaps in Our Lives

Despite being blessed with the potential for spiritual evolution, many of us live disconnected from our true nature. We often become entangled in desires, material pursuits, and the ego, which keep us from realizing the divine potential within. These gaps in our lives arise from:

1. **Ignorance of True Purpose:** We often wander through life without a clear understanding of our higher purpose, which prevents us from experiencing true fulfilment.
2. **Attachment to Material Desires:** Our attachments to worldly possessions and transient pleasures distract us from the path of spiritual growth and inner peace.
3. **Ego and Self-Centeredness:** The ego creates a barrier between us and our divine nature, causing us to act out of selfishness rather than wisdom, leading to confusion and suffering.
4. **Unrefined Mind and Intellect:** A restless mind and unrefined intellect prevent us from discerning the truth and understanding the deeper aspects of life.
5. **Lack of Faith and Devotion:** Without deep faith and devotion, we struggle to surrender ourselves to the divine flow of life, which keeps us from achieving self-realization.

How to Fill These Gaps

As His Holiness Sri Vidyanarayana Theertha teaches, our true purpose is to transcend these limitations and evolve from mere human beings into divine beings. By filling the gaps in our lives with spiritual discipline, self-awareness, and devotion, we can begin the process of transformation:

1. **Self-Reflection and Awareness:**

   The first step in bridging these gaps is self-reflection. By contemplating our purpose and examining the true nature of our being, we can begin to recognize the divine potential within us. Reflect on questions like: *Who am I? What is my higher purpose?* This introspection helps us align with our divine self.

2. **Detachment from Material Desires:**

   Detach from the constant pursuit of material gains. Begin simplifying your life and focus on spiritual growth rather than worldly accumulation. True peace comes not from external possessions but from inner contentment and harmony.

3. **Transcending the Ego:**

The ego is the primary obstacle to divine realization. To transcend it, practice selflessness. Serve others without expecting anything in return, and embrace humility. This will dissolve the ego and open your heart to love and compassion.

4. **Mindfulness and Intellectual Growth:**

A refined mind is crucial for spiritual growth. Engage in mindfulness practices such as meditation to train the mind and intellect. The clearer the mind, the more it can discern divine truths and higher wisdom.

5. **Developing Faith and Devotion:**

Strengthen your connection to the divine through faith and devotion. Engaging in prayer, chanting, and surrendering to divine will helps foster a deeper relationship with God, leading us closer to self-realization.

Question & Answer

Q: What should we learn first in life to achieve spiritual transformation?

A: The first thing we must learn is how to live consciously. It begins with learning to eat and live in a way that honours the sacredness of life. We must discover who we truly are, understand our duties, and align our actions with our higher purpose. Once we gain clarity about our purpose, the intellect begins to evolve naturally. The mind, intellect, and consciousness must merge to create the higher state of wisdom.

Q: How can this wisdom be developed?

A: Wisdom arises when we purify our minds and intellects. Through this process of refinement, analytical power awakens, giving us the ability to discern the truth from illusion. This wisdom is inherent in every human being, but it requires conscious effort to awaken. The more we cultivate wisdom, the more clearly we see the path to self-realization, where the divine light of knowledge illuminates our being, guiding us to our true essence.

Takeaways

- **Purify Your Life:** Begin by cleansing your life of distractions and worldly attachments in order to elevate your spiritual self.
- **Transform Desires:** Recognize that material pursuits are illusions that bind you. True happiness comes from spiritual growth, not worldly possessions.
- **Refine Your Intellect:** The mind and intellect must be refined to develop wisdom that leads to spiritual discernment.
- **Awaken to Your True Self:** By awakening to the wisdom within, you align with your divine nature, experiencing the cosmic connection that binds all.

Challenges

- **Let Go of Attachments:** True spiritual freedom is found by releasing attachment to material things, ego, and desires.
- **Refine Your Actions:** Practice mindfulness in all aspects of life—thoughts, words, and actions—to align with divine truth.
- **Stay Focused:** In a world full of distractions, keep your attention centered on your spiritual journey, seeking inner transformation.

Conclusion

The path to divine realization is a transformative journey that requires sincere effort and deep devotion. As His Holiness Sri Vidyanarayana Theertha beautifully conveys, we must shed the ego and attachments that bind us to the material world. Through the purification of the mind and intellect, we can awaken to the divine light that resides within us. This is not just a lofty ideal but a practical approach to living a life of spiritual fulfilment.

As we walk this path of transformation, let us remain dedicated to the divine guidance that leads us toward self-realization. The more we refine ourselves, the closer we come to embodying our true divine nature. May the wisdom of His Holiness guide us, and may we all strive to live lives that reflect the light of divine truth.

Let us move forward, inspired by Swamy, and be ever mindful of the opportunity to transform ourselves from the mundane to the divine.

CHAPTER-7

FROM FEAR TO FREEDOM: AWAKENING YOUR DIVINE POTENTIAL

Introduction

In the journey of life, two powerful forces often influence our thoughts and actions—**fear** and **forgetfulness**. His Holiness Sri Vidyanarayana Theertha's discourse delves into these profound concepts, revealing how they stem from ignorance and how, through spiritual awareness, one can transcend them. Understanding the true essence of life and our connection with the divine holds the

key to releasing the grip of fear and overcoming the fog of forgetfulness. This discourse aims to illuminate the path towards inner peace and spiritual fulfilment, guiding us to remember our divine nature and live in harmony with the universe.

Question & Answer

Q: What is the root cause of fear and forgetfulness in human life?

A: Fear is born from ignorance. We create walls of protection around ourselves—through possessions, power, and pride—hoping to shield ourselves from the unknown. However, this very act of building walls entangles us in fear. Similarly, forgetfulness arises from our inability to remember our true nature. We forget the essence of who we are and fall into the illusion of separation.

Q: How do we transcend fear and forgetfulness?

A: The answer lies in spiritual awakening—through meditation, self-inquiry, and living in alignment with divine truth. Meditation helps quiet the mind, allowing us to experience the unity of existence and the divine presence within. By practising mindfulness and sincerity, we slowly dissolve the barriers of fear and recall our eternal nature. Truth, compassion, and wisdom become the guiding lights that lead us out of ignorance.

Takeaways

1. **Fear is born from ignorance:** When we forget our true nature, fear takes hold. By reconnecting with the divine, fear fades.
2. **Forgetfulness is the source of suffering:** Our suffering stems from forgetting our divine essence. To find peace, we must remember who we are.
3. **Meditation reveals the divine truth:** Regular practice helps us experience unity with the divine, quieting the mind and heart.
4. **Live by divine truth:** Embrace honesty, humility, and simplicity. These virtues unlock a life free from fear and confusion.

Challenges

1. **Release the ego:** Let go of the need for control and superiority to overcome fear and ego-driven illusions.
2. **Focus on the divine:** Distractions from material pursuits keep us in forgetfulness. Focus on spiritual growth to awaken to your true nature.
3. **Maintain inner peace amidst turmoil:** The world is full of challenges, but peace comes when we remain grounded in meditation and truth.

Conclusion

The path to overcoming fear and forgetfulness is rooted in the realization of our divine self. His Holiness Sri Vidyanarayana Theertha's teachings inspire us to break free from the illusions that hold us captive. Through meditation, self-awareness, and a commitment to living truthfully, we can dissolve the boundaries of fear and remember our connection to the divine.

As we embark on this spiritual journey, let us focus on the present moment, practice inner peace, and remain grounded in the truth. The divine presence within us is the ultimate source of strength, guiding us through life's challenges. The more we align with this truth, the more we transcend fear, forgetfulness, and suffering, stepping into a life of spiritual fulfilment and bliss.

May we all walk the path of remembrance and awaken to the divine light within, for in that awareness lies the ultimate freedom.

CHAPTER-8

THE ILLUMINATING POWER OF PRAYER AND SELF-DISCOVERY

Introduction

Prayer is a transformative act that bridges the human and the divine, illuminating both the mind and heart. His Holiness Sri Vidyanarayana Theertha, in his profound discourse, eloquently emphasizes the essence of prayer, devotion, and the indispensable guidance of a Guru in the journey toward self-realization. Through his insights, he sheds light on the intricate connection between spiritual practices and the awakening of inner consciousness.

As Sri Vidyanarayana Theertha elucidates, prayer is not merely a ritualistic exercise but a deeply personal and transformative experience. It serves as a channel to align the mind with the higher self, fostering clarity, serenity, and purpose. "When you place your mind on the Divine and your hands on diligent work, fatigue cannot touch you," he remarks, urging us to find balance and meaning in every moment.

The teachings further inspire us to dedicate even a small portion of our day to sincere communion with the Divine. This act, though seemingly simple, can yield profound results. The Lord listens, blesses, and paves the way for our spiritual and worldly progress. As Sri Vidyanarayana Theertha wisely observes, "Truth alone triumphs. Let it resonate within you, for it is the foundation of all growth."

Through these reflections, the discourse beautifully conveys that prayer and faith are the timeless treasures that sustain the human spirit amidst life's challenges. When integrated with unwavering devotion and the wisdom imparted by a Guru, these practices elevate us beyond the mundane, revealing our true potential.

Question and Answer Section

Question 1: How does prayer influence the mind and heart?

Answer: Prayer rejuvenates the mind and heart by anchoring one's thoughts to the divine. When hands are engaged in work, and the mind is devoted to a higher power, fatigue does not touch us. Instead, the mind becomes lively, and the heart overflows with joy. Even in moments of lethargy or distress, one should not divert their focus from inner peace and spiritual connection. By dedicating even a small portion of time to prayer, we invite divine blessings into our lives, which pave the way for progress and well-being.

Question 2: What are the two invaluable assets every individual must cultivate?

Answer: The two greatest treasures are:

1. The regular practice of spiritual recitation or reflection.
2. Continuous remembrance of the teachings of spiritual guides and scriptures.

The power of prayer and meditation increases through repetition. This practice forms a protective shield around us, transforming negative tendencies into virtuous ones. It helps overcome anger, jealousy, and hatred, leading us to the ocean of devotion and revealing the divine presence.

Question 3: What is the significance of the Guru's guidance in self-realization?

Answer: A Guru or spiritual guide plays a pivotal role in helping individuals discover their true nature. The Guru dispels ignorance, much like a mentor who awakens a student to their latent potential. By revealing the truth, the Guru empowers the disciples to realize their inherent divinity and embrace their true purpose.

Takeaways

1. **Prayer: A Lamp of Clarity**

   Prayer is a lamp that dispels darkness, filling life with clarity and purpose. A simple, consistent practice can transform ordinary moments into profound experiences.

2. **Consistency Shapes Character**

   Like a water-shaping stone, consistent spiritual practice refines character and reveals inner strength, leading to harmony and wisdom.

3. **Guidance: The Sunlight of Truth**

   The Guru's guidance is like sunlight for a hidden gem—it reveals brilliance and helps us transcend illusions to embrace our true essence.

4. **Path to Resilience**

   Prayer cleanses the mind of doubts and fears, fostering inner strength and confidence. It serves as an anchor in times of uncertainty, reviving the spirit and building resilience.

5. **Trust the Process**

   Growth is not always visible. Trust the process and continue with faith; transformation unfolds in its own time.

6. **The Right Guide at the Right Time**

   The right spiritual guide often appears when the seeker is genuinely ready and sincere.

Insights and Dilemmas of Sadhakas

1. **Dilemma:** "I often struggle to maintain focus during prayer. How can I feel more connected?"

   Resolution: Focus on the intention behind prayer rather than its form. Even a brief, heartfelt connection can be deeply transformative.

2. **Dilemma:** "I feel stagnation despite regular practices. Is it enough?"

   Resolution: Growth is not always visible. Trust the process and continue with faith; transformation unfolds in its own time.

3. **Dilemma:** "How do I find the right Guru or guide?"

   Resolution: Be patient and open. The right guide often appears when the seeker is genuinely ready and sincere.

Conclusion

Prayer, devotion, and the wisdom of spiritual mentors form the trinity of spiritual growth. His Holiness Sri Vidyanarayana Theertha's discourse urges us to nurture these practices with sincerity and perseverance. By holding onto the teachings of spiritual guides and dedicating ourselves to the divine, we can transcend ignorance and achieve liberation. Each step on this path is a testament to the universal truth that within every heart lies the potential for self-realization and boundless joy.

CHAPTER-9

THE ESSENCE OF DIVINE EXPERIENCE: SEEKING PEACE THROUGH THE HEART

Introduction

In this discourse, His Holiness Sri Vidyanarayana Theertha enlightens us about the profound connection between humans and the Divine. Though we cannot see the Lord with our physical eyes, His presence is felt in every particle of existence. True knowledge is attained not through mere perception but through direct experience, which leads to divine understanding and peace.

The key to spiritual awakening lies within our hearts. The heart, being the seat of the soul, is the true laboratory for spiritual research where we can connect with the Divine. In this sacred space, we discover the essence of divine peace, which transcends the limits of physical perception and reaches the core of our being. As we begin to awaken to this truth, we embark on the path of understanding and experiencing the Divine in every moment of our lives.

Questions and Answers

Q1: Can we truly experience God?

- While we cannot see God with our physical eyes, we can experience His divine energy in every aspect of life. True knowledge arises from experiences that bring us closer to understanding the Divine. The heart is the true laboratory where we can study and connect with the Divine, as it is intrinsically linked to the soul.

Q2: Why do we fail to realize God's existence in our lives?

- Even the most ardent atheists cannot escape the cycles of birth and death, which are governed by God's will. Regardless of our acknowledgement, we are all bound by a divine connection that transcends time and life. It is only through the guidance of the Guru that we can begin to truly understand this eternal bond and experience God in our lives.

Q3: How can one attain peace in a chaotic world?

- The key to peace lies in focusing on the Divine. Though the world is often filled with strife, contemplation of God brings tranquility to the heart. The Guru, having recognized God's presence, guides us toward inner peace, helping us rise above the external turbulence of life.

Q4: What is the role of the Guru in experiencing the Divine?

- The Guru is the guiding light that leads us from darkness to light. By offering wisdom and spiritual guidance, the Guru helps us unlock the hidden potential of our hearts, where the Divine resides. Through surrendering to the Guru's teachings, we are able to transcend ignorance and align with the Divine presence that pervades our lives.

Q5: Why do we often feel disconnected from the Divine, despite our efforts?

- Our disconnect arises from the distractions of the material world, the grip of ego, and our constant yearning for external validation. Through focused practice of mindfulness and meditation, under the guidance of the Guru, we can learn to quiet the mind and open our hearts to the Divine presence that always exists within us.

Q6: How does contemplation on the Divine lead to inner peace?

- Contemplation on the Divine brings us into harmony with the universe. By meditating on the Divine form or mantra, we align ourselves with the higher consciousness. This alignment quiets the turbulent waves of the mind, allowing peace to settle within. When we dwell in this peaceful state, we transcend worldly chaos and experience the purity of divine tranquility.

Key Insights

- The heart is the true laboratory for spiritual research, where divine understanding flourishes.
- God's presence is constant, whether we perceive it or not. This connection is eternal and beyond human comprehension.
- Contemplating God brings inner peace; with the Guru's guidance, we transcend worldly struggles.

Challenges on the Path to Divine Realization

1. Material Distractions: The world constantly pulls us away from our spiritual focus with its demands, desires, and distractions. Overcoming these requires detachment and the ability to stay grounded in spiritual practice.
2. Ego: The ego fosters pride, attachment, and separation, creating a barrier between us and the Divine. Surrendering to the Divine will helps transcend ego and opens the heart to true peace.
3. Doubt: Periods of doubt can shake faith, but they are part of the journey. Faith grows through persistence, and the Guru's guidance helps keep us grounded during uncertain times.
4. Suffering: Pain and hardship are inevitable but necessary for spiritual growth. Through suffering, we learn to detach from worldly attachments and deepen our connection with the Divine.
5. Impatience: The spiritual path requires patience. Instant results are unrealistic, and only through steady progress and trust in Divine timing can true transformation occur.

Conclusion

Ultimately, the highest blessing is to live with a pure heart, continuously remembering the Divine presence. The teachings of the Guru provide a lifeline, guiding us through life's challenges toward spiritual fulfillment and lasting peace. By embracing these teachings with sincerity, we can live in harmony with the Divine and achieve true contentment.

In the end, peace and divine experience do not lie in seeking something external but in awakening to the presence of the Divine within. Through sincere devotion, contemplation, and the guidance of the Guru, we can cultivate an enduring connection with the Divine, filling our hearts with peace and transforming our lives. Let this journey be one of continuous remembrance and realization, for in the heart lies the true path to divine peace.

CHAPTER-10

Beyond Illusion: The Path of Service, Self-Realization, and Divine Union

Introduction

Life is full of contradictions and paradoxes that challenge our understanding of the world around us. His Holiness Sri Vidyanarayana Theertha provides profound teachings that offer clarity on these contradictions, helping us navigate the complexities of existence with wisdom. Through his discourse, we explore various aspects of life—differentiating between the concept of "serve and ask," understanding karma's multifaceted nature, and emphasizing the importance of inner consciousness. His Holiness teaches us how to find balance, overcome distractions like Maya (illusion), and cultivate a deeper connection with the Divine.

Questions and Answers

Question 1: Swamiji, what is the difference between "serve" and "ask" in spiritual life?

Swamy:

Serving and asking are two different aspects of spiritual growth, but both are interdependent. Serving is a way of surrendering the ego, as you give without expecting anything in return. On the other hand, asking comes from a place of humility, acknowledging that there is something you don't know or don't have. However, there is an important distinction: to serve is to offer without thought of the self, while to ask is to seek guidance with the understanding that the answer already exists within the universe. When you serve, you are open; when you ask, you are ready to receive. It is through both that we discover our true path.

Question 2: Swamiji, why do different karmas exist, and is it only for perception?

Swamy:

Karma manifests in different forms because life is multi-dimensional, and each action has its own effect. The world around us is perceived through our senses, and how we perceive events influences our actions. The varying types of karma—whether good, bad, or neutral—are often shaped by our perceptions of the world. However, in truth, karma is not defined by perception alone. It is a universal law that operates regardless of our understanding, and it teaches us that our actions have consequences. The real question is not about why different karmas exist, but how we respond to them. By aligning our actions with dharma, we can purify our karma and ultimately transcend its effects.

Question 3: How do we reconcile the paradox of "everything is in me, but I am at his feet"?

Swamy:

This paradox lies at the heart of true spirituality. While we may feel that everything exists within us—the knowledge, the power, the capacity—it is essential to remember that we are but instruments of the Divine. The realization that "I am at his feet" means acknowledging the Divine as the source of all power and wisdom. The duality between "everything is in me" and "I am at his feet" is part of our spiritual journey. On one hand, we are individuals with unique experiences, and on the other, we are connected to the divine essence that permeates all. This balance is the key to understanding and transcending ego.

Question 4: Swamiji, you often speak of "one side we are two, inside we are one." Could you elaborate on this?

Swamy:

This concept refers to the duality and oneness inherent in our existence. Outwardly, we are two—there is the 'individual' self and the 'universal' self. We experience ourselves as separate from others and the world. However, inwardly, there is a deeper realization that all is one, as we are manifestations of the same Divine energy. The ultimate truth is that the soul within us is not separate from the Divine; it is the same essence. This realization can only be attained through meditation and introspection, where we transcend the boundaries of our ego and merge with the Divine.

Question 5: Swamiji, why is questioning important in spiritual growth?

Swamy:

Questioning is essential because it awakens the intellect and leads us to deeper understanding. It is through questioning that we challenge our assumptions, expand our awareness, and break free from the limits of ignorance. However, there is a difference between questioning with doubt and questioning with the intent to understand. When we ask with an open heart and mind, we invite wisdom into our lives. But remember, the answers may not always be immediate, and the journey of seeking is as important as the answer itself.

Question 6: How can we distance ourselves from Maya (illusion) and focus on the Divine?

Swamy:

Maya is the illusion that clouds our perception of reality. It pulls us towards worldly desires and distractions, making us forget the higher purpose of our existence. To overcome Maya, one must cultivate detachment and mindfulness. Understand that the world, with all its attractions, is temporary. For example, a child may be fascinated by a shiny toy, but as it matures, it realizes that the toy is not important. Similarly, when we grow spiritually, we begin to see through the illusion of Maya and turn our attention toward the eternal truth. The key is not to be caught in the illusion but to remain focused on the higher purpose of life—union with the Divine.

Question 7: Swamiji, what is the importance of "giving" in relation to dharma and karma?

Swamy:

Giving is a fundamental aspect of dharma. It is through selfless giving that we practice the essence of dharma—acting with compassion, humility, and responsibility. Giving is not just about material wealth; it includes offering our time, love, and kindness to others. When we give, we are acting in alignment with the universe's flow, and karma purifies us through the act of selflessness. It is the commitment to give from the heart, without expecting anything in return, that aligns us with the Divine will.

Question 8: How do we prepare ourselves for the inevitable challenges of life?

Swamy:

Challenges will come, whether we are prepared or not. The key to handling these challenges lies in inner readiness. When energy or external forces attack us, we may feel unprepared, but in truth, we are always prepared—because our inner consciousness is connected to the Divine. Life is unpredictable, and as the saying goes, "I am not prepared, but I am prepared." There is no need for debate or discussion when challenges arise. Accept them with grace and remain firm in your commitment to dharma. It is through acceptance and action that we overcome life's obstacles.

Takeaways

- Serving and asking are two complementary aspects of spiritual growth—service is selfless giving, and asking is seeking wisdom with humility.
- Karma manifests in different forms, and it is through our actions that we shape our destiny.
- Realize the duality of existence: outwardly we are two, but inwardly we are one with the Divine.
- Questioning is an essential tool for spiritual growth, as it helps expand understanding and break free from ignorance.
- Maya (illusion) can be overcome by detaching from worldly desires and focusing on the eternal truth.
- Giving is dharma in action, and it purifies our karma, aligning us with the Divine.
- Life's challenges are inevitable, but by accepting them with inner readiness and without fear, we can navigate them with grace.

Conclusion

His Holiness Sri Vidyanarayana Theertha's teachings offer deep insights into the path of spiritual growth, guiding us through life's paradoxes and challenges. By embracing the concepts of selfless service, questioning with purpose, and cultivating inner readiness, we can transcend the illusions of the material world and connect with the Divine. Let us walk this path with awareness, understanding, and dedication, for the true purpose of life lies in realizing our oneness with the Divine and living in alignment with dharma and karma.

AWAKENING WISDOM

*"Awakening wisdom is not about knowing more, but realizing deeper.
It is the light that dawns when silence speaks louder than words.
True wisdom is not gathered—it unfolds, like the sky revealing the sun.
Beyond thought, beyond learning, the eternal knowing already exists.
The awakened one sees not with the eyes, but with the soul that
remembers."*

– His Holiness Sri Vidyanarayana Theertha

CHAPTER-11

FROM IMPURITY TO PURITY: A SPIRITUAL JOURNEY GUIDED BY HIS HOLINESS SRI VIDYANARAYANA THEERTHA

Introduction

The path from impurity to purity is not just a matter of external actions or appearances but a profound inner transformation. It is a journey that requires deep self-awareness, where we learn to purify not just our actions, but our thoughts, emotions, and intentions. His Holiness Sri Vidyanarayana Theertha, through his profound wisdom and teachings, has shown us that purity begins within and radiates outward. This journey involves embracing a life of discipline and divinity, where we learn to recognize and overcome the attachments and distractions that bind us to the material world. His teachings encourage us to look beyond the surface and see the divine essence that exists in every form, every action, and every being.

As we walk this path, we come to understand the true nature of sharing, discipline, and detachment. Sharing is not just about giving outwardly, but about sharing from a place of purity and intention, whether it's in our thoughts, words, or actions. Our behaviour, like our attire, should reflect the purity within, for when we mix with the world, we should maintain our divine discipline without losing our essence. His Holiness often emphasizes the importance of not being swayed by the external world but rather engaging with it without attachment, performing our duties with love, and maintaining an open heart towards all beings. This balance between mingling with society and retaining inner detachment is the core of His teachings.

In this transformative process, mistakes and errors are not obstacles but opportunities for growth and learning. His Holiness teaches us that mistakes are energies that accumulate in the body and mind, and through awareness, humility, and divine remembrance, we can purify them. The energy of mantras such as *Mangalam Vasudevaya* invokes divine blessings and assists us in this purification process, helping us align with the divine will. The journey from impure to pure is not about renouncing the world but about transforming ourselves from within. By practicing self-awareness, compassion, and unwavering dedication to the divine, we move closer to our true essence and experience the purity that lies at the core of our being.

Disciple

Swamy, could you explain the path from impure to pure and how we can apply the teachings of purity in our daily lives?

Swamy: The journey from impure to pure is a gradual process. It begins with recognizing that purity is not just about external appearances but about internal transformation. One cannot share everything, for not all things are meant to be shared. To truly share, you must share with intention, with purity of heart.

Just as you dress yourself in clean clothes, you must also adorn your behaviour and qualities with goodness. Your conduct, like your clothes, should reflect purity. When you mingle with others, maintain your discipline in divinity, for true mingling is not about losing your essence in society but about retaining your purity while engaging with the world. Dislike is not divinity.

Hatred and ill-will only bind you further. Remember, attachment is karma—it keeps you tied to the cycles of birth and rebirth. The practice of **Sahavasa Sarvya Nasanaha**, as taught by His Holiness Sri Vidyanarayana Theertha, emphasizes that living harmoniously with others is a path to transcend the impurities of the mind. It could be understood as the concept that through the association with noble, virtuous beings, one can purify oneself, transcend worldly attachments, and remove the impurities that hinder spiritual growth. This association helps one rise above the distractions of the material world, fostering inner peace, clarity, and spiritual wisdom.

Disciple: Swamy, how can we balance mixing with society without getting attached to it?

Swamy: Life is full of paradoxes, and the balance lies in understanding that while you must mix with society, you must not fix it in your mind. Face society with compassion and understanding, but do not let its distractions entangle your spirit. Society will always be there, but your task is to perform your duties with grace and not get attached to the results or judgments.

Just as a protocol is followed to maintain order, there is a divine protocol that guides our actions—acting with mindfulness, understanding, and a heart full of compassion. Every action, every word, every gesture should be a reflection of your commitment to service and love, not expectation or attachment. This teaching of detachment in action is central to the guidance given by His Holiness Sri Vidyanarayana Theertha, who exemplifies the balance between worldly engagement and spiritual discipline.

Disciple: Swamy, how do we handle mistakes and errors on this journey?

Swamy: Mistakes, like everything else in life, are part of the divine play. When we make mistakes, we must accept them with humility and compassion for ourselves. Mistakes are energies that accumulate, and when they are unrecognized or unresolved, they remain with us. It is through self-awareness and self-correction that we can release this energy.

The divine body of the Swamy, as a vessel of cosmic energy, absorbs and transforms these energies into higher consciousness. When you chant mantras like *Mangalam Vasudevaya* or *Mangalam Nanda Sootane*, you are invoking this transformative energy, helping to purify your mind and spirit. The energy of *Mangalam* brings auspiciousness, peace, and harmony, both within and outside. This purification process requires dedication, mindfulness, and the constant remembrance of the divine. Through the teachings of His Holiness Sri Vidyanarayana Theertha, we understand that mistakes are not to be feared but embraced as opportunities for spiritual growth and cleansing.

Key Takeaways

- **Purity**: The journey to purity is internal, reflecting in both your actions and thoughts. Begin with self-awareness and purity of intention.
- **Attachment and Karma**: Attachment keeps you bound in the cycle of karma. Practice detachment by engaging with the world without becoming emotionally entangled in its outcomes.
- **Discipline in Divinity**: Follow the divine protocol, maintaining discipline while engaging with society. The key is to perform your duties with love, not attachment.
- **Mistakes as Energy**: Mistakes are part of growth. Embrace them with humility, and transform the energy through self-awareness and divine remembrance.
- **Divine Presence**: Chanting and invoking divine mantras brings purity and auspiciousness to your life, helping to align you with the divine will.

Inspiring Conclusion

The path from impurity to purity, as imparted by His Holiness Sri Vidyanarayana Theertha, is not about renouncing the external world but about transforming the internal world. It requires us to engage with society while maintaining inner detachment, to serve with love, and to purify ourselves from the attachments that bind us. Mistakes and errors are opportunities for growth, and through humility and self-awareness, we can cleanse our hearts and minds. The energy of divine mantras, like *Mangalam Vasudevaya*, supports us on this journey of transformation, leading us from the impure to the pure. May we walk this path with grace, compassion, and unwavering dedication to the divine will, embracing every step as a step toward spiritual growth and purity.

CHAPTER-12

TRANSFORMING LIFE THROUGH SPIRITUAL FOUNDATION AND MATERIAL HARMONY"

Introduction

As we stand at the threshold of a new year, transitioning from 2024 into 2025, His Holiness Sri Vidyanarayana Theertha's discourse provides profound insight into the balance between material wealth and spiritual growth. In a world that is increasingly caught in a rush for material pleasures, Swamiji's teachings offer a timely reminder that while wealth is an undeniable  necessity in today's age, it must be viewed as a tool for spiritual growth, not an end in itself.

In the ever-evolving rhythm of life, each moment is significant. Time moves forward relentlessly, but it is the choices we make in every second that truly shape the course of our lives. Swamiji's message calls upon us to reflect on the dual aspects of life—the material and the spiritual—and to seek harmony between the two.

In today's world, where there is an incessant rush toward material pleasures and accumulation, it's essential to remember why we are born. We are not merely meant to gather wealth or achievements; we are here to grow, cultivate wisdom, and fulfil our deeper purpose.

Swamiji's teachings remind us that wealth is not inherently wrong, but when it becomes the sole focus, it leads us away from the true essence of life. Rather, wealth should serve as the foundation upon which spiritual growth and wisdom can be built.

As the Bhagavad Gita beautifully says, "Your right is to perform your duty only, but never to its fruits. Let not the fruits of action be your motive, nor let your attachment be to inaction" (Chapter 2, Verse 47). This verse urges us to focus on the actions we take in life—whether in creating wealth or seeking spiritual growth—without being overly attached to the results. The path to fulfilment lies in the process, not the outcome.

Wealth as a Foundation for Spiritual Growth

In Kali Yuga, wealth has acquired an essential role. While past epochs like Dwapara and Treta Yuga saw wealth as irrelevant to spiritual practices, today, it is almost a necessity. Without a solid financial foundation, it becomes challenging to focus on spiritual pursuits. Swamiji explains that wealth is not to be idolized but viewed as a resource that facilitates spiritual growth. Just as we need a strong material base for survival, we also need spiritual practice to nurture our inner selves.

Swamiji's insight reflects the timeless wisdom of the Mahabharata: "A person should not be too attached to worldly wealth, for it is fleeting. True wealth lies in wisdom, kindness, and virtue." Wealth, while necessary, must never overshadow the pursuit of spiritual wisdom. It is a tool for fulfilling our material needs but should not be the end goal.

The need to "build a base" in life—material, cultural, educational, and spiritual—is emphasized. This base offers the stability and independence necessary to lead a balanced life. When wealth and spirituality coexist harmoniously, we find fulfilment, not just in survival but in thriving with purpose.

The Role of Tradition and Spirituality

Swamiji delves into the paradox of tradition and spirituality. Tradition is vital for external accomplishments in the material world, but spirituality must be conquered within. The real challenge lies in cultivating the internal state that leads to wisdom and enlightenment. Wealth management helps shape the external world, but the spiritual journey shapes our inner world.

As the Yoga Vasistha states, "Wealth and fame are like fleeting clouds in the sky. The true wealth is the knowledge of the Self." This highlights the transient nature of material wealth, emphasizing that true success lies in the cultivation of wisdom and self-awareness.

Swamiji teaches that integrating material success with spiritual wisdom is essential for a well-rounded life. When wealth and spirituality are aligned, we can live fully—not just for survival but with deeper fulfilment, understanding that life is a precious gift that should be used in service of the divine.

Parents, Teachers, and the Path of Dharma

Swamiji reflects on the essential roles played by parents and teachers in an individual's journey. While parents equip us with the tools to navigate life, it is the teachers—especially those who integrate material and spiritual education—who truly guide us toward realizing the harmony between these two aspects. The rarest of teachers instil in their students the understanding that material success, when aligned with spiritual principles, becomes a tool for a higher purpose.

As Lord Krishna says in the Bhagavad Gita, "Whenever there is a decline in righteousness and a predominance of unrighteousness, O Arjuna, at that time I manifest myself on earth" (Chapter 4, Verse 7). Teachers who merge material and spiritual wisdom are divinely inspired messengers, guiding us toward the righteous path that leads to holistic success.

Swamiji's reflections on his own life show that even without a strong material base in the beginning, he was able to build wealth and spiritual wisdom over fifty years. His life reminds us that without a foundation, spiritual practice can often be misguided or incomplete. A well-established base—material, intellectual, and spiritual—is necessary to navigate life's challenges.

Mechanical Life Transformed Through Wealth Management

Swamiji also addresses the issue of "mechanical life," the routine existence many people lead. In this existence, material pursuits dominate without a deeper connection to the soul. He suggests that when managed wisely, wealth can help transform this mechanical existence into a more spiritually centred life.

Swamiji notes that retirees are blessed, as they have the financial security to focus on spiritual growth. This balance of independence and dependence is key in navigating the complexities of life, creating a harmonious life where material needs are met and spiritual growth continues.

As the Mahabharata says, "The ultimate purpose of life is to seek knowledge, and with knowledge comes wisdom, which leads to liberation." This reinforces the idea that when used wisely, material wealth supports the pursuit of spiritual wisdom and liberation.

Dharma: The Path to Secure a Base

Swamiji's teachings on Dharma emphasize that it is not merely a set of external rules but a living, dynamic force that shapes every moment of our lives. Dharma is the ethical and spiritual compass that aligns our actions with the deeper purpose of existence. It calls us to live consciously and harmoniously, ensuring that our thoughts, words, and deeds are aligned with the higher good.

Dharma is not a rigid concept but a path that adapts to the circumstances of our lives while upholding universal values. In today's world, where distractions abound and the pursuit of material wealth often takes precedence over spiritual growth, following Dharma becomes all the more crucial. Dharma teaches us to live with intention, not merely for survival or material gain, but with an awareness that each action holds spiritual significance.

Dharma leads us to a balanced life. By following its path, we can create a foundation that is not only material but deeply rooted in spiritual values. It is through Dharma that we cultivate inner strength and clarity, enabling us to navigate the complexities of modern life with wisdom and peace. **It is the essence of our existence—a guiding force that ensures we remain anchored in our values, regardless of external circumstances.**

Thus, Dharma reminds us that wealth, fame, and success are fleeting. It is the strength of our inner character, our devotion to higher principles, and our commitment to truth and compassion that define true success. Dharma is the lens through which we see life and make decisions that align with our highest purpose.

Challenges

- **Material Distractions:** External pressures prioritize wealth and success, making it difficult to focus on spiritual growth.
- **Time Management:** Balancing a busy life with spiritual practices requires integrating moments of mindfulness into daily routines.
- **Attachment to Results:** Focusing too much on outcomes can lead to disappointment; the key is to embrace the process without attachment.
- **Financial Stress:** Financial challenges can hinder spiritual pursuits, but viewing wealth as a tool, not the goal, shifts focus from scarcity to abundance.
- **Overemphasis on Wealth:** Focusing solely on material wealth can overshadow the pursuit of wisdom and inner growth.

Takeaways/Insights

- **Balance is Key:** True prosperity is not defined by material wealth alone but by the balance we strike between material and spiritual growth.
- **Purpose of Wealth:** Wealth is a means to an end, not the end itself. It serves as a foundation for spiritual practice and wisdom.
- **Dharma as a Guide:** Dharma is not just a set of rules but a guiding force that shapes our actions and decisions, leading us toward holistic fulfilment.
- **Transformation of Life:** By using wealth to secure a stable foundation, we transform our mechanical existence into a life of purpose and spiritual growth.
- **Living in the Present:** Every second counts. The present moment is an opportunity to live with intention and to align ourselves with our higher purpose.

Conclusion: The Path is Now

Each moment, each second of our lives is a precious opportunity for growth and transformation. **True change does not happen over a year or decade; it happens in the choices we make in each fleeting moment.** This moment, right now, is as significant as any other, for it is in the present that we shape our future and grow in wisdom.

Swamiji's teachings invite us to recognize the impermanence of external wealth and success. These are tools that support a deeper purpose—the enrichment of our spirit through Dharma, selfless action, and the constant quest for inner wisdom. With every decision we make, let us remember that each second holds infinite potential for spiritual realization.

The future is built in the present. Let us not wait for an arbitrary date on the calendar to begin our journey of transformation. **Every moment**

is a call to action. By living in accordance with Dharma, using our resources wisely, and constantly striving to elevate our consciousness, we will find that every day becomes a step toward spiritual fulfilment.

True growth is not measured by the calendar but by the depth of our inner transformation. May we all cultivate an awareness that transcends time, recognizing the sacredness of every moment, and walk the path of Dharma with full commitment. The journey is not in the future—it is now, in this very instant.

CHAPTER-13

THE MYSTIC PRINCE: JOURNEY BEYOND THE ORDINARY

Introduction

In an intimate and reflective gathering, His Holiness shared with his chosen disciples not only his own journey but also the subtle truths of life that transcend the ordinary. The disciples, eager to understand the deeper essence of existence, engaged in a series of thought-provoking questions. The answers they received were not just philosophical but spiritual revelations—guiding lights to the path of self-realization. Through this informal yet sacred dialogue, His Holiness illuminated the core of spiritual teaching, offering insights on how to navigate life's challenges, find peace amidst distractions, and awaken to one's divine nature.

His Holiness, who often referred to himself as a "mystic prince," explained that this title was not an expression of pride or status but rather a reflection of his unique path—one that combined deep mystical experiences with the noble responsibility of guiding others. As a mystic, he had journeyed beyond the confines of conventional understanding, diving into the mysteries of existence. As a prince, he held the weight of responsibility to lead and uplift others through wisdom, compassion, and grace. This self-chosen title symbolized his embodiment of both the hidden depths of spiritual truth and the noble duty to share that wisdom with the world.

This session became a pivotal moment, as His Holiness's wisdom resonated deeply, offering clarity on the path of enlightenment for all who were present.

The Mystic Prince

Part 1

Disciples: Swamy, could you share with us the significance of India's ancient culture?

Swamy: Our Vedic Sanatana Dharma stands as an eternal testament to the highest wisdom ever bestowed upon humanity. India's spiritual and intellectual prowess has never faltered through the ages. From the depths of metaphysics to the pinnacles of science, from governance to artistic brilliance, every facet of life was nurtured with divine wisdom. Our land has been home to rishis, seers, and sages whose silent contributions continue to uplift the world. The ancient way of life was not merely about existence—it was about harmony, where the cosmos and consciousness intertwined seamlessly.

Disciples: Swamy, could you explain the nature of belief in saints?

Swamy: Saints are not to be analysed; they are to be experienced. Faith in a saint is not a conditioned belief but an inner resonance—a knowing that transcends the intellect. Just as the vast ocean cannot be contained in a single wave, saints cannot be defined by mere words. They are embodiments of divine grace, illuminating the path for those who seek truth. Faith in them is akin to surrendering to the infinite, allowing oneself to be carried by the current of divine wisdom.

Disciples: Who was the mystic who embodied these qualities, Swamy?

Swamy: In every era, there arises a soul who walks among us yet remains untouched by worldly illusions. One such being was born into wealth and privilege but chose renunciation over riches, wisdom over comfort. This extraordinary soul was none other than the beloved Master Dr. Chandrashekar Kaipa, who later embraced the path of monkhood as Swami Sri Vidyanarayana Thirtha. His journey was not of abandonment but of realization—a transition from the fleeting to the eternal.

Disciples: Swamy, can you tell us about your birth and early life?

Swamy: I was born in a sacred land on the eastern coast of Andhra Pradesh, a region graced by the presence of Siddhapurushas (enlightened beings). My arrival was more than a birth—it was an unfolding of cosmic intent. My maternal grandfather, a retired ICS officer, sought the blessings of the great Avadhuta Sri Venkaya Swamy of Nellore. Upon hearing of my birth, the holy sage smiled and uttered, *"Oh... Oh... Oh... A luminous pearl has emerged from the shell. Good... Good... Go... Go... and attend to the work."* Thus, I was named Chandrashekar Kaipu.

Disciples: Swamy, how did you grow up during your early years?

Swamy: My early life was privileged, disciplined, and refined. I was nurtured with the utmost care by Smt. Rathnabai Aaya is a woman of immense kindness. Shielded from hardship, my world was one of ease and comfort. My parents were influential figures—politicians and tea estate owners—deeply engaged in their affairs. But it was my paternal grandfather, Justice K.S., a retired judge of the Madras High Court, who played a defining role in shaping my early years. His wisdom was my first glimpse into the world beyond material existence. My loving grandparents were my anchors, offering not just affection but timeless teachings.

Disciples: Swamy, how did you perform in your early education?

Swamy: Though I lived amidst luxury, life had already begun revealing the stark contrasts of human existence. I was admitted to the prestigious Bishop Cotton School in Bangalore in 1954, an institution modelled after the esteemed Eton Bishop School in the UK. Academically, I soared—topping my class, receiving a double promotion from the 5th to the 7th standard, and completing my Senior Cambridge between 1964 and 1965.

Disciples: Were you always focused on spiritual matters, Swamy?

Swamy: Not consciously. My intellect thrived, yet the deeper purpose of my life remained veiled. The world I knew was one of grandeur, yet an inner yearning, an unspoken pull, persisted. My grandfather's spiritual guidance kept my spirit grounded. My home was a meeting place for some of the greatest minds—President Dr. S. Radhakrishnan, Prime Minister Lal Bahadur Shastri, and other luminaries blessed me with their wisdom. My father, late R.K. Rao, was a Member of Parliament, yet I never felt drawn to political life. Instead, I cherished the warmth of my grandparents, their teachings, and the quiet strength of devotion.

Disciples: Did any other spiritual figures influence your early life, Swamy?

Swamy: Many. Between 1963 and 1973, an elderly sage from the Reddy community, known for his mystical insights, became a guiding presence in my life. He blessed me often, shaping my understanding of the unseen. Our home was graced by Shankara and Madhva saints, whose words carried the weight of timeless wisdom. I was also blessed by towering spiritual figures—Swami Sivananda, Swami Chinmayananda, and Sri Sri Prabhupada, the visionary behind ISKCON. The great scholar Sri Veda Brahma Anantharama Dixitar instilled in me the power of divine names, urging me to chant Lord Rama's name and delve into the depths of the Vishnusahasranama.

Disciples: How did music play a role in your life, Swamy?

Swamy: Music was not just an art for me—it was devotion, an offering of the soul. Under the tutelage of the legendary Sri Semmangudi Srinivasa Iyer, I immersed myself in the celestial compositions of Thyagaraja, Purandaradasa, and Muthuswami Dikshitar. Their music was not mere melody; it was a sacred bridge to the divine.

Disciples: Swamy, what was your life like between 1950 and 1965?

Swamy: It was a life of royalty, discipline, and dignity, untouched by hardship. But destiny had other plans. I pursued medicine at the esteemed School of Medicine in Manipal, where I excelled, completing my MBBS with distinction. Teaching became second nature—I imparted knowledge of chemistry, biology, and English to my juniors. My dream was to heal, to serve as a doctor, and so I continued my studies, specializing in General Medicine while mentoring undergraduate students.

Disciples: Swamy, was there a turning point in your life that shifted your focus?

Swamy: Yes. The tides of destiny are often unseen, but when they arrive, they leave no room for doubt. My journey was about to take an irreversible turn—one that would strip away the illusion of the material world and lead me to the boundless expanse of the spiritual realm. What awaited me was not an end, but a beginning...

The Mystic Prince – Part 2:

Disciples: Swamy, could you share with us the defining moment when your life took a spiritual turn?

Swamy: In 1970, after completing my postgraduate medical exams, I stood on the precipice of a promising career, one that the world eagerly awaited me to step into. The expectations were clear: I was to be a doctor, a healer of the body. But within me, there lingered an insistent sense of emptiness, a quiet unrest. No matter how much I learned, no matter how many lives I helped, my soul felt unfulfilled. I began to question: what is the true essence of life? Is success truly found in worldly accomplishments, or is there a deeper, hidden truth awaiting discovery? During this internal turmoil, a divine experience unfolded, reshaping my destiny forever.

Disciples: Swamy, could you elaborate on this transformative divine experience?

Swamy: The turning point arrived during a solitary pilgrimage to the Himalayas. Surrounded by towering peaks and enveloped in sacred silence, I found a sanctuary for my restless soul. In deep meditation, a profound stillness enveloped me. It was not a mere absence of sound, but a presence—a surge of divine energy that communicated beyond words, unveiling an eternal truth. In that moment, I felt myself dissolve into something vast, boundless, and radiant. The illusions of the material world faded into nothingness, and the realization struck me—I was not merely a physician for the body, but a seeker of the infinite, called to heal through wisdom, not just medicine. That experience marked the true beginning of my spiritual journey.

Disciples: Swamy, did this realization lead you to renounce your medical career?

Swamy: Yes. Medicine had taught me how to diagnose the ailments of the body, but this experience revealed to me the root of human suffering: our separation from the divine. Despite years of rigorous training, I came to understand that no physical cure could heal the emptiness within. The realization was not one of rejection, but transcendence. I saw my true purpose—not in practicing medicine, but in guiding souls toward inner healing, toward the eternal truth. And so, I chose the path of renunciation, surrendering my medical profession to embrace a life dedicated to spiritual service.

Disciples: Swamy, was this decision difficult for you?

Swamy: The mind resists change, and the world questions every step, but the soul knows. Initially, the decision was heavy upon my heart. Years of study, the expectations of family and society, the security of a respected career—all of these weighed on me. But when the soul hears the divine call, everything else pales in comparison. The voice of the eternal is far louder than the noise of the world. When I finally surrendered, I felt an immense sense of liberation—as though a great burden had been lifted. In letting go of the material ties, I became one with the universe. The world became my home, my teacher, and my guide.

Disciples: What challenges did you face after renouncing everything, Swamy?

Swamy: Renunciation is not about abandoning possessions but transcending the self. The greatest challenge lay not in the external world, but within—battling the ego, the attachments, and the lingering doubts. In the beginning, there were moments of hardship—solitude, uncertainty, and the test of detachment. Yet, the divine always provides. The more I surrendered, the more grace flowed into my life. Every hardship became a lesson, every difficulty an opportunity for deeper realization. I wandered sacred lands, met enlightened sages, and learned that selfless service is the highest form of devotion. In surrender, I found strength; in simplicity, I found abundance; in service, I found my true purpose.

Disciples: Swamy, how did you begin your journey as a spiritual teacher?

Swamy: The journey of a teacher begins as a disciple. After renouncing my medical career, I became a seeker, travelling across India to learn from great saints and immerse myself in the timeless wisdom of the scriptures. Every moment of silence and word of wisdom from the enlightened deepened my understanding. But knowledge alone is not enough—it must be lived, shared, and experienced. Gradually, people began seeking my guidance, drawn not by my words, but by the truth I had been blessed to receive. The universe orchestrated the next step, and I became a humble servant, sharing the light I had received and helping others navigate their own spiritual journeys.

Disciples: Swamy, how did you come to be known as Sri Vidyanarayana Thirtha?

Swamy: Names are vessels, carrying the essence they represent. Along this path, I was blessed to receive the guidance of many revered saints. One such master, seeing the depth of my devotion to wisdom and truth, bestowed upon me the name Sri Vidyanarayana Thirtha. 'Vidya' means knowledge—both worldly and transcendental. 'Narayana' represents the supreme source, the infinite consciousness that permeates all. And 'Thirtha' refers to the sacred river of wisdom that purifies all who seek its waters. This name is not an identity but a reminder—that my life's purpose is to bridge knowledge and divine realization.

Disciples: Swamy, what do you consider to be the key to a spiritual life?

Swamy: The key to a spiritual life is not found in rituals, renunciation, or knowledge. It lies in awareness. True spirituality is the art of perceiving the divine in all things, of living with an open heart and a mind free from illusion. It is about transcending the ego—not by fleeing the world, but by living within it with wisdom, love, and compassion. A spiritual life is not about withdrawal but harmony—aligning oneself with the universe's rhythm. The real question is not whether one should renounce the world but whether one can transcend attachment while still being part of it.

Disciples: Swamy, how do we begin our own spiritual journey?

Swamy: Begin where you are, with what you have. The journey is not about reaching distant lands—it is about turning inward. Cultivate awareness in every breath, every thought, every action. Meditate not just in silence, but in every moment of life. Serve others, for in their happiness, you will find your own. Seek wisdom—not for the sake of knowledge, but to dissolve ignorance. And above all, surrender. Surrender your doubts, your fears, and your false identities. The divine is not separate from you; it is you. Walk this path with humility, love, and unwavering faith, and the universe will reveal the way.

The Mystic Prince – Part 3:

Disciples: Swamy, what was your next step after establishing yourself as a spiritual teacher?

Swamy: After stepping into my role as a spiritual teacher, I embarked on journeys across India, spreading the teachings of great saints and sages. I immersed myself in profound philosophical study and spiritual practices, diving into the mysteries of the universe and the nature of reality. This period of deep contemplation transformed my understanding of the divine, enriching my capacity to guide others on their own spiritual paths. I began to help my disciples discover peace and purpose, allowing them to awaken to their higher selves.

Disciples: Swamy, what is the role of a guru in the life of a disciple?

Swamy: A guru is not just a teacher; a true guru embodies the divine truth in every aspect of their being. The guru's role is to guide the disciple on the path of self-realization, illuminating the way through life's challenges. A guru dispels ignorance and shows the disciple how to achieve inner peace and enlightenment. The relationship between guru and disciple is sacred, built on trust, love, and mutual respect. Through the guru's grace, a disciple awakens to their true nature, which is the gateway to spiritual liberation.

Disciples: Swamy, how can we overcome the distractions of the material world?

Swamy: Overcoming distractions is a gradual and conscious process. The key lies in cultivating inner peace and practising self-discipline. Through regular meditation, reflection, and mindfulness, we can centre our minds and reduce distractions. Detach from worldly desires and focus on your spiritual purpose. Remember, true happiness comes not from material possessions but from realizing your essence. Let go of the illusions that bind you, and allow the light of truth to guide you inward.

Disciples: Swamy, what is your message to the world today?

Swamy: My message is simple yet profound: Seek the truth within yourself. Understand that you are not separate from the divine but a part of it. Live with compassion, humility, and wisdom. Serve others selflessly; in doing so, you will discover the peace and fulfilment you seek. The world is in desperate need of love, understanding, and harmony. Our collective responsibility is to create a world that reflects divine qualities such as truth, kindness, and compassion.

Disciples: Swamy, what do you see as the future of humanity?

Swamy: The future of humanity is tied to the awakening of each individual's divine nature. As more people realize their true essence, the world will shift towards peace, love, and unity. Spiritual awakening is the key to overcoming the challenges we face today. By embracing collective wisdom and compassion, we can create a world where all beings live in harmony, not only with each other but with the earth as well.

The Mystic Prince – Part 4:

Disciples: Swamy, you often speak of the importance of selfless service. Could you elaborate on why it is so crucial?

Swamy: Selfless service is the heart of true spirituality. When we serve without expecting anything in return, we transcend the ego and experience the unity of all beings. Service allows us to detach from our desires and connect with the whole. Through selfless action, we experience the divine presence in every encounter and task. The more we serve, the more we purify our hearts and grow spiritually, for service is a path to divinity itself.

Disciples: Swamy, what role do prayer and meditation play in the life of a devotee?

Swamy: Prayer and meditation are fundamental to spiritual growth. Prayer expresses gratitude, seeks guidance, and strengthens our connection with the divine. Meditation, on the other hand, quiets the mind, allowing us to transcend thoughts and connect with our true self. Both practices are essential in cultivating mindfulness, clarity, and deeper understanding. They are tools that help us maintain our inner peace and keep us anchored in the divine presence at all times.

Disciples: Swamy, how can we deal with negative emotions like anger and jealousy?

Swamy: Negative emotions arise when we are disconnected from our true self. The key to overcoming them is self-awareness and mindfulness. When anger or jealousy arise, observe them without judgment and try to understand their root cause. These emotions stem from attachment, fear, and insecurity. By cultivating compassion, patience, and acceptance, we can transform these emotions into opportunities for spiritual growth. Through regular meditation, self-reflection, and prayer, we detach from these lower energies and return to peace.

Disciples: Swamy, you often emphasize the importance of wisdom. How can one cultivate true wisdom?

Swamy: True wisdom arises from deep inner awareness and self-reflection. It cannot be acquired solely from books or external sources; it must be experienced first-hand through spiritual practice. Wisdom grows when we understand life's impermanence and recognise all beings' interconnectedness. It comes when we align our lives with truth, free from ego and desires. To cultivate wisdom, be humble, open to learning, and receptive to divine guidance.

Disciples: Swamy, what advice would you give to someone who is just beginning their spiritual journey?

Swamy: Approach your journey with patience and humility. Spiritual growth is not immediate but a gradual unfolding that requires consistent practice. Begin with a daily routine of prayer, meditation, and reflection. Surround yourself with like-minded individuals who can support and inspire you along the way. Understand that the journey is not about perfection but about progress. Be kind to yourself and stay committed to your practice, for every step you take brings you closer to the divine.

Disciples: Swamy, do you believe that all paths lead to the same ultimate truth?

Swamy: Yes, all paths ultimately lead to the same truth—the realization of the divine within. The external forms of spiritual practices may differ, but the essence of every true path is the same: to awaken to our true nature and unite with the divine. Whether through devotion, knowledge, or meditation, the ultimate goal remains self-realization and divine union. All paths are valid, and we must honour and respect each one as a way to reach the ultimate truth.

Disciples: Swamy, how can we find peace in the midst of chaos and uncertainty in the world?

Swamy: Peace is found within. When we are rooted in our true self, we are undisturbed by external circumstances. In times of chaos, detach from the noise of the world and turn inward. Practices like meditation, prayer, and mindfulness can help you remain centred amidst any storm. When you realize that everything in this world is temporary and that your essence is eternal, you can face life's challenges with equanimity and inner peace.

Disciples: Swamy, what is your vision for the future of spirituality?

Swamy: The future of spirituality lies in the awakening of human consciousness. As more individuals seek the divine within, the world will become more peaceful and harmonious. Spirituality will no longer be seen as separate from daily life but will be integrated into every aspect of existence. It is a future where wisdom, compassion, and love guide every action—where the material and spiritual coexist in harmony. It will be a world where the welfare of all beings is prioritized and where divine truth leads the way.

The Mystic Prince – Part 5

Disciples: Swamy, you often speak of the importance of love and compassion. How can we cultivate these qualities in our daily lives?

Swamy: Love and compassion are not qualities that are acquired; they are the essence of our true nature. To nurture them, we must first recognize the interconnectedness of all beings. Every action we take should reflect the light of kindness and empathy. When you see someone in pain, reach out without hesitation; when you witness joy, share it wholeheartedly. Patience, forgiveness, and humility act as the soil in which these virtues take root. When we serve others with an open heart, love and compassion blossom naturally.

Disciples: Swamy, what is the role of faith in spiritual practice?

Swamy: Faith is the very bedrock of spiritual growth. It is the unwavering trust in the divine, in forces greater than ourselves. Without faith, the spiritual path becomes a labyrinth with no direction. Faith is the fuel that keeps us moving forward through the storms of doubt. It is the invisible thread that connects us to the divine and provides the strength to persevere, even when the journey seems long and difficult. Through faith, we unlock divine grace, which guides us through every step of our path.

Disciples: Swamy, how can we overcome the fear of death?

Swamy: Fear of death comes from ignorance of our true nature. The body is a temporary vessel, but the soul is eternal. When we understand that we are not the body, but the unchanging essence within, death no longer holds any terror. It is not an end, but a transition—a change of form. By contemplating the eternal, we learn to live fearlessly, embracing life with full awareness of its impermanence. In the light of this understanding, death becomes a release, not something to fear.

Disciples: Swamy, can you share your thoughts on the importance of silence?

Swamy: Silence is the gateway to the deepest realms of spirituality. In silence, we connect with our inner self and the divine. The world around us is filled with noise, but it is only in stillness that we can hear the subtle whispers of wisdom. Silence is not mere absence of sound; it is the presence of peace. In moments of quiet, we quiet the mind, clear away distractions, and make space for the divine to speak to us. It is through silence that we find clarity, and in that clarity, we touch the profound mysteries of existence.

Disciples: Swamy, how can we apply your teachings in our everyday life?

Swamy: My teachings are not mere words; they are practices to be woven into the very fabric of your daily life. Begin by cultivating mindfulness in every action, no matter how small. Be present in every moment, aware of the impact of your thoughts, words, and deeds. Live with compassion, humility, and love. Seek opportunities to serve others without expectation. Practice gratitude for the simple blessings you have, and align your actions with your highest truth. When you make these practices part of your life, you will find transformation unfolding naturally, leading you to a life of peace, joy, and divine connection.

The Mystic Prince – Part 6

Disciples: Swamy, you speak often of integrity. How can we live an authentic life?

Swamy: Integrity is the alignment of your thoughts, words, and actions with your highest values. To live authentically, one must first come to know one's true self—one's strengths, weaknesses, and desires. Authenticity arises from self-awareness and an unwavering commitment to truth. It is living in harmony with your soul's calling rather than conforming to external pressures. When you act with integrity, there is no internal conflict; your heart is at peace. Authenticity brings clarity, freedom, and strength, allowing you to navigate life confidently and gracefully.

Disciples: Swamy, why is discipline essential on the spiritual path?

Swamy: Discipline is the bridge between aspiration and realization. Without discipline, our minds become scattered, and we lose focus. Spiritual growth demands regular practice, focus, and consistency.

Discipline helps us master the mind and keeps us on the path despite the distractions of the material world. It is through discipline that we build the inner strength needed to face challenges. Just as a tree requires a strong trunk to withstand the wind, our spiritual practice requires discipline to create stability and sustain progress.

Disciples: Swamy, how can we detach from material desires without becoming indifferent?

Swamy: Detachment is not renunciation of life but liberation from the attachments that bind us. It is the ability to enjoy life fully without clinging to outcomes. Detachment is a recognition that true happiness lies not in external possessions or achievements but in the inner peace that comes from living in the present moment. It does not mean indifference but a wise perspective that sees the impermanence of material things. When we detach from desires, we free ourselves from their control, finding peace in the simplicity of being.

Disciples: Swamy, how can we overcome loneliness?

Swamy: Loneliness arises when we see ourselves as separate from others. In truth, we are all interconnected, part of a vast web of existence. The divine presence is within and around us, and it is in this divine connection that we find true companionship. To overcome loneliness, we must turn inward, recognizing that our soul is never alone. Meditation, service, and connecting with like-minded individuals can help ease feelings of isolation. The key is cultivating a deep relationship with your higher self and seeing the divine in all those around you.

Disciples: Swamy, how do we handle setbacks and failures on the spiritual path?

Swamy: Setbacks and failures are not roadblocks; they are stepping stones to growth. Every challenge you face is an opportunity to learn, to refine your character, and to deepen your spiritual understanding. When you encounter difficulties, don't resist them. Embrace them with patience, for they are part of the divine plan. Remember, every failure is temporary, and it carries the seed of wisdom. A true spiritual seeker never gives up. Setbacks are simply detours on the path to success, helping you build the resilience needed to progress further.

Disciples: Swamy, what role does gratitude play in the spiritual journey?

Swamy: Gratitude is one of the most powerful spiritual practices. It shifts our focus from lack to abundance, from what we don't have to what we do have. A heart full of gratitude is a heart that is at peace, for it recognizes the divine presence in every moment, no matter how small. Gratitude brings us closer to the divine because it opens our hearts to the blessings we have received, whether they come in the form of love, challenges, or guidance. By practising gratitude, we align ourselves with the flow of divine grace.

Disciples: Swamy, you often speak of surrender. What does it mean to surrender to the divine?

Swamy: Surrender is not about weakness or giving up but about releasing the illusion of control. To surrender is to accept that a greater plan is unfolding, one that is always for our highest good. It is an act of trust and humility, recognizing that we are instruments of the divine. Surrender does not mean passivity but the willingness to align our will with the divine will. When we surrender, we stop resisting and allow ourselves to flow with life, trusting that everything is unfolding exactly as it should. In this surrender, we find peace, freedom, and divine guidance.

Disciples: Swamy, how can we find purpose in our lives?

Swamy: Purpose is not something we chase externally; it is something that emerges from within. To find your purpose, you must first understand who you truly are and how you can serve others. Purpose arises when you align your actions with your highest values and the divine plan. It is found in the small, everyday acts of kindness, love, and service. When you live with compassion and selflessness, purpose naturally manifests in your life. Your true purpose is revealed when you connect deeply with the divine and live in harmony with the greater whole.

Disciples: Swamy, how can we strengthen our relationship with God?

Swamy: Strengthening our relationship with God requires devotion, sincerity, and constant remembrance. It is cultivated through prayer, meditation, and selfless service. The more we focus on the divine presence in our lives, the stronger our connection becomes. It is important to see the divine in all things—within yourself, in others, and in nature. God is not distant but present in every aspect of life. By living with humility, love, and gratitude, we deepen our relationship with God and experience the divine in every moment of our existence.

UNIVERSAL TRUTHS

Universal truths are not written—they are realized in the depths of silence.
They do not change with time, for they are beyond time, beyond mind.
Truth is not bound by belief, nor confined to words—it simply is.
To see the truth, one must unsee the illusion, dissolving the self in the infinite.
The one who lives in truth is neither seeker nor knower, but truth itself."

– His Holiness Sri Vidyanarayana Theertha

CHAPTER-14

THE ESSENCE OF TRUTH: MERGING SCIENCE AND SPIRITUALITY

<u>A Discourse with His Holiness Sri Vidyanarayana Theertha</u>

In a world that is increasingly defined by rapid technological advancements and scientific breakthroughs, the pursuit of spirituality often takes a backseat. Yet, as His Holiness Sri Vidyanarayana Theertha so wisely teaches, the true meaning of life cannot be understood through science alone; it requires the depth of spiritual insight.

The modern world often perceives science and spirituality as opposing forces—science is grounded in logic, reason, and empirical evidence, while spirituality focuses on faith, inner experience, and transcendence. However, His Holiness asserts that these two realms are not at odds but complement each other in the quest for truth. Science addresses the *how* of the universe, explaining its mechanics, while spirituality addresses the *why*, offering purpose and meaning beyond the material.

Sri Vidyanarayana Theertha invites us to see that it is only through the fusion of scientific understanding and spiritual wisdom that humanity can achieve a complete understanding of the self and the cosmos. He often quotes, "True knowledge is not the mere accumulation of facts; it is the awakening of the soul through insight and experience."

Question and Answer: Bridging Science with Spirituality

Q: How can one reconcile the findings of modern science with the wisdom of spirituality in daily life?

His Holiness responds, "Science explains the *how* of the universe—how nature operates and how life functions. Spirituality explains the *why*—why we exist and what our purpose is. Both must be woven together to form a complete fabric of understanding."

This fusion is essential not only for intellectual growth but for personal transformation. Modern science tells us how the universe operates, while spiritual teachings provide us with a roadmap to navigate this vast existence. It is through the convergence of these two forces that we find balance and harmony.

Q: What role does spirituality play in achieving mental and emotional well-being?

Sri Vidyanarayana Theertha answers, "Spirituality is the means to inner peace. Science may explain how stress affects the body, but it is through spiritual practices like meditation and mindfulness that we can heal and find tranquillity."

Modern science mirrors the significance of this teaching. Research has shown that mindfulness and meditation—rooted in spiritual traditions—can reduce stress, improve concentration, and even enhance physical health. By cultivating inner peace through spiritual practices, we can counterbalance the pressures and stressors of modern life, leading to greater emotional well-being.

Insights and Takeaways: Integrating Science and Spirituality

1. **Science of Meditation:**
   - Spiritual practices like meditation, passed down through generations, are now backed by scientific research confirming

their benefits in reducing stress and enhancing emotional stability. Meditation not only calms the mind but also has tangible effects on brain structure and function, leading to improved mental health.

2. **The Healing Power of Spirituality:**

   - Science has long acknowledged the connection between the mind and the body. The spiritual practice of self-reflection and awareness strengthens this mind-body connection. Studies show positive mental states, such as gratitude and forgiveness, can enhance physical health and improve overall well-being.

3. **The Role of Consciousness:**

   - Consciousness, a key theme in spirituality, is also a subject of scientific inquiry. Neuroscientists are increasingly exploring how consciousness affects cognition and behaviour. Spiritual practices that foster heightened awareness, such as deep meditation, have been shown to enhance cognitive function and promote mental clarity.

4. **Science and Spirituality in Harmony:**

   - True wisdom is achieved when we integrate scientific knowledge with spiritual insight. Science teaches us how to live longer, healthier lives; spirituality teaches us how to live more meaningful lives. Together, they guide us towards a holistic understanding of existence, helping us not only to survive but to thrive.

Challenges to Overcome: Navigating the Modern World with Wisdom

1. **The Disconnection from Nature:**

   - In today's digital age, many people have become disconnected from nature. Sri Vidyanarayana Theertha advises, "Reconnect with nature, for it is through nature that we connect with the divine." Science has shown that time spent in natural surroundings can reduce stress and improve mental health, yet modern lifestyles often isolate individuals from the natural world.

2. **Materialism vs. Spirituality:**

   o The overwhelming focus on material success often leads individuals to neglect their spiritual growth. His Holiness reminds us, "Material wealth is transient, but spiritual wealth is eternal." While science helps us understand the material world, it is through spirituality that we learn to navigate the inner dimensions of our existence and find lasting fulfilment.

3. **Mindset and Perception:**

   o Negative thought patterns can cloud our judgment and reduce our quality of life. Spiritual practices like mindfulness and self-reflection provide tools to break free from these patterns. Scientific studies have shown that changing one's mindset can improve mental health, demonstrating the powerful intersection of science and spirituality.

Conclusion: A Unified Path Forward

The teachings of Sri Vidyanarayana Theertha guide us towards a path that harmonizes science and spirituality. In today's fast-paced world, we mustn't view these two domains as separate or contradictory but rather as complementary forces that work together to enhance our understanding of the universe and our place within it.

His Holiness beautifully states, "When knowledge and wisdom unite when the scientific and the spiritual are woven together, we transcend the limitations of the mind and experience the boundless potential of the soul." This integration of science and spirituality is not just a lofty ideal but a practical approach that leads to inner peace, personal growth, and a more harmonious world.

By embracing both scientific knowledge and spiritual wisdom, we embark on a journey of holistic growth, transforming ourselves and the world around us. This is the true path to enlightenment—a path where science and spirituality walk hand in hand.

CHAPTER-15

THE DIVINE INCARNATION: UNVEILING THE NATURE OF DIVINE BIRTHS

Introduction

In every era, divine incarnations emerge, not as mere coincidences but as profound cosmic events. These souls, chosen by the divine, are born with a singular purpose: to guide humanity toward truth, love, and enlightenment. Their lives serve as eternal beacons, illuminating the path for those seeking spiritual awakening. These divine personalities are often not  understood by the masses during their lifetimes, yet their impact is timeless, transcending generations.

One such divine soul is His Holiness Sri Vidyanarayana Theertha, a living embodiment of love, wisdom, and divine grace. Swamiji's extraordinary life story is a reflection of the divine plan, an intricate weave of experiences that have shaped him into the compassionate and enlightened guide that he is today. A doctor by profession, a philosopher by spirit, and a yogi by essence, Swamiji's journey is not merely about spiritual growth but about a deep transformation—one that transcends the physical world and touches the very core of the soul.

Swamiji's spiritual journey mirrors the essence of many divine avatars. Like Sai Baba, who transcended all boundaries and embraced all beings with love and compassion, Swamiji, too, has inspired countless individuals. His teachings, deeply rooted in the timeless wisdom of Sanatana Dharma, encourage us to rise above ego and desires and to live in harmony with our higher selves. Swamiji's presence continues to touch lives, leading all who come to him with devotion and faith toward spiritual liberation.

A Divine Dialogue: Reflections on Swamiji's Teachings

Q: What makes His Holiness Sri Vidyanarayana Theertha unique as a spiritual guide?

A: Swamiji embodies the highest qualities of love, wisdom, and compassion. Much like Sai Baba, his teachings transcend distinctions, urging us to recognize the divinity within all beings. His spiritual guidance is not just for the intellectual but for the heart and soul, helping each individual find their way back to their true divine nature.

Q: Why are Swamiji's teachings sometimes difficult to comprehend?

A: Divine wisdom often surpasses human intellect. Swamiji's teachings, rooted in eternal truths, require humility, faith, and deep devotion to understanding. His insights, though simple, are profound and require surrender to grasp their depth fully. True understanding comes when we let go of our ego and approach with an open heart.

Q: What is the significance of Swamiji's statement, "Time is the answer, and the answer is time"?

A: This statement reflects the divine orchestration of the universe. Swamiji teaches that patience and trust in divine timing are essential for spiritual growth. Though desires may arise, the divine plan unfolds at the perfect moment. This teaches us to trust that everything will happen when the soul is truly ready to receive it.

Q: How has Swamiji's life journey influenced his spiritual mission?

A: Swamiji's early life, marked by privilege and abundance, provided him with a rich foundation, but it was his transformative spiritual awakening at the age of 24 that set him on the path of selfless service. Meeting great souls like Dr. Sarvepalli Radhakrishnan, MS Subbulakshmi, Ananta Rama Dikshitar, and others deepened his understanding and reinforced his divine purpose—to lead humanity back to truth.

Q: How does a doctor with an MD choose to take sannyasa?

A: Swamiji's transition from a doctor of medicine to a sannyasi reflects his deeper understanding of the limitations of the material world. His experiences as a physician, where he witnessed the fragility of human life, awakened him to the higher calling of healing souls and guiding them toward spiritual liberation.

Q: What qualities does Swamiji emphasize for spiritual growth?

A: Swamiji's teachings emphasize the importance of patience, trust, humility, and love. He guides his followers to rise above ego, envy, and worldly desires, encouraging them to cultivate selfless devotion, unconditional love, and unwavering faith in the divine.

Key Takeaways and Insights

- **Patience and Divine Timing:** Trust in the divine plan; blessings come when the soul is prepared. Swamiji's adage, "Time is the answer," teaches us to wait with faith.
- **Universal Love:** Like Sai Baba, Swamiji's embrace transcends boundaries, urging us to love unconditionally.
- **Surrender and Wisdom:** True understanding arises when we relinquish ego and trust the guru's guidance.
- **Resilience Through Trials:** Challenges are divine opportunities to deepen faith and devotion.

- **Living Dharma:** Swamiji's life is a testament to living in alignment with higher principles, radiating love and purpose.

Swamiji's Life Journey: A Story of Divine Renunciation

Swamiji's early life was filled with joys and privileges. Born into a family of great cultural and spiritual heritage, he had the extraordinary opportunity to meet many eminent personalities. Among them were the esteemed Dr. Sarvepalli Radhakrishnan, the revered MS Subbulakshmi, and other influential figures like Ananta Rama Dikshitar, Justice Krishnaswamy, and Kittappa. These encounters helped shape his understanding of life, spirituality, and the deeper purpose of existence.

Swamiji's deep reverence for his parents and grandmother was the foundation of his early development. He always acknowledged the significant role they played in his formative years. His gratitude towards his family was evident, and he often expressed profound respect for their love and guidance. As a young man, Swamiji had the opportunity to pay his respects to great saints such as Prabhupada, Chinmayananda Swami, and Sivananda. These meetings left an indelible mark on Swamiji's spiritual journey.

At the age of 24, after experiencing a profound spiritual awakening, Swamiji chose to renounce his worldly life. This marked the beginning of his journey as a sannyasi, a path dedicated to self-realization and the service of humanity. During his previous ashram life, he was taught the Sandhyavandanam ritual by Ananta Rama Dikshitar, and it was these teachings that further deepened his spiritual connection. In this period, Swamiji also encountered figures like B.V. Narasimha Swami, who introduced Shirdi Sai Baba to the southern region, and learned valuable lessons in humility and devotion.

Swamiji's divine renunciation was a turning point in his life. His earlier experiences of joy, pleasure, and privilege became stepping stones leading him to a higher purpose. He transitioned from being a seeker of worldly happiness to a guide who would help others discover the eternal joy of divine connection.

The Divine Miracles and Healing Presence

Swamiji's life has been marked by numerous divine miracles, echoing the miraculous stories of Sai Baba. He is known to have manifested sacred ash (vibhuti) during prayers, and his ability to intuitively understand the needs of his devotees speaks of his divine connection. His healing presence goes beyond physical ailments, extending to the healing of souls. Swamiji's compassion is boundless, and he is known for embracing people from all walks of life, irrespective of caste, creed, or status.

Through his divine grace, Swamiji guides his followers on the path of spiritual growth, helping them overcome obstacles and embrace their higher purpose. His teachings continue to inspire millions, reminding them that the divine is always with them, guiding them with love and wisdom.

Divine Guidance

Swamiji often shares profound wisdom through his simple yet transformative words, offering us timeless insights that resonate with the core of our being. As a revered guru and torchbearer of Sanatana Dharma, he embodies the spirit of Sai Baba, symbolizing true love, unwavering devotion, and boundless compassion. Swamiji's grace transcends all distinctions of caste, creed, and status, blessing us unconditionally and showering us with divine love. His teachings, though vast and profound, unfold clarity and illumination to those who surrender themselves with an open heart.

"To trust and follow Swamiji's guidance without question is to embrace a path of divine wisdom. He knows the depths of our soul and understands our innermost needs. The blessings He bestows are not always immediate, but they come in the perfect divine moment, attuned to the rhythm of the universe. Let us rise above jealousy and ego, embracing humility and cultivating unwavering faith in His wisdom. Remember his words: 'Time is the answer, and the answer is time.' It is in the divine timing of things that all is revealed. Let us surrender ourselves at His holy feet, aligning with the divine and walking the sacred path of love, devotion, and wisdom."

Conclusion: The Path of Devotion and Wisdom

Swamiji's life stands as a luminous example of divine grace in action, a living testament to the power of love and devotion. His teachings illuminate the path to eternal truth, guiding us toward the realization that the divine resides within us all. As a living embodiment of love,  humility, and wisdom, Swamiji offers us the path of surrender—an invitation to trust in His guidance, cultivate patience, and embrace the unfolding of life with devotion. His connection with Shirdi Sai Baba reflects the timeless lineage of pure devotion that transcends generations.

Let us bow humbly at Swamiji's lotus feet, embracing His teachings with a heart full of love and reverence. By aligning ourselves with His divine guidance, we embark on a journey toward inner peace, purpose, and fulfilment, realizing that we are part of the greater cosmic plan. Through devotion and wisdom, we are elevated to a state of harmony with the divine, fulfilling our highest potential in service to the greater good.

CHAPTER-16

UNITY OF ALL PATHS: THE UNIVERSAL JOURNEY TO TRUTH

Introduction

In a world filled with different religions, philosophies, and spiritual practices, it's easy to perceive divisions. However, beneath the surface of every belief system lies an underlying unity—a common truth that connects all paths. His Holiness Sri Vidyanarayana Theertha teaches that while the practices and outward forms may vary, they all ultimately lead to the same divine truth. Just as rivers, though they flow in different directions, eventually merge into the ocean, all spiritual paths, despite their differences, converge at the same ultimate reality. This profound teaching encourages us to embrace unity and respect the various ways in which the divine is experienced and expressed.

Disciple: *Swamiji, is it true that all spiritual paths lead to the same truth?*

Swamy:

Yes, all paths lead to the same truth, just as many rivers flow toward the same ocean. The outward forms and rituals of different religions may differ, but the core truth remains the same. Think of the sun—its rays may touch the earth in many different ways, but it is the same sun that shines on all. Similarly, whether one practices meditation, prayer, or selfless service, the ultimate goal is to experience the same divine presence.

Disciple: *Swamiji, are different spiritual practices just different expressions of the same truth?*

Swamy:

Exactly. Each spiritual practice is a unique expression of the same divine reality. Consider the example of music—there are many instruments, but the same melody can be played on each. Similarly, different practices like chanting, yoga, or devotion are simply different instruments through which one can experience the divine. Just as a river may have different paths but still lead to the same ocean, each spiritual practice, no matter how different it may seem, is just a different expression of the infinite divine.

Disciple: *Swamiji, should we respect all spiritual paths even if they seem different from ours?*

Swamy:

Absolutely. Respecting all spiritual approaches is essential. Each path is valid in its own right, just as every tree in a forest is unique, yet all contribute to the overall health of the forest. Different paths suit different temperaments and backgrounds. For instance, one person may find peace in the teachings of the Buddha, while another may find it in devotion to Lord Krishna. Both paths, though different, lead to the same ultimate truth. It is like different roads leading to the same destination—each one is valid and valuable.

Disciple: *Swamiji, does the unity of all religions reflect the universality of truth?*

Swamy:

Indeed. The unity of all religions reflects the universality of truth. Truth is not confined to any one belief system or culture. It transcends boundaries, much like the sky that covers the entire world. Whether one calls the divine by the name of Allah, God, or the Supreme Being, the essence of the divine is the same. It is the same divine energy that pervades all creation. The outward forms may differ, but the truth they point to is universal and eternal.

Disciple: *Swamiji, is the truth the same regardless of the outward forms of religion?*

Swamy:

Yes, truth remains the same, regardless of the outward forms. Think of the example of a diamond—its value does not change depending on the shape or cut. Similarly, the truth is one, though expressed through different forms. A person may approach truth through the path of knowledge (jnana yoga), devotion (bhakti yoga), or selfless action (karma yoga), yet all are seeking the same divine reality. The essence of the divine is not altered by how we choose to approach it.

Disciple: *Swamiji, can you explain how each path is a unique expression of the infinite divine?*

Swamy:

Each path is indeed a unique expression of the infinite divine. Think of the divine as a vast, limitless ocean, and each path as a wave rising from that ocean. The waves may take different shapes, but they all arise from the same water. Similarly, the infinite divine manifests in various forms and each spiritual path is one such manifestation. Whether one follows the path of devotion, knowledge, or service, they are all expressions of the same divine reality. Like a single tree that bears different fruits, the divine expresses itself uniquely through each path.

Takeaways

- All spiritual paths, despite their differences, lead to the same truth, much like different rivers merging into the same ocean.
- Different spiritual practices are unique expressions of the same divine reality, similar to how different musical instruments can play the same melody.

- Respecting all spiritual paths is important, as each path is valid and suits different temperaments, like the unique trees of a forest contributing to its overall health.
- The unity of all religions reflects the universality of truth, which transcends boundaries, just as the sky covers the entire world.
- Truth remains the same regardless of the outward forms of religion, much like the value of a diamond is not affected by its shape or cut.
- Each spiritual path uniquely expresses the infinite divine, just as waves rise from the same ocean but take different forms.

Conclusion

The wisdom imparted by His Holiness Sri Vidyanarayana Theertha invites us to see unity amidst diversity. In the vast ocean of spiritual practices, each wave, whether large or small, is part of the same water. No matter how varied they seem, all paths ultimately lead to the same divine truth. Just as different instruments play the same song, all spiritual practices are expressions of the same universal reality. Understanding and respecting the unity of all paths is the key to fostering peace, harmony, and spiritual growth. The truth that we seek is not confined to any one tradition but is present in every path that leads us to the divine. Embrace the diversity of spiritual paths, for they all lead to the same ultimate destination: the realization of the eternal truth within.

CHAPTER-17

The Divine Symphony: Unlocking Peace and Transformation through the Vishnu Sahasranama

(A Discourse by His Holiness Sri Vidyanarayana Theertha Swamy)

"Chanting the Vishnu Sahasranama nurtures peace, health, and prosperity, transforming negativity into positivity. It is the divine key to transcend life's challenges and find inner peace."

— *Swamy Sri Vidyanarayana Theertha*

Introduction

In the rapidly changing world of today, where distractions like idle chatter, excessive television watching, and constant use of smartphones dominate our lives, the profound wisdom of Sri Vishnu Sahasranama offers a path to spiritual clarity and peace. His Holiness Sri Vidyanarayana Theertha Swamy, a living embodiment of divine knowledge, shares the transformative power of this sacred text. He highlights how chanting the thousand names of Lord Vishnu can help us reconnect with our higher selves, bring us closer to the divine, and guide us in overcoming the struggles of life. Through His Holiness's teachings, we are reminded of the essential role of spiritual

practices like the Vishnu Sahasranama in nurturing inner peace and aligning our lives with the divine will.

In today's world, where distractions are endless and material pursuits often overshadow spiritual practices, many people find themselves caught in the relentless demands of modern life. With the advent of technology, social pressures, and increasing mental health challenges, we often lose sight of our deeper selves and the wisdom that can guide us through turbulent times. In the midst of this chaos, ancient spiritual practices like the Vishnu Sahasranama stand as an oasis of peace, offering us not just solace but a transformative journey toward inner peace and connection with the divine.

The Vishnu Sahasranama, a thousand sacred names of Lord Vishnu, is not merely a devotional recitation but a powerful tool for personal and spiritual transformation. Each name in this sacred text embodies a divine attribute that offers protection, guidance, and a means to navigate the complexities of life. For those seeking to elevate their spiritual practice or bring calm amidst chaos, the Vishnu Sahasranama offers a roadmap for peace, wisdom, and spiritual awakening.

The Divine Intention Behind Vishnu Sahasranama

The Vishnu Sahasranama, composed by the sage Bhishma on the battlefield of Kurukshetra, holds timeless spiritual significance. In his final moments, lying on a bed of arrows, Bhishma imparted the divine wisdom of Lord Vishnu's thousand sacred names to Yudhishthira. This profound scripture is not merely a prayer; it is a guide to living righteously and a means of connecting with the Supreme Being. The Vishnu Sahasranama encapsulates the essence of the Vedas and Upanishads, offering a comprehensive understanding of Lord Vishnu's divine qualities. Each name reflects His infinite attributes—compassion, protection, justice, and love for all beings—giving devotees a powerful tool for spiritual growth.

His Holiness Sri Vidyanarayana Theertha Swamy explains that the Vishnu Sahasranama is an invitation to dwell on the Supreme Being's attributes, not merely to chant names, but to internalize their deeper meanings and transform our lives. Through the act of reciting these names, we align ourselves with the divine, purifying our minds, hearts, and actions. The practice transcends ritual, offering an accessible way for every seeker to experience the divine presence in their lives.

The Power of Divine Names in Our Lives

The names of Lord Vishnu, when chanted with reverence and profound understanding, carry an immense transformative power. These names are not mere words; they are divine frequencies that align our thoughts, words, and actions with the cosmic rhythm of the universe. Each name encapsulates a sacred attribute of the divine, an aspect of Lord Vishnu that we can invoke to elevate our spiritual awareness and bring about personal and collective transformation.

Let us explore some of these divine names and uncover their profound significance in our lives:

- **Vishvam** (The All-Pervading One): This name serves as a gentle reminder that Lord Vishnu's presence transcends all boundaries. Just as space is all-encompassing and omnipresent, His divine essence pervades every corner of existence. Whether we are in moments of solitude, surrounded by challenges, or grappling with inner struggles, chanting "Vishvam" reassures us that we are never separated from the divine presence. It nurtures the realization that the universe is interwoven with His grace, making us feel eternally connected to the divine.

- **Govinda** (The Protector of the Earth): In today's fast-paced world, where stress, anxiety, and uncertainty often dominate, "Govinda" offers a sense of divine security and protection. This name invokes Lord Vishnu's safeguarding energy, reminding us that despite the chaos around us, we are always in His care. In times of emotional or physical vulnerability, chanting "Govinda" becomes a means to reconnect with our inherent strength and find peace, knowing that we are enveloped in divine protection.

- **Vasudeva** (The Son of Vasudeva, The One Who Dwells in All Beings): "Vasudeva" is a name that draws attention to the interconnectedness of all life forms. By meditating on this divine name, we awaken the consciousness that the divine resides within all beings. It fosters an attitude of compassion, love, and empathy towards others, encouraging us to see beyond superficial divisions and recognize the oneness that binds all existence. In a world fraught with divisions, "Vasudeva" urges us to live in harmony, understanding that the same divine spark resides in every living being.

- **Ananta** (The Infinite): "Ananta" reflects the boundless, eternal nature of the divine. It calls us to transcend the limitations of the material world and to aspire for the infinite. While our lives may be restricted by time, space, and circumstances, chanting "Ananta" helps us focus on the limitless nature of the divine and the infinite potential within ourselves. It reminds us to move beyond the mundane and explore the vastness of spiritual possibility, allowing us to experience freedom from the constraints of worldly attachments.

When these names are chanted with focus, devotion, and understanding, they reverberate through our consciousness, influencing our mental and emotional states. The power of sound, as seen through both ancient wisdom and modern science, has a profound impact on the mind and body. Sound vibrations, particularly when they resonate with divine energy, can alter brain waves, promote healing, and enhance mental clarity. Therefore, chanting the Vishnu Sahasranama is not just a devotional act; it is a holistic practice that aligns our inner world with the divine, helping us become more attuned to spiritual truths and experience inner peace.

Relevance of Vishnu Sahasranama in the Modern World

While the Vishnu Sahasranama is rooted in ancient tradition, its relevance is undiminished in the modern world. In fact, its wisdom is more crucial than ever. Today, as we face unprecedented global challenges—whether it's mental health issues, societal pressures, or existential crises—the teachings embedded in these divine names offer much-needed guidance.

The practice of chanting the Vishnu Sahasranama can help in overcoming stress and anxiety, fostering a sense of inner peace. The rhythmic chanting of the names allows the mind to focus and release distractions, providing a meditative state that is both calming and enlightening. In our fast-paced world, where many feel overwhelmed, the process of reciting these sacred names brings a moment of stillness and reflection.

Moreover, chanting the Vishnu Sahasranama is an exercise in surrender and trust. It reminds us that while we can control certain aspects of our lives, there are many things beyond our comprehension or control. By acknowledging the divine's omnipresence and omnipotence, we learn to trust the unfolding of life, surrendering our ego and finding peace in the divine plan.

The Role of the Guru and Divine Guidance

As with any spiritual practice, the guidance of a guru or spiritual teacher is invaluable in helping us understand the deeper significance of these names and how to integrate them into our lives. A guru helps us interpret the divine wisdom embedded in the names of Vishnu and directs us on how to channel this wisdom for personal and collective transformation.

The guru's role is not just to teach but to empower us to connect directly with the divine, cultivating an inner experience that transcends intellectual understanding. It is through such guidance that we learn not just to chant but to live the essence of the Vishnu Sahasranama.

Vishnu Sahasranama as a Universal Practice

The beauty of the Vishnu Sahasranama is that it transcends religious and cultural boundaries. It is a universal practice that can be embraced by anyone, regardless of their background, seeking inner peace, strength, and wisdom. Whether you are a devout practitioner of Hinduism or simply someone on a quest for spiritual truth, the Vishnu Sahasranama serves as a bridge that connects us to the divine.

In the modern context, it serves not just as a religious ritual but as a holistic practice for mental, emotional, and spiritual well-being. The profound wisdom contained in these thousand names guides us through the complexities of life, offering protection, direction, and clarity.

Scientific and Psychological Insights

The power of sound vibrations in the Vishnu Sahasranama has been affirmed not only in spiritual terms but also by modern science. Recent studies in sound therapy and neuroscience reveal that sound waves have the potential to alter our brainwaves, enhance cognitive function, reduce stress, and improve overall mental health. Chanting the Vishnu Sahasranama with understanding is thus not just a spiritual activity but one that has measurable benefits on our well-being.

The chanting creates a frequency that resonates deeply within us, aligning our thoughts with higher vibrations. This alignment can lead to mental clarity, emotional balance, and a sense of deep connection to the divine. In this way, the Vishnu Sahasranama serves as a practical tool for managing the demands of modern life, especially in an age characterized by stress, anxiety, and constant distraction.

The Timeless Essence of Vishnu Sahasranama

The Vishnu Sahasranama also finds resonance in deeper philosophical contexts such as Vedanta and Sankhya. These philosophies speak of the oneness of all creation, and the divine attributes of Lord Vishnu reflect the same principles. Each name in the Vishnu Sahasranama can be seen as a microcosm of the eternal truth that underlies the universe. By meditating on these names, we align ourselves with the ultimate reality and come closer to realizing our true nature.

Takeaways

- **Timeless Wisdom**: The Vishnu Sahasranama offers universal guidance, transcending religious and cultural boundaries.
- **Spiritual Power**: Chanting the divine names connects us to higher consciousness and purifies the mind.
- **Mental Clarity**: Regular recitation promotes inner peace and mental well-being, reducing stress and anxiety.
- **Divine Attributes**: Each name of Lord Vishnu reflects a unique quality that we can embody in our lives.
- **Holistic Practice**: The Vishnu Sahasranama is not just a prayer, but a comprehensive tool for spiritual growth and personal transformation.
- **Science & Spirit**: Chanting has measurable benefits, with sound vibrations positively influencing brainwaves and emotional health.

Conclusion: Embracing the Divine Names in Our Lives

As we stand at the crossroads of modernity and tradition, the Vishnu Sahasranama offers a pathway to reconnect with the eternal truths that govern the universe. The divine attributes of Lord Vishnu, encapsulated in these thousand names, remind us of the higher potential within ourselves. By embracing this practice, we can bring about a shift in our consciousness, moving from confusion to clarity, from fragmentation to unity, and from chaos to inner peace.

In conclusion, the Vishnu Sahasranama is more than just a devotional recitation; it is a profound tool for self-realization. It is a timeless practice that transcends the ages, offering peace and guidance in a world that often feels disconnected and chaotic. When chanted with devotion, understanding, and the guidance of a guru, these names serve as a powerful reminder of the divine presence that pervades all of existence—bringing light to our journey, no matter where we are on the spiritual path.

CHAPTER-18

MAYA: THE ILLUSION AND DIVINE ENERGY ON THE PATH TO LIBERATION

Introduction

The concept of *Maya*, or illusion, has been integral to Hindu philosophy, offering profound insights into the nature of reality. Traditionally, *Maya* is understood as the veil that distorts our perception of the ultimate truth, often described as the source of the duality we experience in the material world. However, in the teachings of His Holiness Sri Vidyanarayana Theertha Swamy, *Maya* is not merely an illusion  to be renounced but a divine energy to be understood and integrated into spiritual practice. His discourse offers a unique perspective on the dual nature of *Maya*, as both an illusion and a transformative energy, guiding spiritual seekers toward balance, detachment, and surrender. This article explores these teachings and their implications for modern seekers.

Understanding Maya in the Context of Spiritual Growth

In traditional Hindu thought, *Maya* is often seen as the illusion that keeps us trapped in the cycle of birth, death, and rebirth (samsara). It creates a false sense of separateness from the divine and clouds our understanding of the true nature of reality. However, His Holiness Sri

Vidyanarayana Theertha Swamy presents a nuanced view, describing *Maya* as both the void (zero) and Mystic Energy. This dual aspect highlights the paradox that while *Maya* creates an illusion, it is also the energy that can guide one to spiritual realization.

Swamy Vidyanarayana Theertha emphasizes that we should *be near Maya, but be away from Maya.* This instruction invites seekers to engage with the material world, recognizing it as an essential part of our spiritual journey, but without becoming overly attached to it. The key to transcending *Maya* is not in complete rejection of the world but in maintaining a balance between desire (want) and detachment (reject). He teaches that through the practice of *satisfaction*—finding contentment and peace within—one can navigate this delicate balance. The seeker is called to recognize the divine presence in all things, accepting the world as it is, without being consumed by its transient nature.

The practice of *satisfaction* involves cultivating an attitude of contentment, regardless of external circumstances. In doing so, one transcends the need for constant craving or rejection and finds inner peace. This balance between engagement and detachment allows one to experience the world without becoming ensnared by its illusions and, in turn, progress on the spiritual path.

The Path of Surrender and Realization

Swamy Vidyanarayana Theertha further elaborates on the concept of surrender, using the example of a *bachelor* to convey its spiritual significance. In this context, being a *bachelor* means surrendering to the Lord who resides within. It symbolizes a state of purity and detachment, where one relinquishes personal desires and recognizes the divine energy that moves through all creation. According to Swamy Vidyanarayana Theertha, the Lord within "came out from you, enjoyed, suffered, and merged with Mystic Energy," highlighting the inherent connection between the individual and the divine.

This surrender is not a passive act but an active realization of one's true nature. By surrendering to the divine force within, the practitioner acknowledges that the ultimate truth lies beyond the ego and the material world. This understanding leads to liberation from the illusions of *Maya* and a deeper connection with the divine. Surrendering to the Lord within does not imply renunciation of worldly life but rather a transformation in how one perceives and engages with the world. Through this surrender, one becomes attuned to the divine presence in all things, both material and spiritual.

Doctors, Teachers, and the Divine Presence

Swamy Vidyanarayana Theertha also uses the metaphor of doctors, teachers, and students to illustrate the role of divine energy in healing and teaching. In a spiritual sense, he asserts that doctors are embodiments of Mystic Energy, channelling divine wisdom and healing. Teachers, who guide the seeker on the path of knowledge, also function as spiritual doctors, providing the necessary guidance for the student to overcome ignorance and negativity.

In this metaphor, students are seen as patients, not in the physical sense of illness, but as individuals in need of healing from the "disease" of ignorance, desire, and attachment. Negative qualities, such as greed, anger, and attachment, are viewed as patients requiring treatment, while positive qualities, such as wisdom, compassion, and truth, are considered avatars—divine manifestations that help elevate the individual toward spiritual awakening.

By recognizing that all beings are vessels for Mystic Energy, whether they are doctors, teachers, or students, the seeker understands the interconnectedness of all existence. This realization emphasizes that the healer or teacher is not separate from the student but is a channel through which divine energy flows, offering wisdom and healing.

Becoming One with Maya

Swamy Vidyanarayana Theertha concludes his discourse with the profound teaching to *become one with Maya*. To the untrained mind, this might seem contradictory, as *Maya* is often seen as something to transcend or escape. However, in Swamy Vidyanarayana Theertha's teachings, becoming one with *Maya* means recognizing the divine energy within it and understanding that it is both an illusion and a pathway to spiritual realization. The seeker does not reject *Maya*, but embraces it as an integral part of their spiritual journey. By doing so, they come to see the world not as an illusion to be avoided but as a reflection of the divine.

To become one with *Maya* is to transcend the illusion of separation and to embrace the unity that exists between the material and spiritual realms. It signifies a deep awareness that the divine presence pervades everything, and through this understanding, the seeker experiences liberation from the ego and the limitations of the material world. This oneness with *Maya* leads to a profound realization that everything in the universe is interconnected, and the divine resides within all things.

Sai Baba's Divine Connection: Overcoming Maya through the Power of Hari Nama"

Swamy Vidyanarayana Theertha often reflects on the profound teachings of Shirdi Sai Baba, particularly his unique relationship with the divine. Although Baba never married or had a family, he spoke of an unbreakable bond with the divine that transcended all worldly attachments. Despite living a life of renunciation, Sai Baba admitted that he could not forget *Her*—the divine essence, the eternal presence that resides within all.

Swamy Vidyanarayana Theertha explains that for Baba, the only way to remain connected with this divine presence was through the practice of *Hari Nama*. Baba emphasized that the repetition of God's name was not just a spiritual practice but the key to liberation from the illusion of

Maya. Through *Hari Nama*, one could rise above the distractions of the material world and experience the supreme truth.

According to Swamy, Sai Baba's teachings highlighted that true attachment is not to the material world, but to the divine presence within. By surrendering to the sacred name of God, Baba guided his followers to transcend the bonds of *Maya* and attain spiritual realization. In this way, Sai Baba's life and teachings serve as a reminder that the path to liberation is found through devotion, particularly in the constant remembrance of the divine name.

Takeaways

- **Maya as Illusion and Energy**

Maya is both an illusion that veils the truth and a divine energy that can guide the seeker toward spiritual awakening.

- **Balance Between Want and Reject**

Achieving a balance between desire and detachment is key to transcending the effects of *Maya.*

- **Power of Satisfaction**

Practicing *satisfaction* transforms the seeker, fostering peace and contentment despite external circumstances.

- **Surrender to the Divine Within**

Surrendering to the Lord within is the path to spiritual awakening, freeing one from the ego and illusions.

- **Doctors and Teachers as Channels of Mystic Energy**

Embodying Maya as Mystic Energy, doctors and teachers guide seekers toward wisdom and healing.

- **Oneness with Maya**

Becoming one with *Maya* means recognizing the divine presence in all aspects of life, both material and spiritual.

Conclusion

Swamy Vidyanarayana Theertha's teachings on *Maya* offer a transformative perspective on the nature of existence. Rather than rejecting the material world, he invites us to engage with it consciously, finding a balance between desire and detachment through the practice of satisfaction. By surrendering to the Lord within, we transcend the limitations of the ego and the illusions of *Maya*, recognizing the divine presence in all aspects of life. Doctors, teachers, and students, as embodiments of Mystic Energy, guide us toward spiritual growth and healing. Ultimately, by becoming one with *Maya*, we experience the oneness of all existence and attain spiritual liberation. This wisdom, when applied in our daily lives, leads to a deeper connection with the divine and a more harmonious existence within the world.

Chapter-19

The Spiritual Spectrum: Prepaid, Post-paid, and Unlimited Paths to Divine Evolution

Introduction

Spirituality is often viewed as a lifelong journey shaped by numerous stages of growth and self-discovery. To understand this journey, we can look at three key stages: Prepaid, Postpaid, and Unlimited. These stages serve as metaphors, offering insights into the progression of spiritual realization, starting from the initial seeking to the ultimate state of divine union. In today's fast-paced world, where instant gratification often takes precedence, the pursuit of spirituality can sometimes seem like a distant priority.

Many spiritual seekers switch between gurus, beliefs, or practices, hoping for immediate transformation. However, as His Holiness Sri Vidya Narayana Theertha reminds us, true spiritual evolution is not an instant fix but a lifelong journey that requires patience, dedication, and a deep connection with the Divine. Like modern service plans—prepaid, post-paid, and unlimited—spirituality offers distinct paths to self-realization, each guiding us toward divine evolution in different ways.

The Prepaid Path: Preparing for Life's Trials

Prepaid spirituality is the first stage of preparation, where the disciple cultivates inner strength and resilience. Like a soldier training before battle, this stage involves practices such as meditation, prayer, and self-discipline to develop virtues like patience, humility, and wisdom. By nurturing these practices, the disciple becomes equipped to face life's challenges. Lord Rama and Arjuna from the *Ramayana* and *Mahabharata* exemplify prepaid spirituality through their discipline and unwavering commitment to their spiritual practices, preparing them for the trials that lay ahead.

The first stage of spiritual evolution is often described as Prepaid Spirituality. Much like a prepaid plan where one pays in advance for a limited set of services, a person begins their spiritual journey with specific expectations and preparations. The seeker is filled with curiosity, questions, and perhaps even doubts. They may approach spirituality for personal gain—seeking peace, prosperity, or understanding the mysteries of life. At this stage, the individual is guided by external forces—gurus, teachers, or spiritual texts—that lay the foundation for their spiritual path. The seeker is focused on building a relationship with the divine but still operates within a transactional mindset. This is akin to paying upfront for services without fully understanding what lies ahead. The initial steps are often driven by a desire for external rewards: "What can I get out of this spiritual practice?"

Challenges of Prepaid Spirituality

- A strong attachment to results or outcomes, driven by ego and desires.
- A tendency to view spirituality as a commodity—something that can be purchased or acquired.
- Fear or doubt arising when encountering obstacles on the spiritual path.

Despite these challenges, the individual remains on a crucial path of learning and growth, with the prepaid stage serving as essential preparation for deeper spiritual practices. Bhishma from the *Mahabharata* exemplifies this approach. His lifelong commitment to discipline, celibacy, and loyalty prepared him to endure immense personal suffering and the trials of battle without losing focus on his higher purpose. Like Bhishma, who built his spiritual foundation through consistent practices and vows, we, too, must engage in practices such as meditation, prayer, and mindfulness to develop resilience before life's storms arrive. This preparation fortifies us, helping us remain calm and grounded when life's challenges test us.

Post-paid Spirituality: Learning Through Life's Experiences

Post-paid spirituality is about reflecting on and integrating the lessons learned from life's challenges. Every obstacle becomes an opportunity for growth, and the disciple learns to refine their understanding of dharma. Sita from the *Ramayana* exemplifies post-paid spirituality through her resilience and strength during her abduction by Ravana, turning her suffering into spiritual wisdom. Every challenge faced on the spiritual path is an opportunity to deepen one's connection with the Divine.

In a post-paid plan, the user receives services first and pays later. Similarly, this stage represents a time when the seeker has delved deeper into spirituality and begun to experience the fruits of their labour, often without fully understanding how or why these results come. The seeker begins to sense the presence of divine grace, with an increased awareness of the inner workings of life. This stage marks the transition from a transactional approach to an experiential one, where spirituality is no longer about receiving rewards but about surrendering to divine will. The seeker learns to let go of ego-driven desires and focuses more on serving others and self-transformation.

Challenges of Post-paid Spirituality

- Encountering moments of self-doubt as the seeker questions their experiences and progress.
- The temptation to revert to a transactional mindset when faced with setbacks or challenges.
- A deeper confrontation with one's own ego and attachments.

In this stage, the role of the Guru becomes more significant. The Guru's teachings provide clarity and encouragement to persevere. Postpaid spirituality is about realizing that the universe operates on divine principles beyond human comprehension. As the seeker seeks, they are led toward surrender, making this a transformative phase.

Arjuna in the *Mahabharata* provides a powerful example of postpaid spirituality. Despite his skill as a warrior, Arjuna faced a profound moment of inner turmoil on the battlefield, which led him to seek guidance from Lord Krishna. It was through introspection and reflection during this crisis that Arjuna gained deeper spiritual wisdom, transforming his doubt into a renewed sense of purpose. This concept of learning through experience is mirrored in nature. Consider the river, which carves its path through the landscape over time, adapting and flowing around obstacles. Similarly, our life experiences—both positive and negative—shape our spiritual path. Each challenge becomes an opportunity for growth, helping us evolve.

Unlimited Spirituality: Surrendering to Divine Grace

The final stage is Unlimited Spirituality, where there are no limits—everything is available without constraints. This stage represents the ultimate spiritual realization, where the seeker reaches a state of divine union or moksha. At this point, the individual has transcended all personal desires, ego, and attachments. Their spiritual practices are no longer for personal gain but are a direct expression of divine love and grace. The individual is in a state of complete surrender, accepting that the divine force is not separate from them but is within them. In Unlimited Spirituality, the concepts of time, space, and limitations fade away. The seeker becomes one with the universe, experiencing boundless love, peace, and bliss.

Challenges of Unlimited Spirituality

- The complete transcendence of ego and personal identity.
- Remaining grounded in worldly affairs while experiencing deep spiritual fulfilment.
- Maintaining humility and grace despite profound inner transformation.

At this stage, the Guru's presence is no longer external but becomes an intrinsic part of the seeker's consciousness. The Guru leads the seeker toward the final realization of truth. Lord Rama from the *Ramayana* epitomizes this approach. Despite enduring exile and hardship, Lord Rama's unwavering trust in divine guidance and his surrender to the will of the Divine allowed him to triumph over adversity. His life teaches that we are not alone when we surrender fully to the Divine. Divine love and wisdom flow through us, providing peace and strength in every step. Similarly, the lotus flower rises above the muddy waters to bloom in pristine beauty. It does not strive to escape the mud but grows naturally, allowing the water to nurture it. Similarly, when we surrender to the Divine, we rise above external circumstances, experiencing peace and grace.

The Journey of Spiritual Evolution

Spiritual evolution is a dynamic process that integrates preparation, reflection, and surrender. The stages of prepaid, postpaid, and unlimited spirituality are complementary, guiding us toward deeper wisdom, inner peace, and self-realization. While we build resilience through spiritual practices (prepaid), learn from life's experiences (postpaid), and surrender to divine grace (unlimited), we move closer to the Divine, unlocking our highest potential. True transformation, like the growth of a tree or the flow of a river, occurs over time, step by step.

The Spiritual Journey: From SAD to GURU – A Transformative Path Toward Divine Union

The spiritual journey is not linear but unfolds through disciplined practice, deep reflection, and profound surrender to the Divine. It touches every aspect of a disciple's life and requires preparation, acceptance of challenges, and ultimate surrender. Sri Vidya Narayana Theertha emphasizes this journey through the stages of Prepaid, Postpaid, and Unlimited Spirituality—each representing a significant phase in a disciple's growth toward divine realization.

Guruparampara: The Sacred Lineage of Enlightenment

The journey is rooted in Guruparampara—the sacred lineage of enlightened beings who pass down the torch of wisdom. The Guru is not merely a teacher but a guiding light, leading the disciple from ignorance to wisdom. As Sri Vidya Narayana Theertha beautifully articulates, "Without the Sadguru, the path remains lost." The Guru's role is indispensable in leading the disciple to truth, and the relationship is sacred, demanding surrender, trust, and humility. Through the Guru's teachings, the disciple evolves spiritually, intellectually, and emotionally. It is through this divine guidance that the disciple progresses on their spiritual path.

Key Takeaways

- **Spirituality is a Journey**: Evolving from ego-driven desires to divine union, spirituality is a continuous path of self-discovery.
- **Prepaid Spirituality**: Initially sought for personal gain, spirituality is driven by the ego's need for answers and validation.
- **Postpaid Spirituality**: Over time, spirituality shifts from self-interest to grace, surrendering to the pursuit of truth and divinity.
- **Unlimited Spirituality**: The ultimate stage is union with the divine, transcending the ego and experiencing oneness with all.

- **The Guru's Role**: A spiritual guide illuminates the path, offering wisdom and support throughout the journey.
- **Grace as the Catalyst**: Divine grace propels spiritual growth, helping overcome limitations and connect with the higher self.
- **Science Meets Spirituality**: While science explains the material, spirituality reveals deeper meaning and purpose beyond the physical world.
- **Practical Growth**: Self-awareness, compassion, and discipline fuel spiritual evolution at each stage.

A Journey Beyond Limits

By embracing all three stages—prepaid, postpaid, and unlimited—we align with our divine purpose, attaining spiritual realization that transcends the ordinary to become extraordinary. The path of spirituality is an evolving journey, one that moves from the transactional to the transcendent. As we progress through the stages of Prepaid, Postpaid, and Unlimited, we realize that true growth comes not from external rewards, but from inner transformation.

The spiritual seeker's journey is not about what they gain, but how deeply they surrender, how thoroughly they understand their purpose, and how selflessly they serve the divine. Each phase of this journey challenges us to move beyond our ego, to embrace life's lessons, and to trust in the divine plan that unfolds before us.

In a world that often values instant gratification and material success, the journey toward spiritual realization reminds us that true peace, wisdom, and fulfilment come not from seeking external rewards but from the quiet, steady process of inner growth. Through discipline, reflection, and surrender, we come to understand the divine presence within us, recognizing that we are all part of something greater.

As Sri Vidya Narayana Theertha beautifully says, *"True spirituality is not about seeking but about surrendering, for in surrender, we find our true self and the divine that dwells within us."*

ENERGY AND FLOW

*Energy is not created, nor destroyed—it is the eternal flow of the divine.
When the mind resists, it stagnates; when it surrenders, it moves as grace.
Flow is not about direction, but alignment—where the self dissolves into the infinite.
In stillness, energy is boundless; in surrender, it becomes the dance of existence.
To be in flow is to be in harmony with what always was, is, and will be."*

– His Holiness Sri Vidyanarayana Theertha

CHAPTER-20

DIVINE RHYTHM OF LIFE: EMBRACING THE SUPREME ENERGY

Introduction

"In the grand scheme of existence, nothing happens without divine will. Trust in that supreme power and let it guide your journey," says His Holiness Sri Vidyanarayana Theertha. These words remind us of the timeless truth that life is a harmonious interplay of divine will, human effort, and nature's rhythms. Just as the sun rises to dispel the darkness of the night, divine grace illuminates the path for those who surrender to it with unwavering faith.

Humanity's relationship with the divine is like that between the earth and the rain—one nurtures and sustains the other. The five elements of nature, or Panchabhutas, form the sacred foundation of existence, intricately woven into every being. Yet, they remain under the governance of the Supreme Power, the Parabrahma, who manifests as divine energy in countless forms. Be it Lakshmi, the embodiment of wealth and prosperity, or Parvati, the epitome of wisdom and compassion, this divine energy flows through creation, keeping everything in perfect balance.

By understanding and aligning ourselves with the divine rhythms of nature and the cosmos, we unlock the path to self-realization and ultimate peace. Let us now delve into His Holiness's enlightening discourse and discover the secrets of life's divine orchestration.

Questions and Answers

Q1: How can we understand the concept of divine timing and nature's rhythms in our everyday life?

Answer: From a scientific perspective, everything in nature follows a set of laws and cycles. From the rotation of planets to the seasons, there is an order to the universe. Spiritually, divine timing refers to the belief that everything happens at the right moment according to a higher power. Just as a seed takes time to grow into a tree, our actions and efforts must align with the cosmic flow, guided by divine wisdom, to bear fruit at the right time.

Q2: What is the role of nature and the five elements in our lives?

Answer: The five elements—earth, water, fire, air, and ether—form the foundation of everything in existence. Scientifically, these elements constitute the building blocks of life, with each playing a vital role in sustaining life on Earth. Spiritually, these elements symbolize the interconnectedness of all beings. When we understand and respect these elements, we align ourselves with the forces that shape our world and deepen our connection to the divine.

Q3: How does one cultivate inner peace and spiritual fulfilment in today's fast-paced world?

Answer: In the modern world, where distractions are abundant, it can be challenging to find inner peace. Scientifically, meditation and mindfulness have been shown to calm the mind and reduce stress, allowing individuals to reconnect with themselves. Spiritually, inner peace is attained by surrendering to the divine, trusting in the cosmic order, and living in harmony with the rhythms of nature. When we align our actions with these principles, we experience peace that transcends external circumstances.

Key Takeaways

- Trust in divine timing: Life unfolds according to a greater plan. Be patient and align your efforts with this higher wisdom.

- Understand the interconnectedness of nature: The five elements are foundational to life. Honour them to live in harmony with the universe.
- Seek balance: Spiritual fulfilment and inner peace come from aligning your actions with divine rhythm and embracing the natural cycles.

Challenges to Overcome

- Overcome impatience: Trust in divine timing, even when things don't happen immediately.
- Break free from distractions: Cultivate mindfulness to reconnect with the inner self.
- Balance worldly pursuits with spiritual growth: Strive for harmony in both material and spiritual realms.

Conclusion

In the words of His Holiness Sri Vidyanarayana Theertha, "Trust in the divine timing of life, flow with the natural rhythms around you, and live in harmony with the world. In doing so, you will find not just success, but peace and spiritual fulfillment." By aligning ourselves with divine will and the rhythms of nature, we unlock the path to peace and self-realization. This understanding enables us to live not only in tune with the world around us but also in deep connection with our true selves, ultimately leading us to fulfilment beyond the material world.

CHAPTER-21

THE ETERNAL DANCE: EMBRACING CHANGE WITH GRACE

Introduction

In life, we often encounter moments of hardship that seem overwhelming. When we are in the depths of suffering, it feels as though the weight of the world is upon us. But how can we overcome this seemingly insurmountable pain? His Holiness Sri Vidyanarayana Theertha, a revered spiritual guide, offers profound wisdom in such times of distress. Through his teachings, he emphasizes the importance of understanding the natural flow of life and accepting the inevitable passage of time. Drawing from real-life examples, he highlights the transient nature of all things, from physical appearance to relationships and even positions of power. In this discourse, we explore his compassionate responses to the queries of his disciples, offering practical wisdom that resonates deeply with the human experience.

Questions and Answers

Disciple 1:

Swamiji, I am struggling with great pain and hardship. It feels as though I cannot bear the weight of my suffering. How can I overcome this?

Swamiji's Response:

The universe operates according to the principles of time. Everything in this world is governed by time, and thus, change is inevitable. The pain you are experiencing is part of this natural process. Just as you do not desire old age, yet age comes with time, we must learn to move with the flow of time. Your suffering will pass just as the seasons change and the body goes through different phases. It is through understanding and accepting the passage of time that we find peace.

Disciple 2:

Swamiji, we often desire permanence—whether it be in our relationships, wealth, or status. But nothing seems to last. Why is this so?

Swamiji's Response:

No worldly possession, be it wealth, power, or even relationships, is permanent. Just as seasons change, so too does everything in life. The desire for permanence in such things causes suffering. When we realize that all things are transient, we can begin to accept them as they come and go without clinging to them. This acceptance leads to peace and liberation from the bondage of attachment.

Disciple 3:

Swamiji, how can we find joy in the face of inevitable change and suffering?

Swamiji's Response:

The key is to accept the flow of life with a joyful heart. As Krishna Paramaatma said, whatever happens, accept it as it is. By cultivating a mindset of equanimity, we can find joy even in the face of adversity. When we embrace life as it comes, with all its ups and downs, we naturally invite health, happiness, and peace into our lives.

Key Insights

- **Acceptance of Change**: Understanding that time governs all things and that nothing is permanent allows us to let go of attachments, leading to peace and freedom.
- **Equanimity in Suffering**: Instead of resisting suffering, accepting it as part of the natural flow of life can transform our experience.

- **The Power of the Present Moment**: By focusing on the present and embracing life as it is, we open ourselves to greater joy and spiritual growth.

Conclusion

His Holiness Sri Vidyanarayana Theertha's teachings offer profound wisdom for navigating life's challenges. We can cultivate a deeper sense of peace and fulfilment through the acceptance of time's passage, the impermanence of all things, and a joyful embrace of life's ups and downs. In understanding that everything is part of a divine plan, we can rise above the fluctuations of life and find harmony within ourselves. Just as the great yogis perform miraculous feats through deep meditation and selfless service, so too can we unlock the transformative power of accepting life as it is—finding the divine in every moment.

CHAPTER-22

LIVING IN HARMONY: THE PATH OF DHARMA AND DIVINE GUIDANCE

Introduction

Life is a journey where every step is shaped by the choices we make, the values we uphold, and the wisdom we seek. Amidst the chaos of modern living, the timeless teachings of Sri Vidyanarayana Theertha offer a beacon of light, guiding us toward a life of purpose, harmony, and inner peace.

In this profound discourse, His Holiness addresses some of life's most essential questions—questions that resonate with the seeker in all of us. From the righteous approach to earning and spending to understanding the essence of dharma, He reveals the deeper truths that elevate our actions and thoughts. With clarity and compassion, Sri Vidyanarayana Theertha encourages us to align with our conscience, embrace challenges as opportunities, and transcend the illusions of the material world.

Through His words, we are reminded that dharma is not merely a principle—it is the essence of life itself. It is the bridge between our finite existence and the infinite divine. These teachings inspire us to live with integrity, compassion, and wisdom, awakening the divinity within and around us.

Questions and Answers

1. Question: How should one approach earning and spending in life?

Sri Vidyanarayana Theertha's Answer:

"Earning is not just about accumulating wealth; it is a responsibility guided by dharma. Earn through righteous means, and spend wisely to serve a purpose greater than yourself. Spending should uplift not only you but also those around you. It reflects your inner values—your spending shows where your priorities lie. Always remember, wealth is temporary, but the dharma behind its use creates eternal harmony."

2. Question: What does it mean to worship dharma?

Sri Vidyanarayana Theertha's Answer:

"Dharma is the foundation of life. Worshipping dharma doesn't mean bowing before it but living in accordance with its principles. It's about being truthful, fair, and compassionate. When you make every action an offering to dharma, your life becomes a form of worship. Without dharma, even knowledge and power are meaningless."

3. Question: How can we ensure our decisions align with our higher purpose?

Sri Vidyanarayana Theertha's Answer:

"Before you make a decision, engage in deep inquiry. Ask yourself: Does this choice align with dharma? Will it benefit others and not just me? Once you make a decision, commit to it wholeheartedly. Your profession, culture, and wisdom (Gnana) are the fruits of your choices. They shape your journey toward self-realization."

4. Question: Can anyone truly escape karma?

Sri Vidyanarayana Theertha's Answer:

"Karma is inevitable. It's the law of the universe. However, by aligning your actions with dharma, you transcend the cycle of karma. Those who live by dharma do not fear karma, because their actions are pure and selfless. Dharma protects those who protect it. Karma is not a punishment; it's a teacher."

5. Question: Why is it important to avoid criticizing others?

Sri Vidyanarayana Theertha's Answer:

"Criticism arises from ignorance and ego. When you criticize others, you focus on their faults and ignore your own. This creates negativity within you. Instead, observe and learn from others. Absorb their virtues and avoid their mistakes. Criticism divides; understanding unites. Strive to see the divine in everyone."

6. Question: How can we cultivate inner strength to face life's challenges?

Sri Vidyanarayana Theertha's Answer:

"Challenges are life's way of shaping you. Understand the situation fully, withdraw from distractions and withstand the storm with patience and faith. Remember, God has placed within you the strength to endure anything. Trust in Him and in yourself. Challenges are not obstacles—they are opportunities for growth."

7. Question: Who is God, and how can we experience Him?

Sri Vidyanarayana Theertha's Answer:

"God is not confined to temples, mosques, or churches. He is within you, in your conscience, in your love, and in your truth. I am not God, but I bow at His feet. When you surrender to your inner consciousness, you experience the divine within. God is not somewhere else—He is you, beyond your ego."

8. Question: How does time heal wounds and bring transformation?

Sri Vidyanarayana Theertha's Answer:

"Time is the greatest healer and teacher. It gives you perspective, transforms pain into wisdom, and dissolves the ego. Allow time to flow—don't resist it. Healing doesn't mean forgetting; it means growing beyond what hurt you. Trust in time, for it carries the grace of God's will."

9. Question: What role do reasoning and philosophy play in spiritual growth?

Sri Vidyanarayana Theertha's Answer:

"Philosophy is the light that guides you through the darkness of ignorance. Nyaya (logic) sharpens your understanding, Tarka (reasoning) deepens your perspective, and Mimamsa (interpretation) aligns you with dharma. But remember, reasoning is only a tool. True wisdom comes when you live these principles, not merely think about them."

10. Question: How do we align with our inner conscience?

Sri Vidyanarayana Theertha's Answer:

"Obey your inner conscience—it is God speaking within you. Your conscience is pure and knows the truth. Silence the noise of the mind, and you will hear its guidance. When you act in accordance with your conscience, you live in harmony with the divine plan. This is the highest form of dharma."

Closing Words from Sri Vidyanarayana Theertha

"Dharma is the thread that binds your actions, your mind, and your soul. Live it fully, and you will escape the illusions of this world. Remember, God is not outside you—He is in every breath, every thought, and every action. Surrender to Him, and you will find eternal peace."

CHAPTER-23

THE INVISIBLE FUEL: MASTERING YOUR LIFE'S ENERGY

Introduction

Are You Aware of Your Energy Usage?

In today's fast-paced, technology-driven world, we find ourselves constantly rushing from one task to the next, fueled by deadlines, expectations, and the ever-growing need to stay connected. Amidst this relentless motion, one crucial resource often goes unnoticed—the energy that sustains every aspect of our being. We carefully charge our phones, laptops, and other devices, yet how often do we pause to consider the energy that powers us—our bodies, minds, and spirits?

Just as a phone can't function without a charged battery, neither can we thrive if our energy reserves are depleted. Yet, unlike our devices, we don't come with an automatic reminder to recharge. If we neglect our internal energy, we risk running on empty, leading to physical burnout and mental exhaustion. To navigate life with purpose, clarity, and vitality, we must learn to recharge ourselves just as intentionally as we charge our technology. In this world of constant motion, nurturing our inner energy becomes not just a necessity but the key to living a balanced and meaningful life.

Energy as the Core of Existence

Everything around us operates on energy—our actions, thoughts, and even our devices. Energy is the driving force behind everything, and like currency, it must be spent wisely. Lord Krishna's teachings in the Bhagavad Gita offer profound wisdom on managing energy: *"You have the right to perform your prescribed duties, but you are not entitled to the fruits of your actions."* This teaches us the importance of focusing on the present and performing actions with full devotion without becoming overly consumed by the outcomes. By understanding that we control how we expend our energy, we can ensure it serves us in achieving our highest purpose.

Examples of Balance from Legendary Lives

Throughout history, there have been individuals who demonstrated remarkable energy balance. They managed their energy wisely, channelling it toward their goals and inspiring generations:

1. **Swami Vivekananda**: A beacon of spiritual energy and focus, Swami Vivekananda's relentless energy inspired generations. He once said, *"Arise, awake, and stop not till the goal is reached."* His life's work shows how focused energy can transform both the individual and society, providing a lasting legacy that continues to guide spiritual seekers worldwide.

2. **Mahatma Gandhi**: Gandhi's energy was driven by his unwavering commitment to non-violence and truth. His daily practice of recharging his energy through introspection, simplicity, and connection with nature enabled him to lead India's independence movement with profound peace and purpose. His ability to balance his personal and public life allowed him to sustain his mission through difficult times.

3. **Helen Keller**: Despite being both deaf and blind, Helen Keller harnessed her immense inner energy to overcome her disabilities and inspire millions. Her story is a powerful reminder that when energy is channelled with determination and a positive mindset, it can transcend all limitations, unlocking potential even in the most challenging circumstances.

4. **Dr. A.P.J. Abdul Kalam**: Known as the "Missile Man" of India, Dr. Kalam devoted his life to the advancement of science and education. His ability to channel his energy into research,

leadership, and mentorship proved that no goal is too far-reaching when energy is directed with purpose and passion.

Insights for Reflection

To effectively manage and channel your energy, it's important to pause and reflect on a few guiding questions:

- **Where is your energy going?** Reflect on whether your actions align with your life's purpose. Are your daily choices helping you progress toward your goals, or are you expending energy without direction?
- **Do you take time to replenish your energy?** Just as we plug in our phones to recharge, we must take time for ourselves—through mindful rest, meditation, or introspection. Without regular recharging, you risk burnout, stress, and dissatisfaction.
- **Are you focusing your energy wisely?** In today's distraction-filled world, it's easy to dissipate energy. Prioritize your mental and emotional energy on what matters most—whether that's personal growth, family, or meaningful work.

Life Lessons from Technology

Technology offers a helpful analogy for managing energy. Consider how we use our phones and devices:

- **Devices Need Recharging**: Just as your phone needs to be plugged in, we need to regularly recharge ourselves—whether through sleep, prayer, or simply taking time to reflect.
- **Overuse Leads to Damage**: Constantly using a phone without rest can lead to wear and tear. Similarly, overexerting oneself leads to physical and mental exhaustion. Balancing effort with recovery is key.
- **Energy Conservation**: Phones conserve battery by limiting unnecessary processes. In the same way, focusing on what's

essential and minimizing distractions helps conserve our energy for what truly matters.

The Three-Step Practice: Accept, Adjust, Act

Sri Vidyanarayana Theertha offers a three-step process for balanced energy management:

1. **Accept**: Recognize the importance of conserving energy. Acknowledge that you need to rest and recharge, just as your devices need downtime.
2. **Adjust**: Make conscious changes to your lifestyle. Simplify your habits, prioritize meaningful activities, and avoid overcommitting yourself to unnecessary tasks.
3. **Act**: Focus your energy on purposeful actions. Dedicate yourself to your true calling and channel your energy into creating lasting impact.

Practical Examples for Every Life Stage

Energy management is essential at all stages of life. Here are some practical examples:

- **For Students**: Use your energy wisely by balancing studies with rest. Avoid overloading your mind with excessive information—mental fatigue hinders learning. Take breaks and engage in activities that refresh and rejuvenate you.
- **For Professionals**: Build a balance between work and personal life. Without self-care, your work will suffer, and your well-being will deteriorate. Set boundaries around work hours and make space for activities that recharge you—be it family time, hobbies, or exercise.
- **For Caregivers**: Practicing self-care is crucial when caring for others. Only when you are recharged can you truly give your best to those in need. Make sure to allocate time for rest and

rejuvenation so that you can offer your energy with patience and compassion.

- **For Housewives**: The role of a housewife can often be demanding, involving constant attention to household chores, family needs, and maintaining a nurturing environment. It's important to recognize that, just like any other job, you need moments of rest and personal time to recharge. Taking short breaks throughout the day, engaging in hobbies, or simply enjoying quiet moments can help prevent burnout. Balancing household duties with activities that nourish your body, mind, and spirit ensures that you continue to serve your family with energy and love without depleting yourself.

A Simple Analogy: Life as a Battery

Think of yourself as a battery:

- **Recharge Regularly**: Just as a battery needs periodic recharging, so do you. Make sure you rest, meditate, and take time for yourself to stay energized.
- **Excessive Demands**: If you continue to use energy without recharging, you'll face depletion—leading to exhaustion, stress, and even illness.
- **Energy Tax**: Overexerting yourself without proper recharge incurs an energy "tax" that manifests in challenges like stress, burnout, and health problems.

Conclusion: Unlock Your Potential with Balanced Energy

Energy is your most precious and finite resource. By consciously managing and harmonizing your physical, mental, and spiritual energy, you unlock the transformative potential for a life rich in peace, purpose, and fulfilment. When directed with intention and focus, energy becomes the driving force behind extraordinary achievements and profound personal growth.

As you journey through life, remember that energy is not an endless supply. Just as you would never overcharge your phone, it is equally important not to overextend yourself. Make time to recharge, be mindful of how you invest your energy, and, above all, channel it toward your deepest and most meaningful aspirations.

The key to true success lies within you—it resides in the deliberate and mindful management of your energy. When you align and focus your energy wisely, you cultivate clarity, purpose, and peace, creating a life that reflects your highest potential.

CHAPTER-24

Mystical Unity: Celebrating the Timeless Essence of Love and Divine Energy

Introduction

The teachings of Jesus Christ and Lord Krishna offer timeless wisdom, filled with love, compassion, and divine energy that transcends cultural and religious boundaries. These two avatars, revered in their respective traditions, guide humanity toward spiritual awakening through their messages of unconditional love, selflessness, and unity. His Holiness Sri Vidyanarayana

Theertha calls us to reflect on the shared essence of these teachings, urging us to look beyond the labels of religion and embrace the universal energy that unites us all.

The Universal Thread of Divine Energy

On December 25th, we celebrate the birth of Jesus Christ, the embodiment of mercy, tolerance, and patience. His Holiness Sri Vidyanarayana Theertha reminds us that Jesus represents not just a great teacher, but a mystic who channels divine energy through all creation. "Today, we celebrate not only His birth but the flow of divine mystic energy that touches every heart and soul," His Holiness explains. This mystic energy is not confined to one faith; it is a universal force that unites humanity.

"Why does a Peetadhipathi speak of Jesus?" His Holiness asks. "Because the same divine energy flows through Krishna, Rama, Shiva, and all forms of God. It is the essence of love, forgiveness, and harmony that transcends all divisions. In both the lives of Jesus and Krishna, we see a call to rise above religious and cultural boundaries and embrace the oneness of existence."

Jesus and Krishna: Beacons of Unconditional Love

The teachings of both Jesus and Lord Krishna emphasize love as the highest path to spiritual realization. Jesus proclaimed, "Love one another as I have loved you," while Krishna, in the Bhagavad Gita, encourages surrender to the divine with pure devotion. His Holiness highlights that love is not just a sentiment, but the divine force that connects all beings to each other and to the divine source.

"Jesus' crucifixion," His Holiness notes, "was not just an event; it was a profound demonstration of unconditional love and forgiveness. It is a reminder that divine energy calls us to align with love, no matter the circumstances." This message is echoed in the life of Krishna, whose teachings emphasize selflessness, devotion, and the importance of harmony.

Realizing the Essence of Divine Teachings

To truly understand the essence of Jesus or Krishna, we must go beyond intellectual knowledge. "There is no need to dive into complex theology to grasp their message," His Holiness advises. "Feel their presence, feel their love, and experience their teachings in everyday life." Whether it's Jesus' eyes filled with compassion or Krishna's playful wisdom in the Bhagavad Gita, the essence of these avatars is not confined to scripture—it lives in our hearts and actions.

Both avatars teach us that divine love is not just a concept to be studied but a living truth to be experienced and practiced. Just as we feel Krishna's guidance in moments of devotion or the strength of Rama's resolve in the Ramayana, we must also feel the depth of Jesus' love and sacrifice in our lives today.

Practical Insights for Everyday Life

The teachings of Jesus and Krishna are not distant ideals but practical guides for living a more fulfilling and compassionate life. His Holiness offers simple, actionable steps to embody these teachings:

- **Unconditional Love**: Show kindness to others without expectation. A simple smile to a stranger or a random act of kindness can make a profound impact.
- **Forgiveness**: Let go of grudges and offer forgiveness, even if it is not reciprocated. Consider writing a letter to someone you've struggled to forgive, even if you never send it.
- **Selflessness**: Contribute to the well-being of others. Volunteer your time or resources to help those in need, reflecting the spirit of seva (selfless service).
- **Meditative Reflection**: Dedicate moments of stillness to reflect on divine teachings, finding peace and clarity in simple words of wisdom.

Embracing the Unity of All Faiths

His Holiness reminds us that the divine energy we speak of is not limited to one religion. Whether manifesting as Jesus in Christianity, Krishna in Hinduism, or the Buddha in Buddhism, this energy calls all of us to live in love, forgiveness, and harmony. The common thread is clear: All paths lead to the same divine source. By recognizing the essence of these teachings, we can move beyond religious differences and unite in our shared humanity.

Overcoming Division and Finding Unity

While the teachings of Jesus and Krishna are clear, His Holiness observes that many followers still struggle to fully embody their essence. "The greatness of Jesus lies not only in His words but in His life," His Holiness explains. "Yet many focus on rituals rather than the internal transformation His teachings call for. The same is true for those who revere Krishna, Rama, or other avatars—true devotion lies in action, not just belief."

The root of this disconnection often stems from an attachment to external identity, rather than the essence of the teachings. His Holiness urges us all to introspect, to reconnect with the core message of love, compassion, and unity that these divine figures represent.

Inspiring Conclusion: A Call to Action

In closing, His Holiness Sri Vidyanarayana Theertha beautifully sums up the essence of this celebration:

"Whether it is Jesus, Krishna, Rama, or Shiva, all divine forms transcend human-made boundaries. Their lives and teachings converge on a single truth: the path of love, forgiveness, and harmony leads to divine realization. This mystic energy flows through all, inviting us to awaken to our own divinity."

On this sacred occasion, let us honour the birth of Jesus Christ not just by celebrating but by embodying the virtues of mercy, tolerance, and love in our lives. Let His teachings inspire us to see beyond religious divisions, embrace unity, and align with the universal mystic energy that connects us all. Together, we can create a more harmonious and loving world.

CHAPTER-25

THE DIVINE PULSE: AWAKENING THE HIDDEN MYSTICAL ENERGY

Introduction

In the divine presence of Shirdi, where the spiritual energy of SAI Baba fills the atmosphere, Swamy Vidyanarayana Theertha shares a message of profound inspiration, awakening the hearts of all who gather. He speaks of SAI as a universal, all-pervading force—an energy that transcends religion and form, existing in every being and in every corner of the cosmos. Swamy encourages devotees to embark on a transformative journey of self-realization, urging them to "seek, activate, and induct"—to open their hearts to divine light, awaken their inner potential, and internalize wisdom that leads to spiritual awakening. Through serenity, surrender, and selfless service, he guides seekers to transcend the ego and align with the flow of life's infinite energy. In his powerful words, the choice between liberation and rebirth rests in the hands of each soul, and the path of love, truth, and devotion leads us ever closer to the divine light that unites us all.

The Path to Spiritual Awakening: Embracing the Divine Mystic Energy Within

In the journey of spiritual awakening, the greatest realization is not the pursuit of external achievements but the recognition of the divine energy that resides within every being. Swamy Vidyanarayana Theertha's teachings illuminate the path of self-realization by guiding us to understand the profound and transformative force of mystic energy. This energy is not a foreign or distant concept but a universal, omnipresent force that connects all beings and flows through the entire cosmos. By aligning ourselves with this energy, we embark on a journey of profound self-transformation, peace, and ultimate liberation.

The Concept of Mystic Energy: SAI as the Universal Force

In his wisdom, Swamy describes SAI as an all-pervading, powerful energy that transcends all religious and conceptual boundaries. SAI is not confined to any single deity or form; it exists in all beings and through all things. This universal energy flows through the cosmos, guiding, protecting, and empowering the seeker on their spiritual journey.

This divine energy, symbolized by SAI, calls us to recognize the interconnectedness of all life and the divine essence that lies within and around us. It teaches that all paths lead to the same divine source, and SAI is but a manifestation of that unifying force. In this light, SAI is not just a name or a form but the energy of life itself, manifesting in every heartbeat, every thought, and every breath.

The Essence of SAI: A Pathway to Inner Truth

Swamy's teachings offer a profound blueprint for those seeking spiritual awakening. By understanding and embracing the essence of SAI, one is guided through a transformative journey that leads to inner peace, self-realization, and liberation from the cycle of birth and death.

The journey begins with a deep, sincere quest for truth. To seek is to open oneself to the divine light; to activate is to awaken the dormant potential within; and to induct is to internalize divine wisdom, making it a part of one's being. This process transforms the seeker into a vessel of SAI's boundless energy.

Cultivating inner peace and stillness is essential on this path. SAI calls upon us to embrace serenity and accommodate the wisdom of the divine, allowing tranquility to settle into our hearts. This is where the true work of transformation begins—within the silence of our being.

Mystic Energy: The Divine Inheritance Passed Through Time

Swamy Vidyanarayana Theertha speaks of mystic energy as a divine inheritance, a force passed down through generations, awaiting activation in each soul. Time, as a divine medium, holds the answers to our deepest questions: "Why?" "What?" and "What for?" Through the passage of time, the answers unfold—not from the ego or intellect, but from the very mystic energy that flows through us.

This energy is within us all. It is not something external that must be sought; it is already present, lying dormant, awaiting the right moment to awaken. To activate this divine potential requires patience, effort, and above all, surrender to the flow of time and divine will. Swamy reminds us that answers come not from the mind but from the mystic energy guiding our actions.

Principles for Self-Realization: Giving, Gaining, and Going Forward

The journey of spiritual awakening is not one of passive observation but of active participation. Swamy offers us a simple yet profound principle:

- **Give, Gain, Go Forward**: Through selfless giving, one gains wisdom, and with wisdom, the path forward becomes clear. Giving does not refer merely to material possessions but to giving of oneself—one's time, energy, and love. It is through this selfless giving that one is able to receive the divine wisdom that propels the seeker on their spiritual journey.

- **You Are Empty**: Emptiness is not a void but a sacred space—free from ego, free from material attachment. It is in this emptiness that the mystic energy flows unimpeded, filling the seeker with divine light. To realize this emptiness is to align with the infinite, to surrender to the divine presence that is always with us.

- **Don't Challenge the Self**: The ego-driven self is the greatest obstacle on the path to self-realization. When we challenge the self, we reinforce our attachment to the material world. Swamy teaches that true spiritual growth comes not from striving or resisting but from surrendering the self to the divine flow of mystic energy. By letting go of the self, we allow divine energy to guide us toward the truth.

Liberation Through Mystic Energy

The Choice Between Rebirth and Moksha – A Gentle Path to Inner Peace

In today's fast-moving world, where many feel caught in the chase for success, possessions, and fleeting happiness, the teachings of Swamy offer a profound and reassuring truth: true peace and fulfilment lie not in the external world, but in the awakening of the divine mystic energy within us. Swamy's message is simple and gentle—liberation, or moksha, is not a distant, unattainable goal but a peaceful journey of recognizing the divine light that already resides within us.

As the Bhagavad Gita reminds us, "Surrender unto Me, and I will deliver you from all sinful reactions" (Bhagavad Gita 18.66). This passage is not meant to be a source of fear but a promise of divine grace. Surrendering does not mean losing ourselves, but rather letting go of the burden of ego and worldly attachments, and allowing the mystic energy to guide us toward peace, wisdom, and ultimately, liberation.

This journey towards moksha is not about making a difficult choice but about gradually tuning into the flow of divine energy. It is not a sudden leap but a gradual process of surrender, where we start with small steps of letting go—of our attachments, worries, and fears. As we do so, we begin to experience a deep, inner calm, and a sense of connection to a greater purpose.

The path to liberation is not about renouncing the world, but about transforming how we engage with it. By recognizing and aligning with the mystic energy within us, we move toward a life of inner peace, free from the constant cycle of striving and rebirth. The choice to embrace moksha, then, becomes less about an overwhelming decision and more about the gentle realization that by surrendering to the divine, we unlock a deeper peace and a more fulfilling existence.

Takeaways

- **Liberation as a Gradual Journey**: Moksha is not an immediate, daunting goal, but a gradual process of awakening the divine energy within.

- **Divine Surrender**: Surrendering the ego and worldly attachments allows the mystic energy to guide us, leading to peace and wisdom.

- **Peaceful Path to Liberation**: Moksha is a gentle, peaceful journey towards inner fulfilment, not about renouncing the world but transforming our engagement with it.

- **No Fear in Surrender**: Surrender is not about loss but about gaining deeper connection to the divine and experiencing inner calm.

- **The Flow of Divine Energy**: By aligning with the mystic energy within, we move away from the cycle of rebirth and towards liberation.

- **Small Steps Lead to Big Change**: The choice for liberation comes gradually through letting go of fears and attachments, fostering a sense of peace and fulfilment.

- **Connection to a Greater Purpose**: Embracing moksha leads to a life of inner peace and fulfilment, guided by divine wisdom and love.

Embracing the Divine Mystical Energy Within

As we journey through life, we often seek answers in the external world, searching for fulfilment, meaning, and purpose. Yet, the true essence of life, the key to ultimate peace and liberation, lies not in the world around us but within us. Swamy Vidyanarayana Theertha's teachings invite us to awaken to the divine mystic energy that flows through all of creation, an energy that connects every being, every moment, and every breath to the infinite divine source.

When we embrace SAI—the universal force of divine energy—we align ourselves with the unchanging truth that transcends time, space, and form. This energy is not merely a concept or a distant ideal; it is the very breath of life itself, available to each one of us, waiting to be activated within. Through selfless giving, surrender, and the cultivation of inner peace, we can tap into this powerful flow, transforming our lives and the lives of those around us.

The path of spiritual awakening is not always easy. It requires patience, humility, and the courage to surrender our egos and attachments. Yet, as we walk this path with dedication and trust, we are guided by the divine light of SAI, which illuminates even the darkest corners of our hearts. Each step on this journey brings us closer to the truth of our divine nature, where liberation, peace, and ultimate fulfilment await.

Let us, therefore, embrace the divine mystic energy within us, knowing that by doing so, we are not only transforming ourselves but contributing to the greater good of all beings. As we activate the dormant potential within, we become vessels of divine light, embodying the love, wisdom, and peace that the world so desperately needs. The divine energy of SAI is within us all—let us awaken to it, surrender to its flow, and walk the path of self-realization and liberation with faith, courage, and grace.

The Framework for Spiritual Growth: The Process of Transformation

As we embrace the teachings of Swamy Vidyanarayana Theertha and the divine energy of SAI, it is essential to remember the process of spiritual transformation. In this context, I recall what Bhagwan Sri Ram SIR shared with the participants of a seminar, offering a powerful framework for spiritual growth:

- **Listening**: Truly hearing the divine message, not just with our ears, but with an open heart, receptive to wisdom.
- **Thinking**: Reflecting on what has been heard, allowing the mind to process and find deeper meaning.
- **Contemplating**: Going beyond surface understanding to connect the teachings with one's own inner experiences and life.
- **Digesting**: Internalizing the knowledge so it becomes part of our being rather than just intellectual knowledge.
- **Assimilating**: Integrating this wisdom into our daily lives, allowing it to shape our actions, thoughts, and behaviours.
- **Application**: Living the teachings in the world—transforming knowledge into practical wisdom that guides us toward liberation.

When followed with sincerity, this process helps deepen our understanding and allows the mystic energy to guide our every action, leading us toward self-realization and liberation.

CHAPTER-26

THE ART OF ENERGY BALANCE: TIMELESS WISDOM FOR MODERN LIFE

Introduction

Are You Aware of Your Energy Usage?

In today's fast-paced, technology-driven world, we find ourselves constantly rushing from one task to the next, fueled by deadlines, expectations, and the ever-growing need to stay connected. Amidst this relentless motion, one crucial resource often goes unnoticed—the energy that sustains every aspect of our being. We carefully charge our phones, laptops, and other devices, yet how often do we pause to consider the energy that powers us—our bodies, minds, and spirits?

Just as a phone can't function without a charged battery, neither can we thrive if our energy reserves are depleted. Yet, unlike our devices, we don't come with an automatic reminder to recharge. If we neglect our internal energy, we risk running on empty, leading to physical burnout and mental exhaustion. To navigate life with purpose, clarity, and vitality, we must learn to recharge ourselves just as intentionally as we charge our technology. In this world of constant motion, nurturing our inner energy becomes not just a necessity but the key to living a balanced and meaningful life.

Energy as the Core of Existence

Everything around us operates on energy—our actions, thoughts, and even our devices. Energy is the driving force behind everything, and like currency, it must be spent wisely. Lord Krishna's teachings in the Bhagavad Gita offer profound wisdom on managing energy: *"You have the right to perform your prescribed duties, but you are not entitled to the fruits of your actions."* This teaches us the importance of focusing on the present and performing actions with full devotion without becoming overly consumed by the outcomes. By understanding that we control how we expend our energy, we can ensure it serves us in achieving our highest purpose.

Examples of Balance from Legendary Lives

Throughout history, there have been individuals who demonstrated remarkable energy balance. They managed their energy wisely, channelling it toward their goals and inspiring generations:

1. **Swami Vivekananda**: A beacon of spiritual energy and focus, Swami Vivekananda's relentless energy inspired generations. He once said, *"Arise, awake, and stop not till the goal is reached."* His life's work shows how focused energy can transform both the individual and society, providing a lasting legacy that continues to guide spiritual seekers worldwide.

2. **Mahatma Gandhi**: Gandhi's energy was driven by his unwavering commitment to non-violence and truth. His daily practice of recharging his energy through introspection, simplicity, and connection with nature enabled him to lead India's independence movement with profound peace and purpose. His ability to balance his personal and public life allowed him to sustain his mission through difficult times.

3. **Helen Keller**: Despite being both deaf and blind, Helen Keller harnessed her immense inner energy to overcome her disabilities and inspire millions. Her story is a powerful reminder that when energy is channelled with determination and a positive mindset, it can transcend all limitations, unlocking potential even in the most challenging circumstances.

4. **Dr. A.P.J. Abdul Kalam**: Known as the "Missile Man" of India, Dr. Kalam devoted his life to the advancement of science and education. His ability to channel his energy into research,

leadership, and mentorship proved that no goal is too far-reaching when energy is directed with purpose and passion.

Insights for Reflection

To effectively manage and channel your energy, it's important to pause and reflect on a few guiding questions:

- **Where is your energy going?** Reflect on whether your actions align with your life's purpose. Are your daily choices helping you progress toward your goals, or are you expending energy without direction?
- **Do you take time to replenish your energy?** Just as we plug in our phones to recharge, we must take time for ourselves—through mindful rest, meditation, or introspection. Without regular recharging, you risk burnout, stress, and dissatisfaction.
- **Are you focusing your energy wisely?** In today's distraction-filled world, it's easy to dissipate energy. Prioritize your mental and emotional energy on what matters most—whether that's personal growth, family, or meaningful work.

Life Lessons from Technology

Technology offers a helpful analogy for managing energy. Consider how we use our phones and devices:

- **Devices Need Recharging:** Just as your phone needs to be plugged in, we need to regularly recharge ourselves—whether through sleep, prayer, or simply taking time to reflect.
- **Overuse Leads to Damage:** Constantly using a phone without rest can lead to wear and tear. Similarly, overexerting oneself leads to physical and mental exhaustion. Balancing effort with recovery is key.
- **Energy Conservation:** Phones conserve battery by limiting unnecessary processes. In the same way, focusing on what's

essential and minimizing distractions helps conserve our energy for what truly matters.

The Three-Step Practice: Accept, Adjust, Act

Sri Vidyanarayana Theertha offers a three-step process for balanced energy management:

1. **Accept**: Recognize the importance of conserving energy. Acknowledge that you need to rest and recharge, just as your devices need downtime.
2. **Adjust**: Make conscious changes to your lifestyle. Simplify your habits, prioritize meaningful activities, and avoid overcommitting yourself to unnecessary tasks.
3. **Act**: Focus your energy on purposeful actions. Dedicate yourself to your true calling and channel your energy into creating lasting impact.

Practical Examples for Every Life Stage

Energy management is essential at all stages of life. Here are some practical examples:

- **For Students**: Use your energy wisely by balancing studies with rest. Avoid overloading your mind with excessive information—mental fatigue hinders learning. Take breaks and engage in activities that refresh and rejuvenate you.
- **For Professionals**: Build a balance between work and personal life. Without self-care, your work will suffer, and your well-being will deteriorate. Set boundaries around work hours and make space for activities that recharge you—be it family time, hobbies, or exercise.
- **For Caregivers**: Practicing self-care is crucial when caring for others. Only when you are recharged can you truly give your best to those in need. Make sure to allocate time for rest and

rejuvenation so that you can offer your energy with patience and compassion.

- **For Housewives**: The role of a housewife can often be demanding, involving constant attention to household chores, family needs, and maintaining a nurturing environment. It's important to recognize that, just like any other job, you need moments of rest and personal time to recharge. Taking short breaks throughout the day, engaging in hobbies, or simply enjoying quiet moments can help prevent burnout. Balancing household duties with activities that nourish your body, mind, and spirit ensures that you continue to serve your family with energy and love without depleting yourself.

A Simple Analogy: Life as a Battery

Think of yourself as a battery:

- **Recharge Regularly**: Just as a battery needs periodic recharging, so do you. Make sure you rest, meditate, and take time for yourself to stay energized.
- **Excessive Demands**: If you continue to use energy without recharging, you'll face depletion—leading to exhaustion, stress, and even illness.
- **Energy Tax**: Overexerting yourself without proper recharge incurs an energy "tax" that manifests in challenges like stress, burnout, and health problems.

Conclusion: Unlock Your Potential with Balanced Energy

Energy is your most precious and finite resource. By consciously managing and harmonizing your physical, mental, and spiritual energy, you unlock the transformative potential for a life rich in peace, purpose, and fulfilment. When directed with intention and focus, energy becomes the driving force behind extraordinary achievements and profound personal growth.

As you journey through life, remember that energy is not an endless supply. Just as you would never overcharge your phone, it is equally important not to overextend yourself. Make time to recharge, be mindful of how you invest your energy, and, above all, channel it toward your deepest and most meaningful aspirations.

The key to true success lies within you—it resides in the deliberate and mindful management of your energy. When you align and focus your energy wisely, you cultivate clarity, purpose, and peace, creating a life that reflects your highest potential.

THE GURU'S LIGHT

"The Guru's light is not a flame that burns but a sun that awakens.
It does not command, it reveals; it does not bind, it liberates.
True guidance is not in words spoken, but in silence felt within.
The Guru does not give wisdom—he removes the veils that hide it.
To walk in the Guru's light is to see not him, but the truth he unveils."

– His Holiness Sri Vidyanarayana Theertha

CHAPTER-27

THE GRACE OF THE GURU: CELEBRATING THE JOURNEY OF ENLIGHTENMENT

Introduction

The Sacred Significance of Guru Purnima

Guru Purnima is a day of profound spiritual significance, celebrated by countless seekers of truth and wisdom. It is a day dedicated to honouring our Gurus, who guide us through the labyrinth of life toward spiritual awakening. On this sacred day, we remember the invaluable teachings of our spiritual mentors, whose guidance transcends time and place.

As His Holiness Sri Vidyanarayana Theertha beautifully reminds us, *"The Guru is not merely a teacher but a divine guide who leads us from ignorance to light, from darkness to truth. The Guru is the bridge that connects us to our higher self, to the Divine that resides within us all."* Guru Purnima is not just a day of ritual, but a reminder to reflect on our own spiritual journey and the immense grace that our Gurus bestow upon us.

Sri Vidyanarayana Theertha, in his teachings, has often emphasized the sacredness of this relationship between the Guru and disciple. He teaches us that the Guru, as a representative of the Divine, opens the path to self-realization and spiritual fulfilment. On Guru Purnima, we honour the Guru's role in guiding us through the teachings that are the foundation of our spiritual lives.

Q&A Session: Understanding the Role of the Guru

Q: Why do we honour the Guru on this day, and what is the true significance of their teachings?

A: *"A true Guru does not merely teach; he imparts divine wisdom that has the power to awaken your soul."* As His Holiness Sri Vidyanarayana Theertha teaches, honoring the Guru on Guru Purnima is not only a tradition but a deep acknowledgment of the Guru's power to elevate us beyond our limitations. The Guru embodies divine wisdom that leads us to self-realization, guiding us to discover our true nature and divine potential. The teachings of the Guru, passed down through generations, act as a light to dispel the darkness of ignorance and illuminate the soul.

Q: How does a Guru's influence transform an individual?

A: *"The Guru does not change you. He helps you realize who you truly are, which is divine in essence."* Sri Vidyanarayana Theertha's wisdom teaches us that the transformation brought about by the Guru is not external but internal. It is not the Guru who changes us; it is the Guru's grace that helps us recognize the divinity that already exists within us. By surrendering ourselves to the teachings of the Guru, we awaken to our true spiritual nature, gaining clarity, wisdom, and peace.

The story of Ekalavya serves as a powerful example of how devotion to the Guru can lead to spiritual mastery. Even though Dronacharya never formally taught him, Ekalavya's dedication to his Guru allowed him to master the art of archery. This teaches us that the Guru's influence is not always visible but always profound.

Takeaways: Key Insights on Spirituality from Guru Purnima

1. **The Power of Guru's Blessings:** The Guru's blessings are the key to unlocking our spiritual potential. As Sri Vidyanarayana Theertha says, *"In the presence of the Guru, the soul finds the courage*

to recognize its own divinity." The Guru's role is to dispel the darkness of ignorance and awaken the light of wisdom within us. The true blessing of the Guru is the opening of the spiritual door within, guiding us toward our higher self.

2. **Faith and Trust:** The relationship between the Guru and disciple is rooted in unwavering faith and trust. *"Without faith, the journey to self-realization is incomplete,"* says Sri Vidyanarayana Theertha. To truly benefit from the Guru's teachings, one must cultivate an attitude of humility and trust, knowing that the Guru's wisdom is leading us toward divine realization.

3. **Service to the Guru:** True service to the Guru is not only about physical actions but about embodying the Guru's teachings in daily life. Sri Vidyanarayana Theertha teaches, *"Service to the Guru is not in what you do for them, but in how you live according to their teachings."* When we align our lives with the wisdom imparted by the Guru, we honor them in the truest sense.

4. **Humility and Devotion:** *"To walk the path of the Guru, one must leave behind ego and step forward with devotion."* The wisdom of Sri Vidyanarayana Theertha reminds us that to receive the Guru's teachings, we must come with an open heart, free of pride. Humility is the foundation on which the Guru's wisdom can truly take root in our lives.

5. **Rejection of Ego:** Ego is the greatest barrier to spiritual growth. *"When ego is removed, only truth remains,"* says Sri Vidyanarayana Theertha. By shedding the ego, we create space for the divine wisdom of the Guru to enter and guide us. The Guru helps us see past our false identities, leading us to the realization of our true, divine nature.

6. **The Importance of Inner Transformation:** The Guru's role is to facilitate deep inner transformation, guiding us from ignorance to enlightenment. Sri Vidyanarayana Theertha often teaches, *"True knowledge is not intellectual but experiential; it comes when the heart is open to the divine."* Spiritual awakening is not a mental process

but an experience that touches the core of our being, aligning us with the divine consciousness that permeates all of creation.

Conclusion: The Path to Self-Realization

As we celebrate Guru Purnima, let us reflect on the profound wisdom shared by our Gurus, especially as imparted by His Holiness Sri Vidyanarayana Theertha. His teachings remind us that spirituality is not about external rituals but about internal transformation. The Guru's role is to guide us toward the realization that we are all divine in essence, that the answers we seek lie within us, and that the path to self-realization is one of surrender, devotion, and inner awakening.

"When the heart is pure and the mind is surrendered, the Guru's light will illuminate the soul and guide it toward the divine," says Sri Vidyanarayana Theertha. On this auspicious Guru Purnima, let us renew our commitment to walk the path of spiritual awakening with humility and devotion. By doing so, we align ourselves with the divine grace that the Guru offers, guiding us to the ultimate truth: that we are one with the Divine.

CHAPTER-28

DIVINE EMBRACE: THE SACRED CIRCLE OF LOVE, TRUST, CARE, AND SURRENDER

Introduction

In today's world, where trust is fleeting, love is often conditional, and surrender is seen as a weakness, how do we reconnect with our true divine essence? Love, care, trust, and surrender create an unbroken circle—the Atma Devotee Circle—where the divine and the devotee merge as one. This sacred journey calls us to transcend the ego, embrace humility, and open 

ourselves fully to divine grace, allowing it to guide every aspect of our lives. In this circle, we rediscover our innate connection to the divine and experience the transformative power of unconditional love and trust.

> "To know the divine, one must first shed the layers of ego and embrace the heart of humility. Only then will grace flow, and the "Self-Dissolve" into the Divine."
>
> – His Holiness Sri Vidyanarayana Theertha

His Holiness Sri Vidyanarayana Theertha beautifully explains that each quality in this circle is a stepping stone toward self-realization. Love is the seed, care nurtures it, trust strengthens it, and surrender lets it bloom into divine union. This universal truth applies not just to our relationship with the divine but also to how we live, love, and learn as spiritual beings navigating a material world.

Consider a young student overwhelmed by failure finding solace in the Bhagavad Gita's message of surrendering the fruits of action to the Lord. In such moments, the **atma devotee circle** reveals its transformative power, offering clarity, strength, and peace.

Question and Answer Session

Disciple: Swamiji, why do love and care play such a crucial role in devotion?

Swamy: Love and care are the foundation of any relationship, including the one with the divine. When you love Lord Venkateshwara with all your heart, you begin to see Him not as an entity outside but as the very essence of your being.

Caring for others is an extension of this divine love. For example, when devotees visit Tirumala, they offer not just prayers but also acts of care for the less fortunate around them, embodying the spirit of love in action. Consider Sita in *Ramayana*, whose love for Rama extended beyond words into action. Her sacrifices remind us that true love and care transcend personal comfort, anchoring us in divine connection.

Love and care create the soil where trust and surrender can flourish.

Disciple: Swamiji, how does trust strengthen one's spiritual journey?

Swamy: Trust is the bridge between love and surrender. Without trust, the path becomes shaky, filled with doubts and fears. Lord Venkateshwara is a perfect example of trust embodied—millions of devotees entrust their hopes, dreams, and lives to Him, knowing He will guide them.

Trust is not blind faith; it is the result of a deep connection with the divine. When Draupadi called out to Krishna in her moment of despair, it was her trust that summoned His divine intervention. Her story teaches us that trust in the divine can move mountains and protect us even in our darkest hour.

Disciple: Swamiji, what does surrender truly mean?

Swamy: Surrender is not about giving up; it is about giving in—letting go of ego and allowing the divine to guide your life.

When you surrender to Lord Venkateshwara, you realize who He truly is: not just a deity but the supreme consciousness within you. Surrender is a sacred act that frees you from the bondage of self and aligns you with the universal will.

In the *Bhagavad Gita*, Arjuna's surrender to Krishna transformed his despair into clarity. This surrender wasn't a sign of weakness but of wisdom—letting go of ego to embrace divine will. Just as the Gopis surrendered their lives to Krishna, devotees who surrender to the Lord experience boundless joy and peace.

Disciple: Swamiji, how does the concept of Vidyarthi Guru Mandiram relate to devotion?

Swamy: Vidyarthi Guru Mandiram—the students' temple—represents the idea that we are all eternal learners and that God is the ultimate teacher. In this sacred space, every devotee is a student, seeking wisdom and guidance from the divine.

The hallmarks of true devotion are the humility to learn and the willingness to surrender to the Guru's wisdom. Naming Swamiji centres

Vidyarthi Guru Mandiram to reflect this universal truth: no matter how much we learn, the divine always has more to teach.

The Vanaras' devotion to Rama illustrates the power of collective love, care, trust, and surrender, creating a divine synergy that overcame impossible odds.

Challenges Faced by Youth

In the journey toward embodying love, care, trust, and surrender, the youth of today face several unique challenges:

1. **Lack of Clarity and Purpose**

   In an age of information overload, youth often struggle to discern what truly matters. The constant bombardment of societal expectations, peer pressure, and materialistic goals leaves little room for introspection.

2. **Ego and Overconfidence**

   Youthful vigour sometimes breeds overconfidence, which can hinder the ability to surrender. The ego acts as a barrier, preventing the heart from opening fully to the divine.

3. **Distrust and Skepticism**

   With increasing instances of broken trust in relationships, institutions, and leadership, many young people find it difficult to trust others, let alone surrender to a higher power.

4. **Focus on External Validation**

   The pursuit of likes, followers, and validation on social media can disconnect the youth from their inner self. This focus on outward appearances erodes their ability to connect with deeper truths.

5. **Fear of Openness**

To truly love, care, trust, and surrender, one must embrace openness—a trait often feared by many young people. This fear stems from societal conditioning that misinterprets openness as a weakness. Yet, in reality, openness is the gateway to deeper emotional connection and personal growth. By overcoming the fear of being open, individuals unlock the potential for authentic relationships and true emotional resilience. It is through openness that we discover our greatest strengths and cultivate a life of genuine connection.

6. **Neglect of Spiritual Practices**

In the rush to achieve academic, professional, and personal goals, youth often neglect spiritual practices like meditation, prayer, or self-reflection, which are essential to nurturing the atma devotee circle.

7. **Cynicism in Faith**

Exposure to conflicting ideologies and the commercialization of spirituality sometimes makes the youth skeptical about the authenticity of devotion and surrender.

8. **Disconnection from Tradition**

Many young people, especially in urban settings, feel disconnected from traditional practices and values, viewing them as outdated rather than as pathways to spiritual growth.

Takeaways

- **Love and care** are the foundation of spiritual devotion, fostering connection with the divine. Consider Sita's unwavering devotion to Rama in *Ramayana* as a model of these virtues.

- **Trust** is the bridge that makes surrender possible, leading to inner peace and divine guidance. Draupadi's trust in Krishna during her greatest trial exemplifies this truth.
- **Surrender** is the ultimate act of devotion, aligning the self with the universal will. Arjuna's surrender to Krishna in *Bhagavad Gita* highlights the transformative power of this virtue.
- The **atma devotee circle** unites love, care, trust, and surrender, creating a path to self-realization.
- **Vidyarthi Guru Mandiram** reminds us that we are eternal students, with God as our ultimate Guru.
- Naming spiritual centres Vidyarthi Guru Mandiram reinforces the importance of humility and learning in the spiritual journey.

Conclusion

Love, care, trust, and surrender are not just virtues; they are the pillars of a spiritually fulfilling life. His Holiness Sri Vidyanarayana Theertha's teachings guide us in embracing these qualities and entering the sacred **atma devotee circle**.

When we surrender to Lord Venkateshwara, we uncover the profound truth that He is not separate from us; He is the light within. Just as Sita, Draupadi, and Arjuna navigated their journeys with love, trust, and surrender, so too can we discover our inner light by embracing these eternal virtues.

Life becomes a divine dance when we trust His plan, care for others as extensions of His creation, and love Him with all our hearts. Let every spiritual centre resonate with the spirit of Vidyarthi Guru Mandiram, where seekers come as students and leave as enlightened souls. Remember, devotion is a journey of the heart, where love leads, care sustains, trust strengthens, and surrender completes the circle of divine union.

CHAPTER-29

THE GURU'S LIGHT: GUIDING SOULS AND INSPIRING THE YOUTH

Introduction

The Timeless Wisdom of Gurudev

In a world often engulfed by noise, distractions, and fleeting pursuits, the timeless wisdom of Gurus from the traditional lineage emerges as a radiant beacon of hope. These revered spiritual leaders remind us that true peace and enlightenment are not found in external possessions, status, or transient achievements, but through a deep, transformative connection with a genuine Guru.

In this enriching discourse by His Holiness Sri Vidyanarayana Theertha, we are called to reflect on the profound role of the Guru as a guiding force who transcends the illusions of Maya and unveils the path to self-realization. His Holiness emphasizes that a true Guru is not merely a teacher but a spiritual luminary who illuminates the innermost recesses of the soul, dispelling ignorance and instilling wisdom.

This message holds immense relevance in today's context, particularly for the youth navigating a world rife with distractions, discontent, and uncertainty. By reconnecting with the profound wisdom of the Guru, individuals can rise above these challenges, fostering a life of clarity, purpose, and spiritual harmony.

The Guru-Disciple Relationship: Beyond the Illusion of Maya

Ramakrishna Paramahamsa taught us, "The Guru is the embodiment of divinity, the living presence of truth that leads the disciple beyond illusion." His teachings remind us that the Guru's role is not merely that of a teacher, but a divine force guiding the seeker through every aspect of life. This deep connection is not confined to words; it is felt through every action and interaction.

Swami Vivekananda added, "A man is born great, but only a Guru can awaken the greatness in him." The Guru-disciple relationship is a partnership in which the disciple's inherent greatness is nurtured. However, modern distractions often obscure the deeper purpose of this relationship. His Holiness Sri Vidyanarayana Theertha explains, "The Guru is not just an external figure but an internal awakening, a force that transforms the mind and soul." This transformative guidance is what the modern youth desperately needs to overcome the mental pollution and environmental degradation they face.

Today, Ramakrishna Paramahamsa's reminder, "The mind is everything; what you think, you become," is a powerful call to action for youth everywhere. Whether in rural or urban settings, we are surrounded by mental clutter and external distractions. The true Guru helps us transcend these illusions, allowing us to realize our true potential.

The Role of Youth: Overcoming Modern Challenges

The youth of today are navigating an era defined by unprecedented challenges. The rapid pace of global change, coupled with increasing external pressures, has resulted in widespread mental pollution and emotional turbulence. Urban areas, with their fast-paced lifestyles and overstimulating environments, often leave young people feeling disconnected and overwhelmed. Once thought to be immune to such pressures, rural communities are now grappling with similar issues as the pervasive reach of media and technology encroaches upon even the most remote corners, eroding traditional values and replacing them with a flood of external influences.

Environmental degradation adds another layer to these challenges, affecting both rural and urban populations alike. The awareness of the toll human activity has taken on the planet is growing, particularly among younger generations. Amid these pressing concerns, His Holiness Sri Vidyanarayana Theertha reminds us, "The Guru helps the disciple to break free from the illusions created by the external world and realize the power within." This timeless wisdom is critical for today's youth, enabling them to rise above distractions and cultivate a deeper sense of purpose and responsibility.

Swami Vivekananda's clarion call to the youth—"Arise, awake, and stop not until the goal is reached"—resonates with renewed relevance. The greatest challenge lies not in the external world but in the transformation of the inner self. It is through the light of the Guru that the youth can transcend the illusions of modern life, overcome mental and emotional dissonance, and rediscover their innate strength.

Empowered by this inner clarity, they can take charge of their futures, championing both personal growth and collective well-being in a world that desperately needs their energy, passion, and wisdom.

The Rural-Urban Divide: A Growing Challenge

While urban areas often bear the brunt of rapid technological advancements and the resulting social and environmental issues, rural areas are not immune. The rise of media, internet access, and external cultural influences have made their way into even the most remote villages. Rural youth, who once held onto traditional values, are now being influenced by global trends that promote materialism, instant gratification, and mental distractions. The relentless stream of information has led to mental pollution in both rural and urban landscapes.

In rural villages, the traditional connection with nature and spiritual practices has been overshadowed by the constant barrage of external influences—environmental degradation compounds this, affecting these communities' mental and physical well-being. For rural youth, the lack of guidance and emotional support exacerbates the feeling of being lost amidst the noise of a changing world.

His Holiness Sri Vidyanarayana Theertha underscores the need for spiritual guidance in such times, emphasizing, "The Guru helps the disciple to navigate life's complexities with clarity and focus." The Guru's teachings have the power to heal both the mind and the environment, offering a path of mental clarity and spiritual enlightenment to youth in rural and urban areas alike.

Insights for Action and Reflection: Guiding the Youth Towards Self-Realization

To overcome the challenges faced by today's youth—whether in urban or rural areas—it is essential to develop inner strength, clarity, and purpose. Here are some practical insights for action:

- **Cultivate Self-Awareness:** Take time each day to reflect on your thoughts, actions, and values. A true Guru helps the disciple develop awareness, leading to self-realization.
- **Practice Mindfulness:** In an era filled with distractions, meditation and mindfulness practices can help you reconnect with your inner wisdom and reduce mental pollution.

- **Seek Guidance from a True Guru**: Trust in the wisdom and guidance of your Guru, who will help you see beyond external illusions and align your life with a higher purpose.
- **Serve with Compassion**: Whether in urban or rural settings, service to others is a key teaching of the Guru. Engage with your community in meaningful ways that contribute to collective well-being.
- **Stay Grounded in Values**: The rise of technology and media should not distract you from your core values. Stay rooted in spiritual wisdom and ethical principles that help you navigate the complexities of life.

Conclusion: Embracing the Guru's Light for a Transformed Life

In today's world, where the external world is increasingly noisy and disconnected, the teachings of His Holiness Sri Vidyanarayana Theertha, Ramakrishna Paramahamsa, and Swami Vivekananda offer a guiding light. Through their wisdom, we are reminded that the Guru is not just an external figure but an internal awakening—a force that helps us overcome the illusions of the material world and realize our true potential.

For the youth, this connection to a true Guru is not just about spiritual growth but also about empowerment in the face of external challenges. Whether in rural villages or bustling cities, the wisdom of the Guru has the power to heal, guide, and transform lives.

As His Holiness Sri Vidyanarayana Theertha beautifully put it, "The Guru's presence is the eternal beacon that guides the soul beyond the illusions of the world." It is time for the youth to awaken, embrace their divine potential, and contribute to creating a better, more compassionate world.

Takeaways and Clues for Action

- **Self-Reflection**: Engage in daily reflection to increase self-awareness and clarity.
- **Mental Clarity**: Practice mindfulness and meditation to reduce mental pollution.
- **Guru's Guidance**: Seek a true Guru who can guide you in navigating the illusions of modern life.
- **Service**: Contribute to your community, whether rural or urban, through acts of service and compassion.
- **Stay Rooted in Values**: Let spiritual teachings be your anchor amidst the noise of the world.

By incorporating these insights, both rural and urban youth can find their path to spiritual empowerment, creating lives of meaning, purpose, and inner peace.

CHAPTER-30

THE SACRED BOND: HOW THE GURU-DISCIPLE RELATIONSHIP TRANSFORMS THE SOUL

"The Guru does not lead the disciple to the Divine, they lead the disciple to realize the Divine within themselves."

– His Holiness Sri Vidyanarayana Theertha

The Guru-disciple relationship has stood the test of time, transcending cultures and epochs. This sacred bond is one of profound transformation, offering the seeker not just knowledge but also wisdom, compassion, and the divine light that guides the soul toward its true purpose. In today's world, where spiritual paths often seem fragmented and diluted, the essence of this relationship is more crucial than ever.

The Divine Role of the Guru

In every age, God sends spiritual guides to show the path to truth, guiding those who seek enlightenment. The Guru is not a mere teacher of knowledge, but a divine conduit for the teachings of God. "Just as Rama, Krishna, and even great sages like Vyasa and Valmiki had Gurus, they too recognized the importance of learning from higher wisdom. This highlights that even divine beings and revered sages sought guidance, demonstrating that the pursuit of knowledge and spiritual growth is not limited by one's stature. Vyasa, guided by the sage

Vasistha, and Valmiki, transformed by the wisdom of Narada Muni, exemplify the humility required to learn and grow. The Guru, through their grace and selflessness, imparts wisdom not for personal gain, but to help the disciple align their life with the divine, leading them toward the ultimate truth.

His Holiness Sri Vidyanarayana Theertha often reflects on the fact that a true Guru is someone who does not flaunt their scholarship. A true Guru knows how to reach every disciple at their level of understanding, without imposing rigid concepts. They never see themselves as superior but as humble servants of the divine truth. A True Guru does not simply teach; they live by example, making their life the greatest lesson. In their presence, the disciple is encouraged not just to learn but to experience the teachings in a practical, living way.

The Guru as a Guide for Practical Spirituality

A true Guru does not limit wisdom to complex rituals or hidden teachings. They show that spirituality is woven into daily life, helping the disciple see that every action, when done with love and dedication, becomes a way to connect with the divine. Whether it is cleaning, serving, or creating, every task plays a role in the larger harmony of the world. The Guru teaches us to honour all roles and recognize that every person, no matter their work or status, contributes to the greater purpose of life.

When we contemplate the lives of sages like Valmiki and Vyasa, we are reminded that their enduring greatness was rooted not in their social origins but in their unwavering devotion, profound wisdom, and deep understanding of Sanatana Dharma. Their legacies teach us that the light of truth shines brightest through a pure heart and a disciplined mind. Even Krishna, the Divine incarnate, exemplified humility by seeking the guidance of his Guru, Sandipani, demonstrating that spiritual growth is an unending journey. True wisdom blossoms in those who embrace humility and remain open to learning, regardless of their origins or stature.

The Guru ensures that the disciple understands the sanctity of the body, which is a temple of the divine. "The body is not meant for indulgence but for service," the Guru teaches. It is not enough to worship gods in trees, rivers, or idols if we neglect the temple of our own body. The senses must be used sensibly, for they are instruments of divine service. This is an integral part of the Guru's teachings—to guide the disciple in maintaining the body as an instrument for higher purposes, realizing that true service to God starts with honouring one's own existence.

Spiritual Growth: A Journey of Patience and Waiting

In the current world, where instant gratification dominates, there is often impatience, even in spiritual pursuits. Today's seekers often expect quick results, treating spirituality like a commodity—much like the convenience of a ready-made cup of coffee. This impatience, however, undermines the depth of spiritual practice. As His Holiness Sri Vidyanarayana Theertha states, "To grow spiritually, you must wait. Just as a child takes nine months in the womb before birth, spiritual growth requires time. It cannot be rushed."

Spirituality is not a microwaveable process. The modern desire for everything quick—food, clothing, or even spiritual wisdom—fails to acknowledge the importance of patience, perseverance, and inner work. A true disciple understands that wisdom is not imparted overnight but requires steady sadhana, waiting, and an unwavering commitment to the divine path.

Crossing Boundaries: The Universal Truth of God

In Hinduism, we say **God is Truth, and Truth is one,** though we call it by different names. While Hindus may call God by names like Krishna, Rama, Renuka Ellamma, Lakshmi, and Saraswati, Christians may call God Jesus and others by different names based on their traditions. But the truth remains universal—God is one, though paths may differ. The Guru helps the disciples recognize this truth and urges them to transcend the boundaries of religion, caste, and creed. In fact, the Guru's teachings point to the futility of religious dogma, urging disciples to focus on the essence of truth and love rather than being caught up in the rigid structures that often divide humanity.

The Guru guides the disciple to understand that, regardless of religious identity, **the ultimate goal is to reach God and live a life of harmony, service, and compassion.** The West, in its fascination with the Eastern value system, is beginning to recognize the depth of spirituality that the East offers. But instead of merely imitating the West, the East must reclaim its own values, integrating them with the modern world.

The Modern Guru-Disciple Relationship

The Guru-disciple relationship today faces numerous challenges. With the rise of technology and instant access to spiritual information, many seekers expect immediate answers and quick solutions. Spirituality has been reduced to a commodity in the modern world, with many self-proclaimed gurus offering rapid transformations. However, the true Guru teaches that true spiritual growth cannot be rushed.

The disciple must remain grounded, exercising patience and diligence in their practice. Spirituality is not about instant results but about sustained, focused effort and surrender. True spiritual growth is not about filling one's mind with information but transforming the heart and soul through consistent practice, humility, and devotion. The Guru, in today's world, continues to play the role of guiding the disciple through the illusions of modern distractions, showing them the way to inner peace and divine wisdom.

Conclusion: Walking the Path of the Divine

The Guru-disciple relationship is one of the most sacred and transformative bonds that can exist. It is a journey from ignorance to wisdom, from self-centeredness to selflessness, from separation to union with the Divine. The Guru does not merely teach—he or she lights the path, offers the disciple the strength to walk it, and shows them the way to discover the divinity within themselves.

As we walk this path, let us not forget that every role in society—whether as a washerman, barber, teacher, or doctor—is valuable and has its place in the greater divine order. Every work, if done with devotion and sincerity, becomes a form of worship. The Guru teaches that true spirituality is not about retreating from the world but engaging with it in a way that aligns with the divine purpose.

Let us remember the words of His Holiness Sri Vidyanarayana Theertha: "The Guru does not lead the disciple to the Divine. They lead the disciple to realize the Divine within themselves." May we all strive to recognize the divine wisdom in every act, in every role we play, and in every moment we live. The Guru's light shines bright, guiding us to truth, peace, and the realization of our highest purpose.

THE DHARMA IN ACTION

Dharma in action is living with truth, not just speaking of it.
It is serving without seeking, giving without expecting.
When actions come from the heart, they become a prayer.
True dharma is not about success or failure, but doing what is right.
Walk the path with faith, and the divine will guide your steps."

– His Holiness Sri Vidyanarayana Theertha

CHAPTER-31

Embracing Swadharma: The Path of Selfless Action and Awakening

Introduction

His Holiness Sri Vidyanarayana Theertha, in this discourse, explores the profound concept of *Swadharma*—the inherent duty of an individual in alignment with their true nature and higher purpose. He emphasizes the importance of selfless service, compassion, and the journey toward spiritual awakening. The discourse offers insights into how one's actions, when motivated by genuine love and service to others, lead to spiritual growth and fulfilment. *Swadharma* is not simply about performing one's responsibilities but doing so in a way that leads to the awakening of a higher consciousness and connects individuals to the divine purpose that transcends personal gain.

Question and Answer

Question: What is Swadharma, and why is it important?

- *Swadharma* is defined as the righteous duty or responsibility that an individual must follow, guided by their true nature and the higher calling of humanity. It transcends mundane survival activities such as eating and breathing, reaching into the realm of compassion and service, particularly in times of distress. Swadharma calls for selflessness in relieving suffering and promoting the welfare of others. This is what distinguishes human beings from animals—our capacity to care for one another with empathy and love.

Question: How does Swadharma relate to spiritual growth?

- The essence of *Swadharma* lies in selfless service. When one helps others in distress with a pure heart, it not only brings happiness to the recipient but also fosters spiritual growth in the giver. *Karma*, when done with the intention of self-improvement and spiritual development, becomes the catalyst for awakening one's higher consciousness, propelling one toward deeper self-realization.

Question: What should be the motivation behind our actions?

- Actions must not be driven by selfish desires such as seeking praise, honour, or material gain. Instead, they should be fueled by the desire to serve others and contribute to the well-being of all. This pure form of service fosters the development of spiritual wealth, which elevates the individual to the level of a true yogi, transcending the material attachments that hinder spiritual progress.

Question: What is the role of love in Swadharma?

- Love is the foundation of all spiritual practices. True meditation and wisdom emerge from love, which is the motivating force behind selfless actions. A person who acts with love, integrity, and without ulterior motives will naturally attract spiritual power. Such a person is a true yogi, unaffected by external recognition or honour, driven solely by the love for humanity and the divine.

Key Insights

- *Swadharma* involves actions driven by selfless love and compassion to alleviate the suffering of others.
- It is a spiritual journey where one must engage in work that leads to awakening, not simply for survival or personal gain.

- The true motivation behind actions should be service to others, not seeking fame, wealth, or recognition.
- Love is the foundational force behind both meditation and wisdom, enabling one to connect with higher spiritual energies.
- A true yogi is humble, engaged in their duties without expectation, and does not seek external recognition.

Conclusion

The path of *Swadharma* is not only a route to spiritual growth but also to human evolution. By transcending the mundane aspects of life, it guides us to selflessly serve others and awaken our higher consciousness. Acting with pure love and compassion helps align ourselves with our true nature and contributes to the collective well-being, leading us toward divine realization.

CHAPTER-32

SERVICE TO OTHERS: A PATH TO SPIRITUAL AWAKENING

Introduction

Service, or *Seva*, is more than a moral duty; it is a sacred journey that connects us to our higher selves and the divine. In today's world, where individualism often overshadows community, the act of selfless service stands as a beacon of hope and transformation. His Holiness Sri Vidyanarayana Theertha reminds us that service is the essence of spirituality—a practice that nurtures compassion, bridges divides, and uplifts the soul.

Consider the sun—it gives light and warmth without expecting anything in return, enabling life to thrive. Similarly, selfless service allows us to rise above personal desires, illuminating not just the lives of others but our own path toward spiritual growth. Service is not a grand act of charity but a reflection of our innate divinity, expressed in small, meaningful ways that transform both the giver and the receiver.

Disciple: Swamiji, why is service considered a key aspect of spiritual life?

Swamy:

Service, or *Seva*, is not merely an act of kindness but a profound spiritual practice. When you serve others selflessly, you align yourself with the divine purpose of existence. Just as the river flows tirelessly to nourish the land, a life dedicated to service nourishes the soul. For instance, Mahatma Gandhi's life was rooted in service—not just to individuals but to an entire nation. Through selfless acts, he inspired millions and became a living example of how service leads to spiritual awakening.

Disciple: Swamiji, how does selfless service lead to inner peace and a connection with the divine?

Swamy:

When you serve without expecting anything in return, your heart becomes pure, free from ego and attachment. This purity creates space for divine grace to enter. Take the example of Mother Teresa, who devoted her life to serving the destitute and the dying. Her unwavering commitment to *Seva* brought her peace and a deep connection with the divine, inspiring countless others to walk the same path. Inner peace arises when we transcend self-centeredness and see the divine in every soul we serve.

Disciple: Swamiji, how does helping others purify the heart and mind?

Swamy:

Helping others is like cleansing a mirror—it removes the dirt of selfishness, allowing you to reflect the light of the divine within. Think of Saint Ramanuja, who defied societal norms to uplift those considered untouchable, treating them as equals and children of God. His service purified his heart and mind, enabling him to spread the message of equality and divine love. Through service, we let go of prejudices and expand our hearts to embrace all of creation.

Disciple: Swamiji, why is compassion essential in acts of service?

Swamy:

Compassion is the soul of service. Without it, service becomes mechanical or self-serving. When Swami Vivekananda urged his followers to "serve God in man," he reminded us that true service stems from a heart filled with compassion. Compassion transforms ordinary acts into divine offerings. Whether it is feeding the hungry or comforting the grieving, acts of service born from compassion bring healing not just to others but also to ourselves.

Disciple: Swamiji, how does service to the community reflect divine love?

Swamy:

Community service is an expression of divine love in action. Just as a tree bears fruit not for itself but for others, our lives gain meaning when we contribute to the well-being of the community. Sri Narayana Guru, a reformer and spiritual leader, dedicated his life to uplifting marginalized communities. His service exemplified divine love, as he saw God in every being and worked tirelessly to create a more equitable society. Service to the community is a powerful way to manifest the divine love within us.

Disciple: Swamiji, what defines true service?

Swamy:

True service is selfless and free from the desire for recognition or reward. It is like the rain that nourishes the earth without expecting gratitude. Think of Lord Hanuman, whose devotion to Lord Rama was reflected in his tireless service. He sought neither praise nor personal gain but worked for the greater good. True service is an offering to the divine, done with humility and love, for the benefit of others.

Takeaways

- Service is a sacred path that connects us to the divine and fosters spiritual growth.
- Selfless acts of service purify the heart, removing ego and attachment.
- Compassion is the foundation of meaningful service, transforming ordinary acts into divine offerings.
- Community service reflects divine love, reminding us of our shared humanity.
- True service is selfless, free from the desire for recognition, and an offering to the divine.
- Through acts of service, we uplift others and find inner peace and purpose.

Conclusion

Service is not a mere act of charity but the highest form of worship. His Holiness Sri Vidyanarayana Theertha teaches us that when we serve others, we serve the divine itself. Every act of kindness, no matter how small, brings us closer to our true selves and the ultimate truth.

Imagine a world where everyone embraced service as a way of life—where kindness replaced indifference, and unity triumphed over division. This is not an idealistic dream; it is a reality we can create through our actions. Service to others is the bridge that connects us to the divine and to one another.

Let us dedicate our lives to this noble path, knowing that in serving others, we find ourselves. For it is in giving that we truly receive, and in serving that we become one with the infinite divine.

CHAPTER-33

DHARMA: THE GUIDING MANDATE OF LIFE AND DIVINE FORCES

Introduction

Dharma, the eternal and universal code of righteousness, is both the foundation of life and the essence of existence. It transcends religious and cultural boundaries, serving as the guiding principle for individual and collective well-being. In a rapidly advancing scientific world, where humanity constantly strives to harness the forces of nature, Dharma  bridges the gap between spirituality and science. It unites ethical responsibility with the laws governing the universe, much like the principles of physics that maintain order in the cosmos.

His Holiness Sri Vidyanarayana Theertha explains that Dharma is not a mere philosophical concept but a dynamic, all-encompassing force that harmonizes nature, humanity, and divine will. Similarly, the Bhagavad Gita emerges as a timeless guide, offering practical wisdom that applies equally to modern management and ancient spiritual pursuits. Through an exploration of the cosmic roles assigned to Eswara and demi-gods, this discourse sheds light on how divine forces and human actions intertwine to preserve universal balance.

Questions and Answers

Q: Why is Dharma considered the common mandate for all citizens?

Swamy:

Dharma is the foundation upon which societies thrive, ensuring balance, justice, and harmony. It operates like the laws of nature—consistent and universal. Just as gravity binds objects to the Earth, Dharma binds individuals to righteousness, ensuring order in society. When citizens uphold their responsibilities with sincerity and commitment, they contribute to a sustainable and harmonious world.

Example: A tree provides shade, oxygen, and fruit without expectation—fulfilling its Dharma. Similarly, humans must perform their roles selflessly for the collective good.

Q: What is the significance of the Bhagavad Gita in overcoming life's challenges?

Swamy:

The Bhagavad Gita acts as a spiritual medicine, addressing Tapatraya—the threefold afflictions of physical, mental, and spiritual suffering. Like a scientific manual, it offers precise guidance on how to navigate uncertainties, overcome stress, and maintain equilibrium. By teaching detachment and surrender to the divine, the Gita equips individuals with resilience to face challenges.

Example: A scientist faces failure in experiments but perseveres with clarity and purpose, just as the Gita advises detachment from outcomes while focusing on efforts.

Q: How does the Bhagavad Gita serve as a tool for management?

Swamy:

The Bhagavad Gita integrates the principles of leadership and effective management:

1. **Clarity in Decision-Making:** Just as Krishna guided Arjuna through his inner conflict, leaders must address confusion with purpose and foresight.
2. **Work with Detachment:** Focusing on actions rather than results enhances performance, akin to scientific exploration driven by curiosity, not immediate success.
3. **Empowering Leadership:** Krishna exemplifies mentorship, demonstrating that compassionate guidance fosters growth and teamwork.

The Gita's wisdom aligns with modern practices, proving invaluable in decision-making, emotional intelligence, and ethical leadership.

Q: What are the responsibilities given to Eswara (the Supreme)?

Swamy:

Eswara oversees the preservation of Dharma through four key responsibilities:

1. Protection of Dharmic individuals.
2. Punishment of Adharmic actions to maintain cosmic justice.
3. Rejuvenation of Dharma during crises.
4. Offering solace and support to those in distress.

Eswara, like the laws of nature, operates passively yet profoundly, delegating specific roles to demi-gods. This delegation mirrors the scientific principle of distributed systems, where individual components work harmoniously to achieve a greater purpose.

Q: How do demi-gods and minor cosmic forces contribute to Dharma?

Swamy:

Demi-gods are the cosmic administrators tasked with maintaining natural and universal balance. Each demi-god, such as Indra (rain), Agni (fire), and Vayu (air), fulfils a specific role in sustaining life. Minor forces, like planetary influences and karma, ensure continuity at micro and macro levels.

Analogy: Just as the ecosystem relies on the interplay of organisms for stability, the cosmic order depends on the coordinated efforts of demi-gods under Eswara's guidance.

Q: How can one overcome fear and uncertainty in fulfilling their responsibilities?

Swamy:

Fear stems from ignorance and attachment. By embracing Dharma and surrendering to the divine will, fear dissolves. For instance, a scientist approaching a complex problem with confidence in universal laws finds solutions. Similarly, those walking the path of Dharma transcend fear through faith and self-awareness.

Takeaways

- Dharma is the universal law that binds humanity and sustains cosmic harmony, akin to the physical laws governing the universe.
- The Bhagavad Gita serves as both a spiritual remedy and a practical guide for management, emphasizing clarity, resilience, and ethical responsibility.

- Eswara delegates cosmic responsibilities to demi-gods, reflecting the principles of distributed systems in science.
- Demi-gods, as cosmic forces, collaborate to maintain universal balance, mirroring the interconnectedness of natural systems.
- Fear and uncertainty can be overcome through surrender, faith, and alignment with Dharma.

Conclusion

The teachings of His Holiness Sri Vidyanarayana Theertha remind us that Dharma is not just a spiritual concept but a cosmic principle with profound relevance to modern science and management. By aligning ourselves with Dharma, we bridge the gap between spirituality and scientific understanding, ensuring personal growth and universal harmony.

The Bhagavad Gita, like a scientific manual, provides timeless wisdom that applies across disciplines, guiding individuals to act with clarity, confidence, and responsibility. By reciting its verses and embracing its teachings, we align our actions with the rhythm of the cosmos. In doing so, we transcend fear, achieve balance, and contribute to the greater good, realizing that Dharma is both the mandate of life and the key to liberation.

CHAPTER-34

DETACHMENT AND SERVICE: DIVINE INSIGHTS FROM AN AVADHOOTHA

Introduction

In the journey of spiritual growth, there are individuals who transcend the boundaries of worldly attachment and reveal the true path to inner peace and divine connection. These beings, known as Avadhoothas, live in a state of supreme detachment, yet their hearts overflow with love and compassion for all. They are not bound by material desires, yet they serve humanity with a selflessness  that awakens the soul. Avadhoothas life is not one of renunciation in the traditional sense but one of total surrender to the divine, where every action, every thought, and every breath is an offering to God.

Swami Sivananda, Nisargadatta Maharaj, Ramana Maharshi, and Kanchi Paramacharya are some of the shining examples of Avadhoothas who have walked the earth, leaving behind profound teachings and an unwavering commitment to truth and love. These revered sages and saints have shown us that true freedom is not found in escaping the world but in understanding that the divine is present in every part of it.

His Holiness Sri Vidyanarayana Theertha, with his deep spiritual wisdom, invites us to explore the essence of what it truly means to be an Avadhootha. Through his teachings, we come to realize that an Avadhootha is not someone who shuns life but someone who embraces it fully, with complete awareness of the divine in all things. Whether in the forests of Kanchi, the caves of Arunachala, or the bustling streets of modern cities, the Avadhootha walks with a heart open to all, seeing God in every person, every experience, and every moment.

His Holiness guides us to understand that the path of the Avadhootha is about living without attachment yet being deeply connected to the world through service, love, and the practice of dharma. This divine path is one of purity, where the heart remains untouched by ego, and the mind is free from desires. Through the teachings of the Avadhootha, we are reminded that true liberation comes not from renouncing the world but from loving and serving it with an open heart and a soul surrendered to the divine.

Disciple: Swamy, could you please explain the nature of an Avadhootha and how we can apply the teachings of Avadhoothas in our daily lives?

Swamy: Avadhoothas are exceptional beings who have transcended the worldly attachments and distractions that bind us. They do not seek worldly recognition or possessions, yet they care deeply for others. They live not in isolation but as embodiments of divine love and service.

The mind of an Avadhootha may be filled with countless thoughts, yet they remain unaffected by them. It is as if they have mastered the art of detachment, seeing the divine in every being, in every action, and in every situation.

Wherever they are—whether in the heart of the city or in a remote village—they carry the essence of truth, trust, and compassion. Take, for example, the revered Swamy Sivananda, who, despite his profound wisdom, dedicated his life to the selfless service of humanity, offering unconditional love and care.

Similarly, Ramana Maharshi, living in the hills of Arunachala, taught us that silence itself is a profound teaching, and in that silence, one can experience the divine presence. The Avadhoothas life exemplifies profound detachment from the material world yet deep immersion in serving others, always seeing the divine in all forms.

Disciple: Swamy, how can we embody this state of detachment and service in our own lives?

Swamy: To live as an Avadhootha, you must first understand that true detachment is not about renouncing the world but releasing your attachment to the outcomes and desires. Life will present challenges, but the key is to perform your duties with love and selflessness without becoming attached to the results. Remember, the Avadhootha does not perform actions out of expectation but out of compassion and duty. It is like the lotus flower—it remains untouched by the muddy waters around it, yet it blooms with beauty and grace. Similarly, you must engage fully with life while maintaining inner peace, seeing everything as a reflection of the divine.

Disciple: Swamy, is detachment the same as renunciation?

Swamy: No, detachment is not the same as renunciation. Renunciation is the physical withdrawal from the world, while detachment is the mental and emotional freedom from the attachments to the results of your actions.

Detachment allows you to live fully in the world, fulfil your responsibilities, and serve others without getting entangled in expectations or desires. It is like a flower that offers its fragrance to the world but does not ask for anything in return. Detachment helps you live with a heart open to others while remaining untouched by the material world's fleeting nature.

Disciple: Swamy, how can we ensure we are on the right path without getting distracted?

Swamy: The right path is always within you, hidden deep in your heart. While the mind may get distracted and lead you astray, the heart remains true, guided by inner wisdom. Trust your intuition and let your heart guide you. When you live in alignment with dharma—the divine law—you align yourself with the cosmic order.

Practicing kindness, compassion, and detachment allows you to become a vessel for divine will, fulfilling your purpose in this world. The distractions of life may seem overwhelming at times, but when you trust in the divine presence within, your path will always be illuminated.

Disciple: Swamy, what about the challenges and distractions of life?

Swamy: Challenges and distractions are an inevitable part of life's journey and are meant to test your inner resolve. But when you practice detachment, you will begin to see these challenges for what they truly are: temporary and transient. The divine within you is the constant that remains unaffected by these external distractions. Life is like a river—constantly flowing, sometimes turbulent, sometimes calm—but the divine is the stillness beneath it all. When you trust in the divine presence, you will navigate the challenges gracefully, knowing they are just opportunities to grow stronger in your spiritual journey.

Key Takeaways

- **Detachment**: True detachment is not about renouncing the world but about being free from attachment to outcomes and desires.
- **Service**: Avadhoothas spirit lies in selfless service to others, recognizing the divine in all beings and all actions.
- **Trust in the Divine**: The key to inner peace is trusting in the divine presence within, even amidst life's challenges.
- **Inner Guidance**: The heart, guided by inner wisdom, is the true compass for finding the right path in life.

Inspiring Conclusion

An Avadhootha teaches us that freedom and peace are found not in withdrawing from the world but in living with love, compassion, and unwavering trust in the divine. By aligning ourselves with dharma, practising selfless service, and seeing the divine in every action, we, too, can walk the path of inner peace and spiritual fulfilment. The essence of life is not in accumulating possessions or success but in living with a heart full of love, without attachment to the world. Just like the Avadhoothas, we must embrace life fully while remaining detached from the desires that bind us. Let us walk this path with grace and devotion, trusting that the divine will guide us every step of the way.

CHAPTER-35

THE POWER OF ACTION: NURTURING GLOBAL WELL-BEING AND SPIRITUAL HARMONY

The Divine Path of Faith, Dharma, and Self-Realization

Introduction

In the journey of life, the intricate interplay of **LOKA KSHEMAM** (the well-being of the world) and **KARMA PRABHAVAM** (the influence of actions) shapes our destiny. The teachings of His Holiness Sri Vidyanarayana Theertha guide us to understand how our actions, driven by faith and aligned with Dharma, lead to the path of self-realization.

This discourse, **"LOKA KSHEMAM and KARMA PRABHAVAM: The Divine Path of Faith, Dharma, and Self-Realization,"** delves into the timeless wisdom that encourages individuals to embrace the interconnectedness of all beings, purify the mind, and align one's actions with the divine will. His Holiness Sri Vidyanarayana Theertha emphasizes that true spiritual growth is not merely a pursuit of personal salvation but a collective effort toward the well-being of the world. Through the practice of Dharma and a deep connection to the divine, we come to understand our purpose and the profound influence of our actions on the world around us.

In this journey, we are reminded that faith, when nurtured with sincerity, is the foundation upon which all actions are built. **Karma**, in this context, is not just an action but a conscious choice made in alignment with divine guidance, leading us toward both worldly and spiritual harmony. As we move forward in this exploration, we gain insights into how surrender to the divine, devotion to Dharma, and self-awareness bring about the ultimate realization of our true selves.

Faith as the Shield from Life's Traps

Disciple: Swamy, how does belief in God protect us from the traps of life?

Swamy: The essence of belief in God is like a shield protecting you from the illusions of life. When you believe in God with your heart, you are not trapped by the ever-changing whims of the mind. Imagine the lotus, which floats effortlessly in the pond, untouched by the water around it. This is how your mind must remain—unaffected by external circumstances.

Swamy explained further, "If you allow your thoughts to be swayed by negativity, you will drown in the very illusions that bind you. But, if you turn your thoughts toward God, even negative situations will transform into opportunities for growth. Just as a potter shapes clay with skilful hands, your faith shapes the course of your life. With pure belief, you become the creator of your destiny, untouched by the world's turbulence."

The Role of Mind, Heart, and Guru in Spiritual Life

Disciple: Swamy, how do we align the mind and heart on the spiritual path?

Swamy: The mind can be compared to a father, and the heart to a mother. Together, they play important roles in your spiritual journey—your mind helps you think and reason, while your heart connects you to love and compassion. But there's something even deeper guiding both of them: your inner consciousness, which is the Guru within you.

Think of it like a person driving a car. The mind is like the driver's hands on the steering wheel, and the heart is like the car's wheels, guiding the direction of your life. The Guru, who resides inside you, is like the one who controls the steering wheel, making sure you stay on the right path toward your spiritual growth and ultimate purpose.

Swamy shared a beautiful analogy, "Consider a bird flying with two wings—one represents the mind, the other the heart. If either wing is weak, the bird cannot soar. Similarly, balance between the mind and heart is essential for spiritual progress. Let the Guru within be the wind beneath your wings, allowing you to fly toward liberation."

Vedanta in Action: Karma as the Path to Purification

Disciple: Swamy, can Vedanta be understood through action?

Swamy: Absolutely. Vedanta is not merely a philosophy to be discussed but a reality to be lived. Every action you perform, if done with devotion, becomes a spiritual act. Karma is the practical expression of Vedantic principles.

Swamy continued, "Japa (repetition of God's name) and Dhyana (meditation) are essential to purify the mind. Imagine polishing a mirror; it removes all dirt, allowing you to see your true reflection clearly. Likewise, when you perform your actions with purity and devotion, you remove the inner dirt, revealing your true divine nature."

Advaita, Dvaita, and Vishishtadvaita: The Nature of Divie Unity

Disciple: Swamy, could you explain the concepts of Advaita, Dvaita, and Vishishtadvaita?

Swamy: Advaita teaches that there is no separation between you and God. Everything, in essence, is God. The individual soul and the Supreme Being are one, like the wave and the ocean. When you look at the ocean, you see the waves, but at the core, it is all water. Similarly, in Advaita, the individual soul realizes its oneness with the Supreme Being. There is no duality, no separation—just a unified whole.

Dvaita, on the other hand, recognizes the distinction between the individual soul and God, much like the distinction between the branch of a tree and the trunk. While both are part of the same tree, they retain their individual forms. In Dvaita, the soul acknowledges that it is distinct from God, and even though it seeks union, there remains a difference between the two. God is seen as the Supreme Being, and the soul, though seeking closeness, never loses its individual identity.

Vishishtadvaita, a beautiful synthesis of the two, posits that while the soul is distinct, it is inseparably connected to God. Think of a body and its soul—the soul is distinct, yet it cannot exist without the body. In Vishishtadvaita, the soul is an individual entity that always remains in a relationship with the divine, yet it cannot be separated from it. The soul's nature and the divine essence are always interconnected, like a spark that belongs to the fire.

Swamy beautifully illustrated: "Imagine a tree whose branches are intertwined. To the observer, it might seem like the branches are one with the trunk, but each branch has its distinct form. Similarly, in Advaita, the individual soul realizes its oneness with the Supreme Being, while in Dvaita, the soul acknowledges its individual form but still seeks union with God. In Vishishtadvaita, the soul and God remain distinct but eternally connected, like the body and its soul—inseparable and interdependent."

Disciple: Swamy, how can we recognize and experience the divine in our daily lives?

Swamy: You must see God in every being, in every action. The challenge is not in the external world, but in your perception. When you adjust your view to see the divine in all things, you will experience a sense of unity. Just like the tree embraces the sky, let your heart embrace the divine in all beings. Adjust your thoughts, adjust your life, and you will find divinity everywhere.

Disciple: Swamy, how should we approach surrender in our lives?

Swamy: Surrender is the key to unlocking the divine presence in your life. Just as water surrenders to the ocean, you must surrender your ego to God. But surrender comes in different forms, as exemplified by the divine figures we revere. Rama's love, Sita's care, Lakshman's trust, and Hanuman's unwavering surrender all offer different lessons in surrendering to the divine.

Swamy continued, "Rama's love is without condition; Sita's care is nurturing; Lakshman's trust is steadfast, and Hanuman's surrender is complete. Each form of surrender is a facet of the divine love you must cultivate in your life. Just as the clay allows the potter to shape it, allow the divine to shape your life with love and surrender."

The Balance of Past, Present, and Future

Disciple: Swamy, how do we navigate the past, present, and future in our lives?

Swamy: Focus on the present moment. Do not get lost in the past or obsessed with the future. Just as a warrior does not dwell on past victories or defeats but focuses on the battle at hand, you must focus on the tasks at hand.

Swamy shared, "Imagine a warrior preparing for battle. His past triumphs or failures are irrelevant in the moment of action. Similarly, in life, you must focus on the present and trust that the divine will guide you in the future. The key to spiritual growth is not in the past or future, but in the purity of your actions in the present."

The Role of Family and Society in Spiritual Life

Disciple: Swamy, how do we balance our duties to family and society with our spiritual aspirations?

Swamy: Your duties to family and society are integral to your spiritual growth. Start with honoring your parents. They are the roots that nourish your life. Just as a tree cannot survive without its roots, you cannot progress spiritually without honoring the foundation of your existence—your parents and family.

Swamy concluded with a deep reflection, "A tree, no matter how tall it grows, must remain grounded in its roots. Similarly, no matter how far you travel on the spiritual path, you must stay connected to your duties, especially towards your parents and family. They are the vessels through which you receive divine grace."

Takeaways from the Discourse

1. **Faith as Protection:** True belief in God shields you from the traps of illusion.
2. **Mind and Heart Balance:** The mind (father) and heart (mother) must work in harmony, guided by the Guru.
3. **Living Vedanta:** Every action, when performed with devotion, is an expression of Vedantic wisdom.
4. **Perception of Unity:** See God in every being and situation, and adjust your perception to experience divine unity.
5. **Surrender with Love:** Surrender is the path to divine union— express it through love, care, trust, and unwavering devotion.
6. **Focus on the Present:** Live in the present, for it is in this moment that you shape your spiritual destiny.
7. **Honoring Duties:** Your duties to family and society are vital for spiritual growth and divine grace.

Conclusion

The teachings of His Holiness Sri Vidyanarayana Theertha serve as a beacon of light, guiding us through the intricate layers of life, Dharma, and self-realization. His wisdom reveals that every action, no matter how simple, can be imbued with divinity when performed with the right intention.

In the same way that a sculptor patiently chisels a block of stone to reveal a masterpiece, we must patiently and mindfully shape our lives through devotion, faith, and surrender. The lotus, though submerged in the pond, rises above the water, untouched and pure. So, too, must we rise above the distractions and illusions of the world, guided by the steady hand of the Guru. Let us embrace the divine presence in every moment, every action, and in every being, knowing that the path to liberation lies within.

Chapter-36

The Transformative Power of Service: Embracing Divine Grace

In our modern world, filled with distractions and constant pursuit of personal goals, we often overlook the deeper meaning of life. In the search for success and recognition, we may forget the simple yet profound truths that guide us toward spiritual fulfilment. At the heart of many spiritual traditions lies the practice of Seva—selfless service. Seva, when performed with a pure heart and  genuine humility, becomes a pathway not just to personal growth, but to divine grace. It is through service, both to others and to the Divine, that we experience true transformation.

In addition to Seva, prayer holds a central place in many spiritual practices. But prayer, in its truest form, is not a mere ritualistic recitation or an expectation of personal gain. True prayer is an act of connection—a surrender of the ego and an offering of the heart. As we bow our heads and seek divine blessings, we open ourselves to the divine presence that transcends all barriers, helping us move beyond the self and toward greater unity and love.

The Power of Humility in Prayer

When we approach prayer, humility becomes the key to unlocking its true power. Prayer is not a mere recitation of words or rituals; it is a heartfelt connection with the Divine. But how do we connect with the Divine? The answer lies in humility. True prayer is born when we set aside the ego, drop our expectations, and open our hearts completely to the Divine presence.

In prayer, when we seek nothing but divine grace and surrender our will, it becomes an act of profound transformation. Just like a gardener who tends to his plants with love and patience, we must tend to our hearts with devotion and reverence. When we pray humbly, without expectation, we invite the Divine to heal our inner wounds and transform our hearts.

This transformation is not an overnight process. It is a journey, one that requires dedication, patience, and a willingness to let go of our pride and desires. Just as the river gradually carves its way through rock, prayer, over time, works on the soul, washing away impurities and allowing us to experience a deeper connection with the Divine.

Seva and Prayer: Acts of Divine Love

In many spiritual traditions, service and prayer are viewed as intertwined practices. They are not separate acts but are, in fact, two sides of the same coin. When we serve others selflessly, we are praying through our actions. Similarly, when we pray with pure intentions, we are serving the Divine with our words and thoughts.

A beautiful teaching from Sufi mysticism reminds us: *"True worship is not in the rituals but in the act of surrendering the ego and serving humanity selflessly, becoming a vessel for divine love."* Seva, when performed with humility, becomes a form of worship, and prayer, when done with sincerity, becomes an act of Seva.

Both Seva and prayer are pathways to transcend the self. They help us detach from the ego and unite with the divine essence that resides within each of us and in every being around us. Whether we serve others or pray in solitude, these actions, when done with the right intention, elevate our consciousness and connect us to a higher spiritual plane.

Gratitude as the Key to Spiritual Growth

One of the most powerful aspects of Seva and prayer is gratitude. Gratitude for what we have, for the opportunity to serve, and for the divine blessings that surround us every moment. It is through gratitude that we recognize the divine presence in every action, every breath, and every interaction with others.

In every act of Seva, let us be grateful—not just for what we can give, but for what we have received. It is through gratitude that we recognize the divine gift in every task, no matter how small or insignificant it may seem. The Bhagavad Gita teaches us that even the smallest act of selfless service purifies the heart and brings us closer to the Divine.

A Universal Call to Action

This message is not confined to any one tradition; it is a universal truth. Whether through the teachings of *Ahimsa* in Jainism, the surrender of ego in Buddhism, or the call for charity and compassion in Islam and Christianity, the path of Seva and prayer is a common thread that binds all spiritual practices.

In Buddhism, the Buddha emphasized the importance of selfless acts, stating: *"The greatest wealth is to live content with little."* This echoes the idea that true richness comes not from material gain but from the inner wealth of compassion and humility.

In Jainism, the principle of Ahimsa, or non-violence, extends beyond physical actions to include the words we speak and the thoughts we entertain. By practicing Ahimsa in our service, we are not just serving the world, but we are also cultivating peace within our hearts.

In Islam, the Prophet Muhammad (PBUH) said: *"The best of people are those that bring most benefit to the rest of mankind."* This teaching underscores the transformative power of selfless service and the importance of humility in our actions.

Christianity similarly teaches the value of humility and service. Jesus Christ said: *"Whoever wants to be great among you must be your servant."* This aligns perfectly with the essence of Seva, where the greatest among us are those who serve with humility and love.

Sri Vidyanarayana Theertha's Teachings on Seva and Prayer

As His Holiness Sri Vidyanarayana Theertha beautifully reminds us: *"Seva removes our past negativities in words and deeds. Let us thank Krishna for yesterday, pray for today, and be aware not to repeat the mistakes of yesterday. Let us begin the day with prayers, moving forward with humility and grace."*

These words encapsulate the essence of Seva and prayer—both are means to cleanse ourselves of past mistakes, move forward with humility, and stay open to the divine presence in every moment. Sri Vidyanarayana Theertha's wisdom reminds us that the practice of Seva and prayer is a continual journey toward spiritual awakening.

A Closing Reflection: Walking the Path of Humility

As we engage in Seva and prayer, let us keep in mind the importance of humility. Humility allows us to serve with sincerity and pray with reverence. Without ego, we can truly connect with the Divine, whether through action or contemplation. Let us dedicate ourselves to acts of Seva with no thought of personal gain, offering prayers with a heart open to divine grace.

May our spiritual practices guide us toward greater peace, wisdom, and compassion, and may we always recognize the divine presence in ourselves and in others.

Takeaways

- **Seva** and **prayer** are interconnected, transformative acts that purify the heart and mind.
- **Humility** is key to unlocking the divine power of both Seva and prayer.
- **Gratitude** enhances the spiritual process, allowing us to recognize divine blessings in all actions.
- The universal wisdom of Seva and humility can be found across diverse spiritual traditions, uniting humanity in service and devotion.

Inspiring Conclusion

The practice of Seva and prayer is not just a spiritual duty; it is an opportunity to connect with the Divine in a profound and personal way. As we dedicate ourselves to serving others selflessly and praying with humility, we are reminded that every small act of kindness and reverence contributes to the greater good of humanity. Let us walk this path of service and prayer, knowing that in doing so, we are invited into the divine embrace that transcends all boundaries, elevates our souls, and brings us closer to the light within.

Final Reflection from Sri Vidyanarayana Theertha

"True grace is not in the act itself, but in the humility with which it is offered. Seek not to be praised for your Seva, nor to gain in your prayers. Serve and pray to awaken the divine within, and the universe will shower its grace upon you."

CHAPTER-37

DHARMA IN JUDGMENT: ANCIENT WISDOM FOR MODERN JUSTICE

Invocation to the Divine

"May the divine wisdom of the sages and seers illuminate our minds and hearts, guiding every seeker to discern truth and act in alignment with dharma, ensuring compassion and righteousness prevail in all actions."

Uphold Dharma, Perform Karma.

Introduction

The Spiritual Essence of Justice

What truly defines justice in a world teeming with complexity? Is it merely the enforcement of laws, or does it extend deeper—demanding compassion, understanding, and a commitment to righteousness? In a time when technicalities and legal frameworks often dominate, His Holiness Sri Vidyanarayana Theertha provides a profound perspective that transcends conventional notions of justice. Drawing from the timeless teachings of the four ashramas—Brahmacharya (Effort), Grihasthashrama (Balance), Vanaprastha (Decision), and Sanyasa (Surrender)—Swamiji offers a framework that integrates intellect with compassion, duty with detachment, and action with surrender.

Swamiji's wisdom guides not only judges but all individuals entrusted with decision-making. By aligning with the principles of dharma—the divine law that governs the universe—true justice is realized. It is not merely about delivering judgments, but about acting in accordance with universal righteousness, ensuring fairness, balance, and compassion in all aspects of life.

The Four Ashramas and the Judge's Journey

Swamiji's teachings illuminate the journey of a judge through the four stages of life described in ancient scriptures, offering both a spiritual and practical compass for decision-making. Each stage provides invaluable lessons that apply to the role of a judge and anyone who must navigate moral dilemmas.

1. **Brahmacharya: The Stage of Effort**

   Brahmacharya, or the stage of effort, is defined by discipline, learning, and growth. This stage signifies the importance of rigorous study and self-refinement for anyone seeking truth and justice. Just as a student must master the principles of karma and dharma, one must cultivate wisdom, clarity, and understanding. One can draw inspiration from Ekalavya in the Mahabharata, who, despite being denied formal guidance, mastered archery through relentless dedication. His unwavering focus on his craft mirrors the journey of any seeker, striving for impartiality and integrity, regardless of the challenges faced.

   Swamiji emphasizes that effort is the foundation of wisdom. For all of us, this means continuously refining our understanding of justice, ensuring our decisions transcend personal biases and societal pressures. Only through sustained effort can one approach the truth with clarity.

2. **Grihasthashrama: The Balance Between Duty and Compassion:**

   Grihasthashrama, the householder's life, calls for a delicate balance between personal duties and societal obligations. This balance is critical in any role of responsibility. It means being impartial while recognizing the human experiences and emotions behind each case.

The Ramayana offers a powerful example through King Dasharatha, who, though deeply distressed by the exile of his beloved son Rama, upheld his duty as a ruler above his personal feelings. Similarly, a person in any role of decision-making must maintain impartiality while ensuring that their decisions reflect fairness and compassion, transcending personal emotions to honour their duty to justice.

In this stage, Swamiji teaches that justice requires not only a commitment to righteousness but also an understanding of the human condition. We must balance intellectual duties with emotional capacity for empathy and compassion.

3. Vanaprastha: The Stage of Decision-Making

Vanaprastha, the stage of decision-making, symbolizes the need for introspection, detachment, and wisdom. This stage encourages one to approach each decision with clarity, free from personal biases and external pressures. Bhishma in the Mahabharata exemplifies this principle. Despite his familial ties and emotional conflicts, Bhishma remained neutral during the Kurukshetra War, driven by his commitment to truth and duty. One must align decisions with universal truths and ethical standards, remaining detached from personal allegiances and emotional entanglements.Swamiji teaches that detachment allows us to discern deeper truths, making decisions grounded in righteousness and wisdom, rather than in personal attachments or worldly concerns.

4. Sanyasa: The Stage of Surrender

Sanyasa, the final stage of renunciation, is about selfless action, offering one's actions to the greater good rather than seeking personal gain. For anyone seeking true justice, this stage represents the epitome of selflessness—delivering decisions with integrity, humility, and detachment. Lord Krishna's advice to Arjuna in the Bhagavad Gita mirrors this principle, urging Arjuna to perform his duty as a warrior without attachment to the outcome. Similarly, we must approach our roles with a sense of duty, offering our actions as instruments of divine will rather than seeking personal satisfaction or recognition.

Swamiji emphasizes that actions should not be driven by ego or personal desires. When one acts with pure intentions, their decisions become a channel for divine order, restoring societal balance and righteousness.

Key Takeaways and Insights

- ❖ Effort Counts: True justice begins with constant learning and growth. Dedication to dharma is the key to fair and unbiased decisions.
- ❖ Balance is Key: Fairness comes from blending compassion with wisdom and personal feelings with societal duty.
- ❖ Decisions Build Legacy: Each choice reflects your commitment to truth. What you decide today shapes the future.
- ❖ Selflessness Leads: Justice is at its purest when done without ego or personal gain, serving a higher purpose.
- ❖ Embrace Dharma: Let your actions be guided by the greater good. Live in alignment with the universal truth.
- ❖ Serve with Integrity: True justice isn't about power; it's about serving others with honesty and fairness, creating a ripple of positive change.

True Justice: A Path of Dharma

Swamiji's teachings transcend the judicial profession, offering a profound blueprint for all decision-makers. Whether in the courtroom, the boardroom, or our personal lives, the principles of effort, balance, clarity, and surrender guide us toward dharma. True justice is not merely about following laws but also aligning our actions with dharma—the universal moral order transcending time and place.

As Swamiji articulates, justice is an act of surrender to dharma, where one's role becomes a divine calling. It is not a profession but a path to serve the greater good, uphold truth and righteousness, and restore harmony in the world.

Justice Beyond the Courtroom

Reflecting on the wisdom of our epics and applying these principles to our lives, we move closer to a world where fairness, truth, and dharma reign supreme. True justice is not about power or control but about aligning with the universal moral order and seeking harmony above all else. May we walk the path of dharma with humility, wisdom, and compassion, ensuring that our decisions uphold the divine order and serve the greater good.

In every judgment and decision we make, let us not merely seek fairness but strive to embody dharma—a universal righteousness that transcends time, place, and circumstance. May we approach each choice with unwavering integrity, allowing dharma to guide us toward a future where compassion, truth, and justice are not just ideals but lived realities. Through our actions, let us create a world where these principles take root and where harmony, understanding, and respect flourish for generations to come. Let us be the torchbearers of justice, illuminating the path for others to follow, ensuring that righteousness prevails in every corner of life.

BEYOND THE SELF

"Beyond the self lies true freedom, where the mind is still and the soul shines.
Let go of 'mine' and 'yours,' and see the oneness in all.
The more we release, the more we receive—this is the way of the infinite.
Ego limits, love expands—step beyond, and the whole universe is yours.
In losing the self, we find the truth that was always within."

– His Holiness Sri Vidyanarayana Theertha

CHAPTER-38

THE ESSENCE OF TRUE CONSCIOUSNESS: REVEALING THE ETERNAL SELF

Introduction

In our daily lives, we often feel overwhelmed by the ever-changing circumstances around us—work pressures, relationships, and the pursuit of fleeting goals. But deep within, there lies an unchanging reality, a part of us that is unaffected by these external factors. This is the true nature of the Self. **His Holiness Sri Vidyanarayana Theertha** guides us on a journey to understand that the Self is not confined to the body or mind but is a pure, eternal consciousness. This understanding isn't just an abstract concept; it's a practical key to finding lasting peace and true spiritual freedom. Just like a leaf that moves with the wind yet remains rooted to the tree, the Self remains constant while the external world constantly shifts.

Disciple: *Swamiji, what is the true nature of the Self?*

Swamy:

The Self is eternal and indestructible, beyond the physical form. Consider the example of the sun. When clouds block its light, we may think the sun has disappeared, but it remains constant and unaffected behind the clouds. Similarly, the Self is always present, whether we are aware of it or not. It is pure consciousness, unaffected by birth or death, like the eternal flame that remains unchanged regardless of how much wind or rain it faces.

Disciple: *Swamiji, how can we distinguish the true Self from the body?*

Swamy:

The body is like a vessel—temporary and subject to the laws of nature. It is like wearing clothes that eventually wear out or get replaced. Imagine a person wearing a coat. When the coat gets torn or becomes old, they simply replace it. The person remains unchanged. Similarly, the body is a temporary covering, but the true Self is beyond the body. It is like the screen in a cinema theatre that is not affected by the images projected on it. The images may change, but the screen remains unaffected.

Disciple: *Swamiji, is the true Self-limited by the material world?*

Swamy:

No, the true Self is beyond the material world. It is like the vast ocean that is unaffected by the waves on its surface. While the waves rise and fall, the ocean remains unchanged. Similarly, the body, mind, and senses are subject to the material world's changes, but the true Self is beyond these fluctuations. The material world is like a passing shadow, and the true Self is the sun that shines, irrespective of the clouds.

Disciple: *Swamiji, how does understanding the nature of the Self lead to spiritual awakening?*

Swamy:

When you understand that you are not the body or the mind, but the pure consciousness that exists beyond them, you begin to free yourself from the illusions that create suffering. Imagine a person trapped in a room filled with mirrors. They think they are lost and surrounded by many people. But once they realize that all the reflections are simply illusions, they see the door and walk out to freedom. Similarly, realizing the true nature of the Self removes the illusion of ego and opens the door to spiritual awakening.

Disciple: *Swamiji, what role does the ego play in our perception of the Self?*

Swamy:

The ego creates the illusion of separation. It is like a cloud that temporarily hides the sun. When we identify with the body and mind, we believe we are separate from others and the divine. However, once we transcend the ego, we realize that we are all part of the same essence. Just as a drop of water in the ocean is not separate from the ocean itself, the individual Self is not separate from the universal consciousness. The ego is like the illusion of a person's shadow—the more you chase it, the further it runs away, but when you stop running and simply stand still, the shadow vanishes.

Disciple: *Swamiji, is the Self affected by birth and death?*

Swamy:

No, the Self is not affected by birth or death. Imagine the eternal sky— when a bird flies across it, the sky doesn't change. Similarly, birth and death are events that happen to the body, but the Self remains untouched by these cycles. The Self is like a river that flows eternally, while the individual forms of water droplets may come and go. Birth and death are just transitions for the body, but the Self, like the river, continues its journey uninterrupted.

Disciple: *Swamiji, how does realizing the true Self free us from suffering?*

Swamy:

Suffering arises from ignorance. It is like a person trapped in a dark room, trying to find their way but stumbling over objects because they cannot see. When you realize the true Self, it is like turning on the light in that room. Suddenly, everything is clear. When we understand that we are not our desires, attachments, or fears, we become free from them. The realization of the Self removes the clouds of ignorance and brings peace. Just as a storm may rage outside, but the inner peace of the ocean remains unaffected, realizing the Self brings peace despite external turbulence.

Takeaways

- The Self is eternal, indestructible, and beyond the physical form, like the sun that remains unaffected behind the clouds.
- The true Self is pure consciousness, separate from the body and mind, like the screen in a cinema unaffected by the images projected.
- The Self transcends the material world, like the vast ocean that is unaffected by the waves on its surface.
- Realizing the true nature of the Self leads to spiritual awakening, similar to someone escaping from the illusion of mirrors and finding the door to freedom.
- The ego creates the illusion of separation, like a cloud that hides the sun, but transcending it reveals the unity of all.
- The Self is unaffected by birth and death, like the eternal sky that remains unchanged regardless of the birds that fly across it.
- Realizing the true Self frees us from suffering, just like turning on the light in a dark room that allows us to navigate clearly.

Conclusion

The teachings of **His Holiness Sri Vidyanarayana Theertha** open the doors to understanding our true nature. The Self, which is eternal and beyond the body and mind, offers us a path to peace, freedom, and spiritual awakening. Just as the sun remains unchanged regardless of the clouds or the ocean is untouched by the waves, the Self is always present, unaffected by the fluctuations of the material world. By realizing this, we free ourselves from the illusions that bind us, experiencing life with clarity, purpose, and deep fulfilment. Just like a traveller discovering the true destination after a long journey, realizing the Self is the ultimate discovery—one that brings freedom from suffering and a sense of connection with all of existence. Let this realization guide us to live fully and embrace the eternal truth that resides within each of us.

CHAPTER-39

THE DIVINE TRANSITION: THE PATH FROM KARMA YOGA TO SANYASA

Introduction

In a world driven by material pursuits, the notion of Sanyasa often evokes images of renunciation—discarding worldly possessions and embracing ascetic rituals. Yet, as His Holiness Sri Vidyanarayana Theertha enlightens us, Sanyasa is not about external symbols or mere physical detachment. It is an inward journey, marked by the purification of mind and spirit,  leading to divine wisdom and eternal liberation.

True Sanyasa emerges from Karma Yoga, where every action becomes an offering to the divine. The Karma Yogi begins by transforming self-centred motives into selfless service, progressively shedding the bonds of attachment and ego. Through this sacred process, the Yogi evolves into a Sanyasi, embodying love, equanimity, and unwavering devotion to truth.

In this profound dialogue, His Holiness elucidates the essence of Sanyasa, its foundational roots in Karma Yoga, and the path to achieving Tatvagnana—the ultimate realization of truth. These teachings serve as a timeless guide for seekers navigating the complexities of daily life while striving for spiritual enlightenment.

Dialogue with His Holiness Sri Vidyanarayana Theertha

Disciple: Swamy, how can a Karma Yogi transition to Sanyasa and achieve Tatvagnana?

Swamy: A Karma Yogi dedicated to selfless action can indeed adopt Sanyasa. However, Sanyasa is not attained through mere rituals or external symbols like wearing specific attire. It is a state of being, characterized by the absence of hatred and attachment. A true Sanyasi neither desires nor despises anything. Instead, they embody love, trust, and compassion, freed from sin and worldly cravings.

Disciple: What are the defining traits of a true Sanyasi?

Swamy: A true Sanyasi possesses unwavering clarity and a focused mind. They do not oscillate between belief and doubt. Their knowledge is precise, their actions proactive, and their awareness deeply rooted in divinity. For them, virtues like love, care, and trust become imperishable treasures, while vices like anger and desire are left behind. The Sanyasi's journey unfolds in four stages:

1. **Realization**: Recognizing the impermanence of worldly pursuits.
2. **Differentiation**: Distinguishing between the eternal and the transient.
3. **Seeking Guidance**: Turning to a Guru or divine source for direction.
4. **Graceful Journey**: Embracing the path with humility and resilience.

Disciple: How should a Sanyasi view the world and its challenges?

Swamy: The entire world is the divine unfolding. Every moment, every breath, every encounter—whether seen or unseen—reflects the presence of God. To live in this world, one must align with its divine flow, surrender to the cosmic rhythm, and trust in the will of the Divine. Master the material world by remaining centred, composed, and attuned to your higher purpose. Follow the path of dharma, perform your duties selflessly, and instead of questioning the Divine, turn inward and examine the purity of your own intentions and actions.

Disciple: Swamy, how can one maintain focus amidst worldly distractions?

Swamy: Stand firm in your principles. Struggle for spiritual clarity and embrace challenges as opportunities for growth. Avoid synthesizing falsehoods or settling for mediocrity. Even in bustling places like airports or stations, maintain discipline in your speech and purity in your thoughts. Your composure and mindfulness reflect the divinity within.

Key Takeaways

5. **Sanyasa Beyond Symbols**

   True Sanyasa transcends rituals and attire. It is an inner state of freedom from hatred, attachment, and desires.

6. **Foundation in Karma Yoga**

   Karma Yoga, or selfless action, purifies the mind and lays the groundwork for spiritual realization and divine wisdom.

7. **Divine Perspective**

   See the world as a manifestation of the divine. Accept life's flow, follow its rhythm, and surrender to the higher will.

8. **Navigating Society with Detachment**

   Engage with the world while maintaining inner calm and detachment. Discipline your actions and thoughts to align with dharma.

9. **Resilience in Spirituality**

   Embrace struggles as stepping stones to growth. Stay steadfast in truth and cultivate simplicity, love, and integrity.

Inspiring Conclusion

The transition from Karma Yoga to Sanyasa is not a rejection of the world but a profound embrace of its divine essence. His Holiness Sri Vidyanarayana Theertha's teachings remind us that the journey to liberation begins with selfless action, evolves through detachment, and culminates in the realization of truth.

As we navigate life's challenges, let us embody the virtues of a true Sanyasi—free of hatred, filled with love, and guided by wisdom. By aligning our actions with dharma and surrendering to the divine, we can transcend worldly attachments and experience the eternal bliss of spiritual freedom. Let us walk this sacred path with courage, compassion, and unwavering faith, illuminating our lives and the world around us with the light of divine truth.

CHAPTER-40

FROM THE SHADOW OF COMPARISON TO THE LIGHT OF DIVINE REALIZATION"

"Transform comparison into growth, desires into wisdom, and challenges into grace. The journey from worldly attachments to divine realization is not about striving for more, but about embracing what is eternal within."

The Journey from Comparison to Divine Realization

Life often places us on a path where comparison becomes an inevitable part of our existence. Whether it's professional success, personal achievements, or material possessions, we find ourselves measuring our worth against others. But what if we approached comparison differently? His Holiness Sri Vidyanarayana Theertha Mahaswamiji offers profound insights into transforming the way we perceive comparison and desire, leading us from worldly entanglements to divine realization.

Compare, But Not to Conquer

During a phase of personal struggle, questions arose—why couldn't certain achievements, like top positions or wealth, be attained as easily as others? Comparisons were often tinged with jealousy, and that mindset became a heavy burden. Then, an enlightening Satsang with His Holiness Sri Vidyanarayana Theertha Mahaswamiji shifted this perspective. He emphasized the need to balance life through the grace of the Guru, offering a powerful mantra: *"Compare to compare, but not to conquer."*

Swamiji taught us to admire and learn from others' achievements without envy. Every individual's circumstances are uniquely ordained by God, and our role is to accept our position, put forth honest efforts, and grow without harming others. This revelation shifted the mindset from envy to gratitude. The successes of others became opportunities for learning, and joy replaced the previous sense of competition. For instance, instead of viewing a colleague's promotion as a threat, it was now seen as an opportunity to understand their dedication and skills.

The Endless Cycle of Desires

Swamiji's teachings extend beyond comparison, guiding us to examine the unending chain of desires. He remarked, *"We often tell God, 'Fulfil just this one desire, and I will ask for nothing more,'"* but once that desire is fulfilled, another swiftly takes its place, continuing the cycle of unfulfilled longing.

This endless pursuit of material satisfaction traps us in the illusions of the world. Swamiji emphasized breaking free from this cycle through self-awareness and surrender. Rather than seeking fulfilment in transient objects, we must cultivate contentment and direct our longings toward the eternal. For instance, instead of yearning for a larger house, the focus could shift to creating a loving atmosphere within the current space. As the Bhagavad Gita (2.70) beautifully expresses:

"A person who is not disturbed by the incessant flow of desires—like rivers flowing into the ocean, which is ever being filled but is always still—can achieve peace, and not the person who strives to satisfy such desires."

Gratitude and the Grace of the Guru

Swamiji's words *"We shed tears for worldly relationships, but never shed a tear out of gratitude for either God or Gurudev, who stands behind all our pains, sufferings, and calamities,"* call us to realign our priorities and recognize the divine grace that guides us. Both joy and suffering are tools used by God and the Guru to guide us toward spiritual growth.

To cultivate this gratitude, a daily journal was maintained, listing three instances of divine grace experienced each day. This simple habit transformed the perspective, allowing challenges to be seen as opportunities for growth. The Shrimad Bhagavatam (10.14.8) echoes this sentiment:

"My dear Lord, one who earnestly waits for You to bestow Your causeless mercy upon them while patiently enduring the reactions of their past misdeeds and offering You respectful obeisances with their heart, words, and body is surely eligible for liberation."

Maya and the Mall: A Metaphor for Life

Swamiji often likened the material world to a mall—a place filled with countless attractions designed to captivate the senses. "Mall is Maya," he explained, underscoring the fact that while the material world can trap us, it also offers valuable lessons.

In this metaphor, every shiny object in the mall represents a fleeting desire. While it's easy to be drawn into these distractions, true wisdom lies in discerning what is truly essential. Just as one might resist impulse purchases in a mall, we can resist the pull of unnecessary distractions in life, cultivating discipline and focus to prioritize the eternal over the ephemeral.

Single-Pointed Focus: The Key to Realization

Swamiji's advice to seekers is clear: *"Don't add things. Focus on one."* By dedicating energy to a single goal—whether it's devotion to the

Guru, Krishna, or an eternal principle—clarity and transcendence of distractions are achieved.

To implement this, time was set aside each day for meditation, with a focus solely on Swamiji's teachings. This single-pointed devotion brought immense clarity to the spiritual path. The Bhagavad Gita (9.22) reinforces this approach:

"To those who are constantly devoted and who worship Me with love, I give the understanding by which they can come to Me."

Inspiring Takeaways for Seekers

1. **Compare to Grow**: Observe others' strengths with curiosity and adopt what resonates. For instance, appreciate a colleague's organizational skills and try implementing them in your work.
2. **Redirect Desires**: Identify one recurring desire and write about its true impact on your peace of mind. Reflect on whether pursuing it aligns with your higher purpose.
3. **Practice Gratitude**: Maintain a daily gratitude journal, noting three blessings you received and their spiritual significance.
4. **Embrace Maya as a Teacher**: Use life's distractions to practice detachment and focus on the eternal. For example, when tempted by unnecessary purchases, pause and reflect on their importance.
5. **Focus on One Goal**: Dedicate yourself to a single spiritual pursuit, such as chanting, meditation, or reading scripture, for clarity and growth.

Conclusion: From Comparison to Divine Realization

The teachings of His Holiness Sri Vidyanarayana Theertha Mahaswamiji offer a profound roadmap for spiritual seekers. By transforming our approach to comparison and desire, cultivating gratitude, and focusing on the eternal, we embark on a journey from worldly entanglements to divine realization. As the Upanishads proclaim:

"From delusion, lead me to truth. From darkness, lead me to light. From death, lead me to immortality."

Reflect on your own journey: What comparisons weigh on you? What desires keep you bound? As we walk this sacred path with unwavering faith, guided by the Guru's wisdom and grace, may we find peace, joy, and the ultimate realization of our divine essence.

CHAPTER-41

MASTERING THE MIND: THE PATH TO SELF-REALIZATION

"The greatest victory is not in accumulating wealth or possessions, but in mastering the mind. By calming its storms and finding peace, we discover the divine power within. This is the journey from confusion to clarity, from the self to the Supreme."

— Swamy Vidyanarayana Theertha

Introduction

In a world racing against time, the greatest battles are fought not in the outer world but within the vast expanse of the mind. Amid the hustle and bustle of modern life, where external distractions cloud inner peace, one eternal truth remains: the greatest conquest is not over the world but over one's own mind.

His Holiness Sri Vidyanarayana Theertha Swamy beautifully elaborates on this profound idea, inviting us to explore the essence of balance, the difference between expectation and extension, and the deeper meaning of realization. By weaving timeless lessons from the epics with his teachings, Swamiji lights a path to a balanced, fulfilling life rooted in spiritual awareness and practical wisdom.

The Call to Conquer the Mind

The journey toward spiritual realization begins with mastering the mind. Swamiji teaches that the inherently pure mind becomes imbalanced when mixed with conflicting thoughts. This imbalance mirrors the modern-day struggles of decision-making, emotional stress, and moral dilemmas.

The Bhagavad Gita offers a profound example of this through Arjuna, who stands paralyzed on the battlefield of Kurukshetra. Overwhelmed by doubts and inner turmoil, Arjuna's mind is guided by Lord Krishna to align with dharma through selfless action and unwavering focus. Krishna's message—to conquer inner doubts and act with purpose—remains a beacon for all seekers.

Swamiji's teachings echo this wisdom, emphasizing that balance is achieved by regulating our thoughts and shifting from reaction to pro-action. Fulfilment, he explains, stems not from expecting or extracting but from adjusting and extending. Through this perspective, we learn that the true battleground of life lies within, where harmony is cultivated by regulating the mind and embracing selfless actions.

Balancing Expectations and Extensions

Life's imbalance often arises from unfulfilled expectations—from others, God, or even ourselves. Swamiji highlights that while expectations are impermanent and tied to fleeting desires, extensions—acts rooted in selflessness—are enduring and transformative.

Consider the story of Sudama, Krishna's childhood friend. When Sudama visited the Lord, he brought nothing more than humble rice flakes as an offering. His heart, devoid of expectation, radiated purity.

In response, Krishna's blessings transformed Sudama's life, teaching us that true wealth lies in selfless love and pure intentions.

Swamiji emphasizes focusing on essentials: food, shelter, and support. Approaching these basics with responsibility and commitment forms the foundation of a simple yet spiritually fulfilling life. By extending help to others without anticipating returns, we create a ripple effect of positivity and harmony.

From Conquest to Realization

"Don't conquer, but conquer the mind," Swamiji advises. This profound distinction underscores the essence of realization. While material conquests are transient, a conquered mind leads to spiritual awakening and enduring peace.

Swamiji highlights the mystic energy behind nature, emphasizing that it exists to reveal the divinity within. The Ramayana's episode of Lord Rama seeking counsel from Sage Agastya reflects this truth. The sage's guidance on patience and inner strength reminds us that realization begins with aligning our inner world with the harmony of nature. By observing the world's beauty and reflecting on its deeper meanings, we uncover the divine essence within ourselves.

Practical Steps Toward Balance

1. **Observe to Absorb**: Replace constant questioning with mindful observation and reflection. This practice fosters inner quietness and clarity.
2. **Shift from Expectation to Extension**: Extend selflessly through acts of love, care, or support without anticipating returns.
3. **Prioritize Cleanliness**: Maintain discipline and cleanliness as foundational principles of spiritual and daily life.
4. **Embrace the Basics**: Simplify life by focusing on essentials and avoiding unnecessary complexities.

5. **Follow "Wait, Watch, Win"**: Exercise patience, remain observant, and act wisely to achieve meaningful outcomes.

Takeaways

- **Fulfilment in Simplicity**: Balance fosters contentment (Sampthirpthi), peace (Shanti), and harmony (Samanvayam).
- **Conquer Through Care**: Avadhootas teach that detachment means caring deeply without attachment.
- **Divinity Within**: Nature mirrors mystic energy, guiding us to recognize God within ourselves.
- **Practical Spirituality**: Realization thrives through discipline, selflessness, and harmony.

Conclusion

"I am a mystic energy that flows through you, guiding and transforming your lives. You are all truly blessed. At first glance, my teachings may seem incoherent, especially when filtered through the mind, which is often clouded by the ego. However, when we open our hearts—the true source of love—we experience a profound inner coherence and peace. May you all bathe in my serene love, which is unconditional, untainted, and as pure as the holy waters of the Ganga" Swamy

The wisdom of His Holiness Sri Vidyanarayana Theertha Swamy beckons us to embark on the ultimate journey—the conquest of the mind. Guided by timeless teachings from the epics and Swamiji's profound insights, we learn that balance, simplicity, and selflessness are the keys to realization. As we navigate life's challenges, let us observe, extend, and conquer within. For it is in mastering the mind that we find not just peace but the divine essence that resides in us all.

CHAPTER-42

True Consciousness: Unveiling the Eternal Self

Introduction

In our daily lives, we often feel overwhelmed by the ever-changing circumstances around us—work pressures, relationships, and the pursuit of fleeting goals. But deep within, there lies an unchanging reality, a part of us that is unaffected by these external factors. This is the true nature of the Self. **His Holiness Sri Vidyanarayana Theertha** guides us on a journey to understand that the Self is not confined to the body or mind but is a pure, eternal consciousness. This understanding isn't just an abstract concept; it's a practical key to finding lasting peace and true spiritual freedom. Just like a leaf that moves with the wind yet remains rooted to the tree, the Self remains constant while the external world constantly shifts.

Disciple: *Swamiji, what is the true nature of the Self?*

Swamy: The Self is eternal and indestructible, beyond the physical form. Consider the example of the sun. When clouds block its light, we may think the sun has disappeared, but it remains constant and unaffected behind the clouds. Similarly, the Self is always present, whether we are aware of it or not. It is pure consciousness, unaffected by birth or death, like the eternal flame that remains unchanged regardless of how much wind or rain it faces.

Disciple: *Swamiji, how can we distinguish the true Self from the body?*

Swamy: The body is like a vessel—temporary and subject to the laws of nature. It is like wearing clothes that eventually wear out or get replaced. Imagine a person wearing a coat. When the coat gets torn or becomes old, they simply replace it. The person remains unchanged. Similarly, the body is a temporary covering, but the true Self is beyond the body. It is like the screen in a cinema theatre that is not affected by the images projected on it. The images may change, but the screen remains unaffected.

Disciple: *Swamiji, is the true Self-limited by the material world?*

Swamy: No, the true Self is beyond the material world. It is like the vast ocean that is unaffected by the waves on its surface. While the waves rise and fall, the ocean remains unchanged. Similarly, the body, mind, and senses are subject to the material world's changes, but the true Self is beyond these fluctuations. The material world is like a passing shadow, and the true Self is the sun that shines, irrespective of the clouds.

Disciple: *Swamiji, how does understanding the nature of the Self lead to spiritual awakening?*

Swamy: When you understand that you are not the body or the mind, but the pure consciousness that exists beyond them, you begin to free yourself from the illusions that create suffering. Imagine a person trapped in a room filled with mirrors. They think they are lost and surrounded by many people. But once they realize that all the reflections are simply illusions, they see the door and walk out to freedom. Similarly, realizing the true nature of the Self removes the illusion of ego and opens the door to spiritual awakening.

Disciple: *Swamiji, what role does the ego play in our perception of the Self?*

Swamy: The ego creates the illusion of separation. It is like a cloud that temporarily hides the sun. When we identify with the body and mind, we believe we are separate from others and the divine. However, once we transcend the ego, we realize that we are all part of the same essence. Just as a drop of water in the ocean is not separate from the ocean itself, the individual Self is not separate from the universal consciousness. The ego is like the illusion of a person's shadow—the more you chase it, the further it runs away, but when you stop running and simply stand still, the shadow vanishes.

Disciple: *Swamiji, is the Self affected by birth and death?*

Swamy: No, the Self is not affected by birth or death. Imagine the eternal sky—when a bird flies across it, the sky doesn't change. Similarly, birth and death are events that happen to the body, but the Self remains untouched by these cycles. The Self is like a river that flows eternally, while the individual forms of water droplets may come and go. Birth and death are just transitions for the body, but the Self, like the river, continues its journey uninterrupted.

Disciple: *Swamiji, how does realizing the true Self free us from suffering?*

Swamy: Suffering arises from ignorance. It is like a person trapped in a dark room, trying to find their way but stumbling over objects because they cannot see. When you realize the true Self, it is like turning on the light in that room. Suddenly, everything is clear. When we understand that we are not our desires, attachments, or fears, we become free from them. The realization of the Self removes the clouds of ignorance and brings peace. Just as a storm may rage outside, but the inner peace of the ocean remains unaffected, realizing the Self brings peace despite external turbulence.

Takeaways

- The Self is eternal, indestructible, and beyond the physical form, like the sun that remains unaffected behind the clouds.
- The true Self is pure consciousness, separate from the body and mind, like the screen in a cinema unaffected by the images projected.
- The Self transcends the material world, like the vast ocean that is unaffected by the waves on its surface.
- Realizing the true nature of the Self leads to spiritual awakening, similar to someone escaping from the illusion of mirrors and finding the door to freedom.
- The ego creates the illusion of separation, like a cloud that hides the sun, but transcending it reveals the unity of all.
- The Self is unaffected by birth and death, like the eternal sky that remains unchanged regardless of the birds that fly across it.
- Realizing the true Self frees us from suffering, just like turning on the light in a dark room that allows us to navigate clearly.

Conclusion

The teachings of **His Holiness Sri Vidyanarayana Theertha** open the doors to understanding our true nature. The Self, which is eternal and beyond the body and mind, offers us a path to peace, freedom, and spiritual awakening. Just as the sun remains unchanged regardless of the clouds or the ocean is untouched by the waves, the Self is always present, unaffected by the fluctuations of the material world. By realizing this, we free ourselves from the illusions that bind us, experiencing life with clarity, purpose, and deep fulfilment. Just like a traveller discovering the true destination after a long journey, realizing the Self is the ultimate discovery—one that brings freedom from suffering and a sense of connection with all of existence. Let this realization guide us to live fully and embrace the eternal truth that resides within each of us.

MYSTIC EVOLUTION

*"Mystic evolution is not about becoming, but remembering who you are.
It is the journey from seeking to seeing, from knowing to being.
As the mind dissolves, the soul rises—silent, vast, limitless.
True growth is not upward or outward, but inward—to the eternal core.
When the seeker disappears, only the divine remains."*

– His Holiness Sri Vidyanarayana Theertha

CHAPTER-43

THE UNFOLDING MELODY OF DIVINE WISDOM

Introduction

In the sacred presence of His Holiness Sri Vidyanarayana Theertha, spiritual aspirants gathered to seek clarity on life's profound questions. Through an interactive discourse, Swamy offered answers imbued with wisdom and compassion, blending practical insights with spiritual truths. Each conversation was a guiding light for those seeking to align their lives with divine principles.

This timeless dialogue delves into the essence of Dharma, Karma, Bhakti, and the ultimate purpose of life, inspiring aspirants to walk the path of righteousness with unwavering faith.

Dedication to God and Karma

Disciple: Swamy, how can we make our daily work an offering to God?

Swamy: Any work, when done with sincerity and offered to God, becomes sacred. This is the essence of *"Krishnarpanam."* Whether your task is big or small, its value lies in your dedication.

Swamy elaborated, "Think of a potter shaping clay. The clay may appear lifeless, but in the hands of a dedicated potter, it transforms into something useful and beautiful. Your work, too, when dedicated to Krishna, becomes an expression of divinity."

Disciple: But Swamy, sometimes we feel that our efforts are not enough.

Swamy: Whatever you receive is *Krishnanugraham*—God's grace. Like a farmer who tills the soil but depends on rain for a good harvest, your efforts, combined with God's blessings, yield results. Do your best and leave the rest to Him.

The Role of Dharma and Karma in Life

Disciple: How do Dharma and Karma shape our journey?

Swamy: Dharma is like a compass that provides direction, and Karma is the effort that moves you forward. When these two align, life becomes meaningful.

Swamy explained, "Imagine a river flowing within its banks. The banks are Dharma, and the flowing water is Karma. If the river breaches its banks, it causes destruction. Similarly, actions without Dharma lead to chaos."

Disciple: And what happens when we face obstacles despite following Dharma?

Swamy: Life is a school. Just as a sculptor chisels a stone to reveal the statue within, challenges refine your soul. Embrace them as opportunities for growth.

Atma Rahasya (Secrets of the Soul)

Disciple: Swamy, what is the secret to understanding our true self?

Swamy: Faith in God is the key to self-realization. Yagna is not a mere ritual; it is an offering of your heart. Sacrifice ego and attachment, and you will discover the essence of your soul.

Swamy added, "A sailor trusts the stars to navigate vast oceans. Similarly, trust in God will guide you through life's uncertainties. Just as a lamp lights up a dark room, faith illuminates the soul."

The Essence of Bhakti and Pooja

Disciple: How can we truly please God?

Swamy: God is not pleased by quantity but by quality. A single flower offered with devotion is more valuable than a heap of flowers offered without sincerity.

Swamy continued, "Think of a child presenting a simple drawing to a parent. It may lack perfection, but the love behind it touches the parent's heart. Similarly, God values your heartfelt devotion, not extravagance."

Disciple: So, is it about intention rather than action?

Swamy: Exactly. Time cures time. Dedicate your time and your heart to God, and He will guide you.

Overcoming Illusion and Ignorance

Disciple: How can we overcome life's illusions?

Swamy: Illusions bind us with attachment and ignorance. Sacrifice material desires with wisdom and humility. This lightens the burden on your soul and brings divine joy.

Swamy shared, "A bird flying high carries no baggage. Let go of unnecessary attachments, and you will soar. Like clouds that momentarily obscure the sun, ignorance may veil your soul, but wisdom restores its radiance."

Faith and Inner Growth

Disciple: How does faith shape our journey?

Swamy: Faith is the foundation of spiritual progress. Everything is God. Trust Him, and the path will unfold effortlessly. If you test God, you will fail, but if you trust Him, you will thrive.

Swamy remarked, "A seed trusts the soil and rain to grow into a tree. Your faith is like that seed—nurture it. Like a bird perched on a fragile branch, trust lies not in the branch but in its wings. Place your trust in God, not in circumstances."

Balancing Dharma and Karma in Relationships

Disciple: How should we approach family life?

Swamy: A husband symbolizes Dharma, while a wife represents Karma. Together, they create balance. Relationships thrive when guided by love, respect, and mutual understanding.

Swamy elaborated, "The wheels of a cart must move in sync to carry the load. Similarly, family members must work together to overcome life's challenges. Just as a tree's roots (Dharma) and fruits (Karma) sustain it, harmony in relationships mirrors divine principles."

Takeaways from the Discourse

1. **Dedicate Your Actions to God:** Every action becomes sacred when offered with devotion and sincerity.
2. **Balance Dharma and Karma:** Align your actions with Dharma to achieve harmony.
3. **Faith as a Foundation:** Trust in God as your guiding light.
4. **Devotion Over Extravagance:** Sincerity pleases God more than outward displays.

5. **Let Go of Attachments:** Free yourself from material desires and illusions.
6. **Challenges Purify the Soul:** Embrace difficulties as steps toward spiritual growth.
7. **Family as a Sacred Bond:** Cultivate relationships with love and respect.
8. **Conquer Inner Struggles:** Overcome anger, greed, and ego to realize your true self.

Conclusion

His Holiness Sri Vidyanarayana Theertha's wisdom transcends time, offering spiritual seekers a pathway to enlightenment. By dedicating every action to God, nurturing faith, and letting go of illusions, we can transform life into a journey of divine realization.

Swamy's teachings remind us that life is not about accumulating material wealth but about discovering inner peace. Like a potter shaping clay, we must shape our lives with devotion and purpose, trusting in God's infinite grace.

Let us carry these lessons as treasures in our hearts, walking the path of Dharma and Karma with unwavering faith and a spirit of surrender, ever mindful of the divine symphony that plays within us all.

CHAPTER-44

THE MYSTIC ASCENT: AWAKENING THE INNER DIVINE

"The journey inward unveils the divinity within,
revealing the oneness of the self and the universe."

Introduction

The Inward Journey to Divinity

In an era dominated by rapid technological advancements and material pursuits, many find themselves disconnected from their deeper essence. The true quest of human existence lies not in accumulating external wealth, but in awakening to the divine within. The Bhagavad Gita reminds us, "When meditation is mastered, the mind is unwavering like the flame of  a lamp in a windless place." This metaphor speaks to the clarity and steadiness achieved through spiritual practice, a goal that calls upon each individual to embark on an inward journey of discovery.

His Holiness Sri Vidyanarayana Theertha, a spiritual luminary, has often emphasized that awakening is not a singular event, but a continual process of aligning with one's highest truth. This journey, akin to climbing a mountain, gradually reveals new vistas of consciousness, allowing us to transcend the limitations of our material identity. In this sacred journey, the connection between science and spirituality plays a crucial role, uniting the rational with the transcendent.

The Role of Kundalini in Awakening: Unlocking Hidden Potential

At the heart of the spiritual journey lies Kundalini—an ancient concept of dormant spiritual energy residing at the base of the spine. When awakened, this energy ascends through the body's energy centres, or chakras, unlocking profound transformation. His Holiness Sri Vidyanarayana Theertha explained that the rise of Kundalini parallels the awakening of human potential, aligning body, mind, and spirit in perfect harmony.

Kundalini energy is often misunderstood as merely mystical; however, His Holiness draws a direct parallel between this spiritual concept and modern scientific principles. Just as electrical impulses flow through the nervous system, Kundalini energy flows through the nadis (energy pathways) of the body, activating both physical and spiritual changes. This awakening is not about obtaining supernatural abilities but about becoming aligned with one's true self—experiencing life from a state of purity, balance, and divine awareness.

The Guru's Role in Safeguarding the Awakening Process

The journey of awakening Kundalini requires the guidance of a realized Guru. As His Holiness frequently emphasizes, "A Guru is the catalyst who awakens the latent energy safely and harmoniously." The Guru provides the tools, wisdom, and protection necessary for the aspirant to navigate this profound journey. Without proper guidance, the awakening process can lead to confusion or even imbalance.

The role of the Guru transcends that of a teacher; the Guru is a spiritual mirror, reflecting the true nature of the disciple. His Holiness teaches that through the Guru's blessings, aspirants can attain clarity, wisdom, and divine grace—essential components in awakening Kundalini and achieving self-realization.

Chakras: Energy Centres for Transformation

The flow of energy through the chakras is crucial to spiritual growth and self-realization. Each of the seven energy centres, or chakras, represents a different aspect of our physical, emotional, and spiritual well-being. As the energy ascends from the base of the spine to the crown of the head, it unlocks higher consciousness and fosters healing, balance, and inner peace. The upward movement of energy symbolizes spiritual awakening and enlightenment, while the downward flow would signify stagnation or regression, trapping us in lower, primal instincts.

The Journey Through the Chakras: A Path to Self-Realization

The Root Chakra (Muladhara), located at the base of the spine, serves as the foundation of our existence. It governs our sense of stability, security, and connection to the earth. It anchors us to the physical world and provides the grounding necessary for spiritual growth. When energy flows upward from this chakra, it lays the groundwork for balancing the physical and spiritual aspects of life.

The Sacral Chakra (Svadhisthana), situated just below the navel, governs creativity, emotions, and intimacy. This chakra is connected to our ability to nurture relationships, experience pleasure, and embrace life with fluidity. As the energy rises through this centre, it enhances emotional balance, self-love, and creative expression, enriching both our inner and outer worlds.

The Solar Plexus Chakra (Manipura), located above the navel, is the seat of personal power, confidence, and willpower. It empowers us to take decisive actions aligned with our purpose. When energy ascends through this chakra, it strengthens inner courage and determination, fostering a sense of control over our lives and the ability to act with clarity and confidence.

The Heart Chakra (Anahata), located at the centre of the chest, symbolizes love, compassion, and emotional healing. It bridges the physical and spiritual realms, governing our ability to give and receive love. As energy flows through this chakra, it opens us to unconditional love, empathy, and forgiveness, deepening our emotional connections with ourselves and others.

The Throat Chakra (Vishuddha), positioned at the throat, governs communication and self-expression. This chakra enables us to articulate our truth and express ourselves with authenticity. As energy rises here, it fosters open, honest communication, empowering us to align our words and actions with our higher self.

The Third Eye Chakra (Ajna), located between the eyebrows, represents intuition, insight, and spiritual perception. It allows us to access our inner wisdom and see beyond the physical realm. Energy ascending to this chakra sharpens our intuitive abilities, enhances mental clarity, and helps us make enlightened decisions that resonate with our deeper understanding.

Finally, the Crown Chakra (Sahasrara), located at the top of the head, serves as the gateway to spiritual enlightenment and connection to the divine. It links us to higher consciousness and universal wisdom, facilitating the experience of oneness with the cosmos. When energy flows through this chakra, it unlocks spiritual awakening and a profound sense of unity with all creation.

The Upward Flow: Kundalini and the Koshas

Kundalini energy represents the dormant spiritual power coiled at the base of the spine. Its upward ascent through the chakras parallels its penetration of the five koshas—the layers of human existence—activating and refining their associated qualities:

- Physical Grounding (Annamaya Kosha/Muladhara): The physical sheath associated with the body and survival. Kundalini energy stabilizes the body and anchors the spirit in physical existence.
- Energy Flow (Pranamaya Kosha/Svadhisthana & Manipura): The vital energy sheath connected to the breath and life force. As energy rises through these chakras, it revitalizes vitality, emotional fluidity, and dynamic action.
- Emotional Balance (Manomaya Kosha/Anahata & Vishuddha): The mental sheath linked to emotions and thoughts. Kundalini energy nurtures love, compassion, communication, and emotional harmony.
- Wisdom and Clarity (Vijnanamaya Kosha/Ajna): The intellectual sheath representing insight and discernment. When Kundalini reaches this level, it sharpens intuition, fosters wisdom, and provides clarity of purpose.
- Spiritual Unity (Anandamaya Kosha/Sahasrara): The bliss sheath connected to divine awareness. The culmination of Kundalini's journey brings spiritual enlightenment and the realization of oneness with the universe.

The Transformative Process of Kundalini Awakening

The upward flow of Kundalini energy symbolizes spiritual awakening and self-realization. It nurtures not only physical well-being but also emotional, mental, and spiritual growth.

- Foundation to Fulfilment: The journey from the Root Chakra to the Crown Chakra integrates the koshas, harmonizing the physical, energetic, emotional, intellectual, and spiritual dimensions of being.

- Awakening Potential: Kundalini unlocks dormant capabilities, encouraging the individual to embody their highest potential and live a life of balance and purpose.
- A Path to Unity: By refining each kosha, the journey leads to the ultimate realization of unity with the cosmos, enabling a profound sense of bliss and harmony.

As Kundalini ascends through these chakras, it brings about the realization of each aspect of the self. The process is deeply transformative, and as energy rises, the individual experiences spiritual clarity, emotional healing, and mental balance. However, these transformations require deep awareness and patience.

Energy Flow and Obstructions: Clearing the Path to Awakening

The nadis through which Kundalini flows can become obstructed by negative emotions, past traumas, or unwholesome habits. These blockages create resistance, preventing the free flow of energy and hindering spiritual growth. His Holiness has taught that these obstructions must be cleared through mindfulness, ethical living, and spiritual discipline.

Practices such as meditation, prayer, yoga, and breathwork help dissolve these blockages. In the words of His Holiness, "Kundalini awakening is not about force; it is about allowing the energy to rise naturally, clearing the pathways of the mind and body."

The Interplay of Science and Spirituality

In today's world, science and spirituality are often seen as separate domains, with science focusing on the material world and spirituality concerned with the intangible. However, His Holiness Sri Vidyanarayana Theertha has continually emphasized the harmony between the two. "Science reveals the mechanisms of the universe; spirituality uncovers its meaning," he says.

Through this lens, we can begin to understand Kundalini not only as a spiritual phenomenon but also as a natural force within the body, akin to the nervous system's electrical impulses. Modern neuroscience provides valuable insight into how the brain and nervous system function, just as ancient spiritual wisdom teaches how these systems can be aligned with cosmic energy for self-realization. The union of science and spirituality in this context allows us to approach the spiritual journey with both rational understanding and deep spiritual devotion.

The inseparability of science and spirituality is a profound truth that resonates deeply in the modern world. While science seeks to explain the tangible and measurable, spirituality delves into the intangible and immeasurable aspects of existence. These two realms are not opposites but complementary forces that, when aligned, create a holistic understanding of life. Science provides the tools for exploring the physical universe, while spirituality guides the inner journey towards wisdom, compassion, and transcendence. Together, they offer a balanced perspective, where the exploration of the external world enhances the quest for internal peace and enlightenment.

Practical Steps for Kundalini Awakening: A Guide for the Modern Seeker

The path of Kundalini awakening, while deeply spiritual, also requires practical discipline. As His Holiness often highlights, "Spirituality is not a detachment from life but an engagement with it at a deeper level." Here are key practices to aid in the awakening process:

1. **Mindful Breathing**: The foundation of spiritual awakening begins with the breath. Conscious breathing helps calm the mind, making it receptive to spiritual insights and energetic transformations. Techniques such as Pranayama (breath control) can help activate the dormant energy within.

2. **Living Ethically**: Spiritual practice is built on a foundation of ethical living. Truthfulness, compassion, non-violence, and gratitude are essential values that purify the mind and body. "Sathyam vada, sathyameva jayate" (Speak the truth; truth alone triumphs) is a guiding principle in this process.

3. **Dedication to Practice**: Consistency is key. Just as physical exercise requires regularity, so too does spiritual practice. Dedication to daily meditation, prayer, and mindfulness strengthens the inner connection, allowing for the gradual rise of Kundalini.

4. **The Role of the Guru**: The Guru serves as the guide, offering wisdom and insight on how to safely navigate the spiritual journey. With a Guru's blessings, one can avoid pitfalls and awaken the latent energy with grace.

The Significance of Awakening: Realizing the Divine Within

Awakening Kundalini is not just about attaining spiritual enlightenment but also about living a life of purpose, compassion, and love. By integrating spiritual practices and conscious living, we align ourselves with the divine presence that resides within us all.

As His Holiness Sri Vidyanarayana Theertha teaches, "True awakening is the realization that the divine is not outside, but within. We are all expressions of that divine energy, and our purpose is to awaken to it fully." This realization brings profound peace, clarity, and a sense of unity with all of creation.

The Guru's Universal Wisdom: A Beacon for All

His Holiness teachings transcend all boundaries—religious, cultural, and geographical. The journey of awakening Kundalini is not exclusive to any one tradition or belief system. The Guru's wisdom is universal, offering guidance for anyone seeking spiritual fulfilment.

His Holiness often reminded his followers, "The Guru's light shines in all hearts, regardless of race or religion. The awakening of the divine within is the birthright of every soul." His approach, marked by compassion, simplicity, and deep insight, has inspired countless individuals to embark on their own journey of self-discovery and awakening.

Conclusion: The Divine Ascent Within

In conclusion, Kundalini awakening is not merely a mystical concept but a profound and practical path to self-realization. The integration of science and spirituality, coupled with the wisdom of the Guru, provides the tools necessary for the modern seeker to embark on this transformative journey. As His Holiness Sri Vidyanarayana Theertha profoundly says, "The awakening of Kundalini is not about gaining powers but about realizing your true self and the divine potential within."

Through conscious effort, ethical living, and the guidance of a realized Guru, the dormant energy within us all can rise, leading to the realization of our inner divinity. This path of awakening not only transforms the individual but also has the potential to bring about a collective shift in consciousness—leading to a world that is more peaceful, compassionate, and spiritually aware.

NAVIGATION LIFE'S DUALITIES

"Life's dualities are not to be fought but understood—light and dark, joy and sorrow.
Balance is not in choosing one over the other, but in flowing through both with grace.
When the mind clings, it suffers; when it accepts, it is free.
True wisdom lies in seeing beyond opposites—to the stillness within.
Walk with faith, and life's waves will carry you, not drown you."

– His Holiness Sri Vidyanarayana Theertha

CHAPTER-45

EXPLORING LIFE'S DUALITY: THE ROAD TO SPIRITUAL CLARITY

Introduction

In this discourse, His Holiness Sri Vidyanarayana Theertha reflects on the dual nature of existence and the supreme role of the divine in guiding us through life's challenges. He explores the transient nature of material wealth, relationships, and the body, emphasizing the importance of spiritual wisdom and the guidance of a true guru. By understanding life's impermanence and seeking the divine, one can navigate the hardships of existence and attain true peace and liberation.

Question and Answer

Question: What is the significance of duality in the world?

- The world operates on duality—light and darkness, pleasure and pain, joy and sorrow. This inherent contrast is a reflection of the cosmic order. While we cannot predict what tomorrow holds, and while life brings inevitable challenges, the divine remains our protector. Only the wise are able to recognize the presence of the divine amidst these dualities.

Question: How should we view hardships and struggles in life?

- Hardships are an inseparable part of existence, serving as opportunities for spiritual growth. Just as nature balances itself through elements like wind and fire, our struggles are necessary for the purification of the soul. The true spiritual seeker faces these challenges with patience, understanding, and diligence, knowing that they are steps on the path to salvation.

Question: How should one approach life and ageing?

- In youth, the mind is often consumed by fleeting desires, leaving peace and contentment out of reach. As the body ages and health declines, it is crucial to remember that the body is temporary. True fulfilment lies not in external pleasures but in the wisdom gained through righteous action and spiritual awareness, which transcend the limitations of the physical realm.

Question: What is the lasting legacy one leaves behind?

- After death, material possessions and relationships are left behind. What remains is the accumulated karma—both good and bad. The only true legacy is the soul's journey and the guidance received from the divine. The wisdom of the guru is the key to liberation, for it is through the guru's grace that one attains eternal peace.

Question: How does a true guru guide the disciple?

- A true guru is the ultimate source of spiritual guidance. Their teachings, their presence, and their blessings lead the disciples toward liberation. Seeking refuge in the guru is essential to finding inner peace, as the guru's guidance leads one through life's challenges toward spiritual fulfilment.

Key Insights

- Life's duality is a divine principle where struggles and joys coexist as part of the greater cosmic order.
- Only through wisdom and understanding the impermanence of the body and material life can we navigate challenges.

- True spiritual wisdom is attained by recognizing the transience of relationships, wealth, and possessions.
- The guidance of a true guru is essential for attaining peace and liberation.
- One's karma, not material possessions, is the only legacy that truly follows us beyond death.

Conclusion

The world is transient, filled with dualities that challenge our existence. Yet, through understanding the impermanence of life, the nature of the self, and seeking the guidance of a true guru, we can transcend these challenges. By following the path of wisdom, selfless service, and devotion, we can attain spiritual peace and liberation, overcoming the limitations of the material world.

CHAPTER-46

"Embracing Life's Challenges: The Art of Preparation, Acceptance, and Action"

Introduction

In the ever-evolving journey of life, we often find ourselves confronted with challenges and adversities, akin to an enemy attacking with a force we may not be prepared for. However, the key lies not in being fully prepared for every circumstance, but in the mental readiness and inner strength to face it. By cultivating awareness, embracing our duties, and trusting in  the wisdom of our inner consciousness, we find the power to act with clarity and conviction, just as ancient scriptures and teachings guide us. The principles outlined here combine both the spiritual wisdom of the Bhagavad Gita and practical examples to help us navigate life's uncertainties with resilience and confidence.

Question 1: Swamiji, when the enemy (life's challenges) attacks, how should we be ready to face it?

Swamy: When life's challenges strike, it's essential to understand that preparation is not just about external readiness but about cultivating mental resilience. *"I am not prepared, but I am prepared."* This paradox means that while you may not have all the resources, tools, or knowledge, your readiness comes from inner strength, awareness, and commitment to the task at hand.

For example, consider a sports team preparing for a championship match. Even though they may not know every tactic the opposing team will use, their preparation is built on years of practice, discipline, and teamwork. Similarly, when life presents unexpected trials, our inner discipline and connection to Dharma equip us to face them with courage.

Takeaway: Preparation is not only about external readiness but also cultivating mental resilience and trust in your inner strength.

Question 2: Swamiji, how does one accept their inner conscience amidst challenges?

Swamy: In times of uncertainty, there is no room for debate or dissent. The key is to "accept inner conscience," which guides you toward the right actions. Your inner voice, honed by experience and aligned with your Dharma, will always lead you to the right course of action.

Take the example of a leader facing a tough decision: instead of getting bogged down in debates and external pressures, they turn inward, relying on their values and inner understanding to make the right choice. This decisiveness brings clarity, ensuring actions align with higher principles rather than fleeting desires.

Takeaway: Trust your inner conscience as a guiding force when facing tough decisions, and avoid unnecessary debates.

Question 3: Swamiji, how does "search, seek, select, and settle down" apply in the journey of life?

Swamy: The approach of "search, seek, select, and settle down" is a methodical way to engage with life's challenges. First, you search for solutions, then seek out the best option, select what aligns with your Dharma, and finally settle down in the knowledge of your decision. This process helps you remain grounded and confident.

For instance, a student choosing a career path often faces multiple options. By searching for meaningful work, seeking advice, selecting the right field based on their strengths and values, and settling into that choice, they move forward with clarity and purpose. This process applies to every decision in life, ensuring that we make informed choices that lead to growth.

Takeaway: The methodical approach of searching, seeking, selecting, and settling down brings clarity and commitment to decisions.

Question 4: Swamiji, what does it mean when you say, "Copy means fail"?

Swamy:

When we copy others without understanding or aligning the action with our unique purpose, we fail to grow authentically. "Copy means fail" emphasizes the importance of individuality in action. Each person has their own path, and blindly imitating someone else's success does not lead to personal fulfilment.

For example, a business owner who tries to replicate another successful company's model may find success in the short term but might miss out on the long-term potential of building their unique brand and vision. The lesson here is that authenticity leads to success.

Takeaway: To truly succeed, cultivate your unique path rather than imitating others.

Question 5: Swamiji, how does the concept of "I am begging, but I am not begging" apply to our daily lives?

Swamy: The statement "I am begging, but I am not begging" speaks to the balance between humility and self-reliance. It conveys the idea that while we may seek support or blessings, we do not surrender our dignity or self-worth. This is similar to a student asking for guidance from a teacher—they seek wisdom, but their desire for knowledge is coupled with self-respect and effort.

Think of a person praying for a job. While they seek divine blessings and guidance, they do not beg for it in desperation; instead, they continue working hard, preparing themselves, and contributing positively to their environment. This mindset leads to a sense of dignity even in seeking help.

Takeaway: Seek help when needed, but never lose your self-respect and dignity in the process.

Question 6: Swamiji, what does it mean to "not go when not invited"?

Swamy: This lesson emphasizes the importance of respecting boundaries and knowing when to act and when to refrain. Sometimes, when we force ourselves into situations where we are not invited, we disrupt the natural flow of things. In the Bhagavad Gita, Krishna advises Arjuna not to rush into battle before it is time—timing and appropriateness are crucial in every aspect of life.

For instance, a leader at work knows when to intervene and when to let the team handle things. Overstepping can lead to unnecessary conflict. Just as in life, we must know our place and wait for the right moment to act.

Takeaway: Respect the boundaries and act at the right time for harmony.

Question 7: Swamiji, how does Karma clean the mirror covered by dust?

Swamy: Karma, the principle of cause and effect, acts as a cleansing force, clearing away the dust that clouds our judgment and perception. When we act with pure intentions and righteousness, the dust of ego, desire, and attachment is removed, revealing our true self. Just like a mirror covered in dust cannot reflect clearly, our actions often obscure our true nature. By performing good deeds with selflessness, we purify our hearts and minds.

A simple example is when a person engages in charity or selfless service; not only does this benefit others, but it also brings peace and clarity to the giver's own mind. Their actions reflect their inner state of purity.

Takeaway: Act with integrity and selflessness to purify the mind and clear away the distractions of ego and attachment.

Conclusion

The teachings of His Holiness Sri Vidyanarayana Theertha remind us that life's challenges are inevitable, but our response to them is within our control. By cultivating mental resilience, embracing our inner conscience, and acting with clarity and purpose, we navigate through life's complexities. With the wisdom of Dharma, we can face adversity with a calm mind and a strong heart, ready to grow and thrive. By applying the principles of preparation, authentic action, and self-awareness, we can successfully align ourselves with the flow of life's greater design, overcoming obstacles and embracing opportunities with grace.

CHAPTER-47

Navigating Life's Challenges

Introduction

In a world full of uncertainties and complexities, questions about life's true meaning and purpose often arise. As we strive to make sense of the challenges we face, we look to spiritual wisdom for guidance. His Holiness Sri Vidyanarayana Theertha offers profound teachings that illuminate the path to understanding. Through this enlightening discourse, we delve into the significance of cooperation, karma, dharma, and knowledge, exploring how to navigate life's challenges with a steady mind and a spiritual heart. His Holiness' teachings provide clarity on how to live a life of purpose, inner strength, and wisdom, while remaining connected to the Divine.

Question 1: Swamiji, how should we view cooperation and coordination in our lives?

Swamy: Cooperation and coordination are the pillars upon which we build harmonious relationships and successful endeavours. Everything in life, whether it's working together in a family, collaborating on a project, or simply living in a society, is interconnected. For example, just as the parts of a machine work together to make it function, we, too, must cooperate with the world and others. Life is temporary, and we must understand that the flow of time and circumstances are ever-changing. Observe others, learn from their experiences, and always remain alert in your own journey. Cooperation is not merely about working with others—it's about aligning with the rhythm of life itself.

Question 2: How does karma affect our lives, and how can we respond to it?

Swamy: Karma shapes our existence and its effects are undeniable. Think of karma as the seeds we plant in the soil of life—some grow into beautiful flowers, while others may grow into thorns. Our actions create ripples that influence our present and future. The external powers we rely on—whether wealth, status, or temporary comfort—are fleeting. The internal power, however, comes from self-awareness and spiritual practice, which remains steadfast. Perform your karma with sincerity, without expecting rewards. The true power lies in selfless action. For instance, imagine a farmer who tends to his crops without worrying about the harvest; he knows the harvest will come in due course. Similarly, perform your duties without attachment to outcomes, and wisdom will follow.

Question 3: Swamiji, how can we control the distractions that often impede our spiritual growth?

Swamy: Distractions are a natural part of life—sleep, hunger, desires, and worldly temptations often pull us away from our spiritual path. But true growth comes from discipline and control. Life is like a river; it flows continuously, but we must choose how we navigate it. Take the example of a skilled archer—no matter how noisy or distracting the surroundings, his focus on the target remains unwavering. Similarly, we must perform our duties with detachment, accepting whatever comes our way without hesitation. Indecision only leads to stagnation. Make firm choices and move forward, for each decision shapes your destiny.

Question 4: What is the relationship between dharma, karma, and the pursuit of knowledge?

Swamy: Dharma and karma are two sides of the same coin. Just like a tree needs both roots and branches to grow, dharma (righteous duty) and karma (actions) must work together to guide us on our spiritual journey. Consider the life of a soldier—his duty is to protect his land, and through this action, he earns his honour. Similarly, by fulfilling our personal duties, we cultivate wisdom (Gnana). Life presents countless experiences, and through each one, we must practice karma yoga—acting without attachment. You cannot escape karma; it is inevitable. Our only choice is how we perform our actions in alignment with our Swadharma or personal duty.

Question 5: How should we approach the concept of renunciation and the challenges of age?

Swamy: Renunciation is not about physically abandoning the world; it is the detachment from worldly desires and expectations. Age does not determine your ability to renounce; it is the purity of your intentions that matters. Take the example of a seasoned warrior—he may retire from the battlefield, but his inner strength and wisdom remain intact. Similarly, you are not the first person to encounter the challenges of life. Many have faced them before and emerged victorious. The body is meant to serve others, and through selfless service, the mind is purified. True renunciation is a mental state, not an age-dependent process.

Question 6: Swamiji, how can we cultivate knowledge and wisdom through our actions?

Swamy: Wisdom is not something that can be attained through intellectual pursuit alone; it is earned through the practice of karma.

Think of a blacksmith who hammers metal to shape it—just as the metal becomes stronger through continuous pounding, our wisdom is honed through consistent action. Life is a battlefield where success and failure are part of the journey. Whether we win or lose, the key is to keep moving forward. Knowledge arises through the purification of the mind, which comes from reflection and questioning. By staying humble, we allow true wisdom to unfold. Life may be full of thorns, but we must walk it without fear, for each challenge is an opportunity for growth.

Takeaways

- Cooperation and coordination are essential for spiritual growth and understanding.
- Karma shapes our lives, and we must act selflessly without attachment to the results.
- True power lies within, and we must remain in control of distractions.
- Dharma and karma work hand-in-hand to guide us on our spiritual journey.
- Renunciation is an internal process, not limited by age or circumstances.
- Wisdom is gained through the consistent practice of karma, not by avoiding action.

Conclusion

His Holiness Sri Vidyanarayana Theertha's teachings serve as a guiding light for all who seek to live a life filled with wisdom, purpose, and grace. By embracing the interconnectedness of dharma, karma, and the pursuit of knowledge, we can navigate the challenges of life with clarity and strength. The true purpose of life is not in avoiding difficulties but in how we face them—with awareness, determination, and humility. Let us walk the path of spiritual growth, knowing that each step we take brings us closer to the Divine.

CHAPTER-48

DISCIPLINE: THE PATHWAY TO CLARITY, CONTROL, AND SPIRITUAL GROWTH

<u>Introduction</u>

In today's fast-paced world, particularly among the youth, discipline has never been more crucial. With the overwhelming presence of social media, constant notifications, and the addictive allure of cell phones, the mind is often scattered, distracted, and far from the truth. Though education is widely available, the deeper understanding—true education—is lacking in many aspects of life. This is where spiritual discipline, as taught by His Holiness Sri Vidyanarayana Theertha, becomes indispensable. Discipline is not just about controlling one's actions; it's about regaining control over the mind and steering it toward higher purposes. It helps us break free from the cycle of distraction and addiction, enabling us to channel our energy toward spiritual progress and mental clarity. In a world where external noise dominates, discipline serves as the anchor that keeps us grounded, focused, and on the path to self-realization.

Disciple: *Swamiji, why is discipline so important in today's world, especially with distractions like social media and technology?*

Swamy: Discipline is the key to controlling the mind amidst the distractions of modern life. The constant exposure to social media and the misuse of cell phones can scatter our focus, preventing us from experiencing mental clarity. Imagine trying to study with ten different things pulling your attention—it's impossible to truly learn. Discipline teaches us to focus on what is important, to limit distractions, and to control our impulses. Just as a car cannot function without a driver who guides its path, our mind cannot function effectively without the discipline to guide it. In a world that constantly calls for our attention, discipline becomes the driver, ensuring we stay focused on our higher purpose.

Disciple: *Swamiji, can you explain how discipline can help overcome the addiction to social media and cell phones?*

Swamy: Certainly. Social media and excessive use of technology are powerful forces that can easily take over our lives. The addiction to constant scrolling, likes, and virtual interactions pulls the mind away from reality, leaving little space for meaningful reflection or personal growth. Discipline is the remedy. Just like athletes who train consistently, we must develop self-control over our digital consumption. Set boundaries for when and how much time is spent on devices. This discipline allows you to reclaim your time and energy, which can be better utilized in meaningful practices like study, meditation, or engaging in real-world interactions that contribute to personal growth. When you have control over your technology use, you regain control over your life.

Disciple: *Swamiji, how does discipline relate to the gap between education and true understanding?*

Swamy: Education is widely available today, but true education—understanding the purpose of life, cultivating virtues, and knowing oneself—is often neglected. Discipline bridges this gap. While formal education provides knowledge, spiritual discipline guides us in applying that knowledge wisely. For example, you may learn a subject in school, but true understanding comes when you discipline your mind to focus, reflect, and integrate that knowledge into your life. Discipline allows you to channel your intellectual abilities into wisdom, helping you navigate life's challenges with insight and clarity. Without discipline, even the best education becomes shallow, as it cannot reach the depths of true understanding.

Disciple: *Swamiji, how does spiritual discipline purify the mind, especially when the mind is overwhelmed with distractions?*

Swamy: When the mind is overwhelmed with distractions, spiritual discipline acts as a purifier. Just as a filter cleanses water, discipline clears the mental clutter and brings focus. It is through discipline that we regain our ability to be present in the moment. In the context of today's youth, who are often overwhelmed with information overload, spiritual discipline helps reduce mental noise and creates space for inner peace. Through practices like meditation, self-reflection, and mindful engagement, discipline calms the mind and connects it to its true nature, leading to a state of serenity amidst the chaos.

Disciple: *Swamiji, what role does self-control play in facing these modern-day challenges?*

Swamy: Self-control is a vital virtue, especially in the modern world. With so many distractions at our fingertips, it is easy to succumb to temptation. However, spiritual discipline strengthens self-control, enabling us to make wise choices. It is like a rope that holds the mind steady in the midst of strong winds. Whether it's resisting the urge to check your phone every few minutes or choosing to spend time on more meaningful pursuits, self-control is what keeps us grounded. It allows us to balance our desires with our higher purpose, ensuring that we use our time and energy wisely.

Disciple: *Swamiji, how can the youth today apply discipline to experience peace and spiritual growth?*

Swamy: The youth today can apply discipline by first setting clear intentions for their lives. In the era of distractions, it is important to have a structured routine—whether it's for study, meditation, or self-improvement. Consistency in these practices gradually transforms the mind and brings inner peace. Just as a tree requires consistent care to grow, the mind requires regular discipline to flourish spiritually. By setting aside time for reflection, practice, and positive action, the youth can counter the distractions of social media and technology, using these tools mindfully instead of allowing them to control their lives.

Takeaways

- Discipline helps control the mind and senses, bringing clarity and focus, especially in the face of modern distractions like social media and technology.
- Through self-control and structure, we can break free from digital addictions and reclaim time for personal growth and spiritual practices.
- Education alone does not guarantee wisdom; spiritual discipline bridges the gap between knowledge and true understanding by helping us apply what we learn meaningfully.
- Spiritual discipline purifies the mind and creates space for inner peace, reducing the mental clutter brought on by constant distractions.
- Self-control strengthens our ability to make wise choices, helping us focus on what truly matters in life and avoid unnecessary temptations.
- The youth can apply discipline through consistent routines and practices, leading to spiritual growth and greater inner peace.

Conclusion

In today's world, where distractions are everywhere, discipline is the key to regaining control of our minds and focusing on what truly matters. Just as the mind needs discipline to avoid the scattered path of addiction and distraction, it also requires consistency to nurture spiritual growth. The youth of today face unique challenges, but through self-control, structure, and dedication to spiritual practices, they can achieve mental clarity and peace. By embracing discipline, we can bridge the gap between formal education and true wisdom, ultimately leading us toward a life of purpose, fulfilment, and connection to the divine.

CHAPTER-49

WISDOM FOR LIFE: DIVINE TEACHINGS ON DHARMA, KARMA, AND SPIRITUAL GROWTH

Introduction

In today's fast-paced, constantly changing world, the quest for life's true purpose is more pressing than ever. As we face daily challenges, we are often left questioning the deeper meaning behind our existence. The journey of spiritual growth demands not just external knowledge but an inner awakening—a profound connection with the Divine.

In this connection, we discover clarity amidst the chaos of life. In this illuminating discourse, His Holiness Sri Vidyanarayana Theertha imparts timeless wisdom, guiding us on how to navigate life's complexities while remaining anchored in our spiritual essence. His teachings offer a beacon of light, helping us align our thoughts, actions, and purpose with the higher will of the Divine.

Disciple: In a world where everything seems to have a price, it is often said that God gives us air and water freely. But why is this so?

Swamy: The Divine, in its infinite wisdom, provides essential elements like air and water without any expectation of return because they are not owned by any individual. They belong to the Earth and to the universe as a whole. When we come to recognize that these gifts are divine in nature, we see that life itself is a gift from the Divine. The human tendency to place value and taxes on everything arises from a desire to control. But in truth, life is priceless and not bound by human-created limits. If we learn to appreciate this, we start to understand that the Divine's generosity is not meant to be taxed or quantified.

Disciple: But how do we navigate the world when everything seems to demand our attention, from the mundane to the extraordinary?

Swamy: The world is a manifestation of the Divine, and all its aspects—whether mundane or extraordinary—carry within them the divine essence. The air we breathe, the trains that carry us, the vehicles that move us forward, and even the people we encounter are forms of God. To navigate this world, one must not struggle against its flow. Accept its rhythm, and follow the divine will with humility and wisdom. It is only by surrendering to this divine flow that we align ourselves with the greater purpose of life. In doing so, we free ourselves from unnecessary burdens, remain calm, and stay connected to the higher purpose that guides us.

Disciple: How can one maintain peace in such a busy, often chaotic world?

Swamy: To stay peaceful amidst the chaos, you must practice detachment from the outcome of your actions. Focus instead on performing your duties with devotion, but without expecting anything in return. This is the essence of Dharma—the righteous path—and Karma—the actions we perform in accordance with that path. When you act selflessly, you let go of attachment to the results and, in turn, find peace. One must be like a flower, spreading fragrance without expecting to be admired. By controlling the mind, you can maintain a steady, peaceful state, unaffected by external turbulence.

Disciple: What is the relationship between Dharma and Karma, and why is it important?

Swamy: Dharma and Karma are two sides of the same coin. Dharma refers to the righteous path—the principles that guide our actions and decisions. Karma refers to the actions we take in alignment with those principles. When one follows Dharma, the actions performed (Karma) are selfless and lead to spiritual growth. Without understanding Dharma, our actions are driven by selfish desires and may create negative Karma. Therefore, following the right principles leads to positive, righteous actions; by doing so, one can walk the path of spiritual liberation.

Disciple: The world is divided into different classes—Brahmins, Kshatriyas, Vaishyas, and Shudras. What does this division mean, and how should we view it?

Swamy: The division of society into four varnas—Brahmins, Kshatriyas, Vaishyas, and Shudras—has both spiritual and practical significance. Each class contributes uniquely to the harmony of society. Brahmins hold the knowledge of both material and spiritual worlds, and it is their responsibility to share wisdom. Kshatriyas, the warriors and leaders, ensure the protection and governance of society. Vaishyas, the traders and entrepreneurs, manage the material wealth of society with care and caution. Shudras, the supporting class, are essential in providing service to society. It is important to understand that this system is not about superiority or inferiority but about contributing according to one's abilities and duties. Ultimately, all are equal in the eyes of the Divine, each playing their part in the cosmic order.

Disciple: In today's world, how can one maintain balance and avoid the extremes of attachment and detachment?

Swamy: The key is to maintain, not to hold on. Attachment to things, people, or outcomes causes suffering, while total detachment can lead to isolation. Instead, maintain—earn, respect, and nurture—but do not become attached. Recognize that time is the greatest gift we have, and it is fleeting. Relationships are temporary, but the lessons they bring are eternal. Attach where necessary, detach when required, and choose wisely what to give your energy to. In the end, it is through balance that true peace is found.

Disciple: What is the role of time in our lives, and how can we make the most of it?

Swamy: Time is a divine creation. It is both a measure and a teacher. Each moment is a reflection of God's will, and how we use it determines our spiritual growth. Time should not be seen as something to be controlled but as something to be respected. By living with awareness, focusing on the present moment, and aligning our actions with Dharma, we honour time as a divine gift. Never waste time in the pursuit of fleeting pleasures; instead, use each moment to serve, learn, and grow.

Disciple: How can we practice the teachings of Dharma and Karma in everyday life?

Swamy: Begin by examining your actions. Each choice you make should reflect your higher purpose and be in harmony with the greater good. Ask yourself: Are my thoughts, words, and actions aligned with the Divine will? Are they motivated by selflessness or selfishness? When you act with the understanding that you are part of a greater whole, your actions will naturally follow the path of Dharma and lead to positive Karma. Whether in work, relationships, or personal endeavours, ask yourself, "How can I contribute to the well-being of others?" The answer will guide you on the right path.

Disciple: Is there a practical way to balance worldly life and spiritual life?

Swamy: Yes, the key lies in being present in the world without being attached to it. Engage with life fully, but remember that it is transient. Your spiritual practice is not separate from your everyday actions— it is integrated within them. When you perform your duties, do so with the awareness that your ultimate goal is spiritual growth. In this way, every action, no matter how mundane, becomes a step towards enlightenment.

Disciple: What final advice would you give to those seeking spiritual growth?

Swamy: Remember that the journey of spiritual growth is a personal one, yet it is connected to the whole of existence. Seek knowledge, but not just intellectual knowledge—seek wisdom that leads to compassion, humility, and selfless service. Practice daily mindfulness, keep your thoughts and actions pure, and always align yourself with Dharma. Trust in the Divine, surrender to its will and live each moment as an offering. Ultimately, the greatest truth is that we are all one with the Divine. Realizing this truth brings peace, liberation, and joy.

Takeaways

- **Selfless Action:** True peace is found in selfless action. By acting without attachment to the results, you align yourself with the Divine flow.
- **Balance in Life:** A harmonious life requires both worldly and spiritual pursuits. Balance your duties with wisdom and always remain aware of your higher purpose.
- **Dharma & Karma:** These are the two pillars that guide us. Dharma is the righteous path, and Karma is the action that follows it. Together, they lead to spiritual liberation.
- **Time is Sacred:** Time is a divine gift. Use each moment to learn, grow, and serve others.

Conclusion

In a world full of distractions and struggles, the path to spiritual growth lies in understanding the deeper truths of existence. By following the teachings of Dharma and Karma, practicing detachment, and recognizing the divine presence in everything, we can navigate life with peace, purpose, and joy. As we move forward, let us remember that every action, every thought, and every moment is an opportunity to connect with the Divine. In surrendering to its will, we unlock the path to true freedom and fulfilment.

CHAPTER-50

DISCIPLINE: THE PATHWAY TO CLARITY, CONTROL, AND SPIRITUAL GROWTH

Introduction

In today's fast-paced world, particularly among the youth, discipline has never been more crucial. With the overwhelming presence of social media, constant notifications, and the addictive allure of cell phones, the mind is often scattered, distracted, and far from the truth. Though education is widely available, the deeper understanding—true education—is lacking in many aspects of life. This is where spiritual discipline, as taught by His Holiness Sri Vidyanarayana Theertha, becomes indispensable. Discipline is not just about controlling one's actions; it's about regaining control over the mind and steering it toward higher purposes. It helps us break free from the cycle of distraction and addiction, enabling us to channel our energy toward spiritual progress and mental clarity. In a world where external noise dominates, discipline serves as the anchor that keeps us grounded, focused, and on the path to self-realization.

Disciple: *Swamiji, why is discipline so important in today's world, especially with distractions like social media and technology?*

Swamy: Discipline is the key to controlling the mind amidst the distractions of modern life. The constant exposure to social media and the misuse of cell phones can scatter our focus, preventing us from experiencing mental clarity. Imagine trying to study with ten different things pulling your attention—it's impossible to truly learn. Discipline teaches us to focus on what is important, to limit distractions, and to control our impulses. Just as a car cannot function without a driver who guides its path, our mind cannot function effectively without the discipline to guide it. In a world that constantly calls for our attention, discipline becomes the driver, ensuring we stay focused on our higher purpose.

Disciple: *Swamiji, can you explain how discipline can help overcome the addiction to social media and cell phones?*

Swamy: Certainly. Social media and excessive use of technology are powerful forces that can easily take over our lives. The addiction to constant scrolling, likes, and virtual interactions pulls the mind away from reality, leaving little space for meaningful reflection or personal growth. Discipline is the remedy. Just like athletes who train consistently, we must develop self-control over our digital consumption. Set boundaries for when and how much time is spent on devices. This discipline allows you to reclaim your time and energy, which can be better utilized in meaningful practices like study, meditation, or engaging in real-world interactions that contribute to personal growth. When you have control over your technology use, you regain control over your life.

Disciple: *Swamiji, how does discipline relate to the gap between education and true understanding?*

Swamy: Education is widely available today, but true education—understanding the purpose of life, cultivating virtues, and knowing oneself—is often neglected. Discipline bridges this gap. While formal education provides knowledge, spiritual discipline guides us in applying that knowledge wisely. For example, you may learn a subject in school, but true understanding comes when you discipline your mind to focus, reflect, and integrate that knowledge into your life. Discipline allows you to channel your intellectual abilities into wisdom, helping you navigate life's challenges with insight and clarity. Without discipline, even the best education becomes shallow, as it cannot reach the depths of true understanding.

Disciple: *Swamiji, how does spiritual discipline purify the mind, especially when the mind is overwhelmed with distractions?*

Swamy: When the mind is overwhelmed with distractions, spiritual discipline acts as a purifier. Just as a filter cleanses water, discipline clears the mental clutter and brings focus. It is through discipline that we regain our ability to be present in the moment. In the context of today's youth, who are often overwhelmed with information overload, spiritual discipline helps reduce mental noise and creates space for inner peace. Through practices like meditation, self-reflection, and mindful engagement, discipline calms the mind and connects it to its true nature, leading to a state of serenity amidst the chaos.

Disciple: *Swamiji, what role does self-control play in facing these modern-day challenges?*

Swamy: Self-control is a vital virtue, especially in the modern world. With so many distractions at our fingertips, it is easy to succumb to temptation. However, spiritual discipline strengthens self-control, enabling us to make wise choices. It is like a rope that holds the mind steady in the midst of strong winds. Whether it's resisting the urge to check your phone every few minutes or choosing to spend time on more meaningful pursuits, self-control is what keeps us grounded. It allows us to balance our desires with our higher purpose, ensuring that we use our time and energy wisely.

Disciple: *Swamiji, how can the youth today apply discipline to experience peace and spiritual growth?*

Swamy: The youth today can apply discipline by first setting clear intentions for their lives. In the era of distractions, it is important to have a structured routine—whether it's for study, meditation, or self-improvement. Consistency in these practices gradually transforms the mind and brings inner peace. Just as a tree requires consistent care to grow, the mind requires regular discipline to flourish spiritually. By setting aside time for reflection, practice, and positive action, the youth can counter the distractions of social media and technology, using these tools mindfully instead of allowing them to control their lives.

Takeaways

- Discipline helps control the mind and senses, bringing clarity and focus, especially in the face of modern distractions like social media and technology.
- Through self-control and structure, we can break free from digital addictions and reclaim time for personal growth and spiritual practices.
- Education alone does not guarantee wisdom; spiritual discipline bridges the gap between knowledge and true understanding by helping us apply what we learn meaningfully.
- Spiritual discipline purifies the mind and creates space for inner peace, reducing the mental clutter brought on by constant distractions.
- Self-control strengthens our ability to make wise choices, helping us focus on what truly matters in life and avoid unnecessary temptations.
- The youth can apply discipline through consistent routines and practices, leading to spiritual growth and greater inner peace.

Conclusion

In today's world, where distractions are everywhere, discipline is the key to regaining control of our minds and focusing on what truly matters. Just as the mind needs discipline to avoid the scattered path of addiction and distraction, it also requires consistency to nurture spiritual growth. The youth of today face unique challenges, but through self-control, structure, and dedication to spiritual practices, they can achieve mental clarity and peace. By embracing discipline, we can bridge the gap between formal education and true wisdom, ultimately leading us toward a life of purpose, fulfilment, and connection to the divine.

SACRED CONVERGENCE

"Sacred convergence is where the seeker, the path, and the truth become one.
It is not found in distance but in dissolving—ego fades, the divine remains.
When mind and heart unite, wisdom flows, love shines, silence speaks.
All energies return to their source, where stillness and movement are the same.
In that sacred space, nothing is separate—only oneness prevails."

– His Holiness Sri Vidyanarayana Theertha

CHAPTER-51

Maha Kumbh Mela: A Spiritual, Scientific, and Social Confluence

तस्मात् भारत जन्म प्राप्य स्वर्गोऽपि गरियसि

"To be born in Bharat is itself a great blessing, surpassing even heaven."

In a profound address at the Dwaraka Badarika Ashramam Mutt in Malleshwaram, Bangalore, His Holiness Sri Sri Srividyanarayana Teertha illuminated the sacred significance of the Maha Kumbh Mela. He conveyed that the Kumbh Mela transcends a mere religious gathering; it is a cosmic confluence where faith, wisdom, and divine energy unite in the quest for spiritual liberation. The Mela offers a divine opportunity for purification and self-realization, drawing seekers, ascetics, and devotees worldwide to transcend worldly illusions and immerse themselves in the eternal flow of divine consciousness.

The Maha Kumbh Mela: A Living Testimony of Eternal Wisdom

The Maha Kumbh Mela is not simply a festival but a living testimony to the eternal spiritual wisdom that has guided humanity for millennia. This grand event is held once every twelve years as a confluence of divine grace, spiritual fervour, and cultural unity. Rooted deeply in Hindu Sanatana Dharma, the Mela offers a unique platform for spiritual seekers, ascetics, and devotees to gather in their pursuit of divine realization. The name "Kumbh" is derived from the Sanskrit words "Kum" (earth) and "umbhati" (purity or water-filled), symbolizing the clay pot—a vessel containing the divine nectar of wisdom and grace.

Tracing its origins over 850 years ago, the Kumbh Mela is traditionally linked to the great sage Adi Shankaracharya. Ancient Puranas narrate that during the churning of the ocean (Samudra Manthan), nectar (Amrit) drops fell at four holy locations: Prayag, Haridwar, Nasik, and Ujjain. These sacred places became the epicentres of the Kumbh Mela, where devotees gather to purify their souls and seek liberation from the cycle of birth and death. The sacred waters, believed to have absorbed the nectar of immortality, possess the power to cleanse sins and grant salvation.

The Divine Locations of the Kumbh Mela

The Kumbh Mela unfolds at four sacred locations, each renowned for the purity of its waters during specific time windows. Every twelve years, these locations align with celestial forces, enhancing the purity of the waters and the power of divine energy. Devotees believe that immersion in these waters during the Punya Kaal (auspicious period) purifies the soul, erases past sins, and grants spiritual and material growth blessings. The event rejuvenates the body, mind, and spirit, washing away not just physical impurities but also negative thoughts and emotions.

Types of Kumbh Melas: A Spiritual Journey

There are three major variations of the Kumbh Mela:

1. **Ardha Kumbh Mela**: Held every six years, it represents a partial period of the sacred Kumbh. The last Ardha Kumbh Mela occurred in 2019.
2. **Kumbh Mela**: This main event occurs every 12 years and provides a grand opportunity for spiritual renewal. The next Kumbh will take place in 2025.
3. **Mahakumbh Mela**: This rare event occurs once every 144 years (12 x 12) and marks the alignment of twelve suns. The last Mahakumbh Mela was in 2013; the next one will be held in 2157.

The Divine Origin of the Kumbh Mela

Steeped in legend, the story of the Kumbh Mela begins with the tale of Indra, the king of the gods. After angering the great sage Durvasa, Indra, in his shame, wandered in the form of a donkey seeking redemption. With guidance from Narada Muni, Indra invoked Lakshmi, the goddess of wealth, and regained his divine riches. This was followed by the churning of the ocean of milk (Samudra Manthan), from which drops of nectar fell at four holy sites: Prayag, Haridwar, Nasik, and Ujjain, which later became the focal points of the Kumbh Mela.

A Social Convergence of Faith

The Kumbh Mela, while deeply spiritual, is also a remarkable social phenomenon. Naga Sadhus, mystics, ascetics, Veera Shaiva initiates, and thousands of devotees converge, forming a vibrant tapestry of faith, unity, and devotion. It brings together people from diverse backgrounds—within India and internationally—creating a global community united by the shared quest for spiritual purification and divine grace. The gathering embodies the power of collective belief and energy, inspiring millions in their pursuit of mental peace and spiritual awakening.

A Call to Reflection: Timeless Relevance

As modern society becomes increasingly materialistic, the Kumbh Mela reminds us of our deeper spiritual needs. In a world often distracted by the noise of daily life, it offers an invitation to step back, reflect, and reconnect with our true selves. India, the land of these divine gatherings, holds a unique place in the world—the only place where such profound spiritual phenomena occur. The Maha Kumbh Mela thus offers an unparalleled opportunity for renewal, where individuals can reconnect with the divine essence of existence.

Scientific View: The Healing Power of Sacred Waters

From a scientific perspective, the Maha Kumbh Mela can be understood through the lenses of quantum physics, environmental science, and psychology. The rivers where the Mela is held—especially the Ganges, Yamuna, Godavari, and Shipra—are rich in minerals, and research shows that the Ganges contains higher levels of bacteriophages, which help maintain ecological balance and may contribute to the healing properties attributed to the water during the Mela. Additionally, the collective energy of millions of participants creates a potent environment for spiritual awakening, aligning with the concept of "collective effervescence" in psychology, where large congregations elevate consciousness and create transformative experiences.

A Celebration of Unity in Diversity

The Maha Kumbh Mela symbolizes the inclusivity of Sanatana Dharma, uniting diverse sects and philosophies under its vast umbrella. Whether Shaivas, Vaishnavas, Shaktas, or followers of various yogic paths, all come together in a unified spiritual experience. The presence of Naga Sadhus, Aghoris, and other ascetics adds depth to the spiritual landscape, challenging conventional notions of purity and illustrating the many paths to liberation.

A Cultural and Social Reawakening

The Mela also acts as a cultural and social event, fostering unity among people of all social backgrounds. It serves as an occasion to reassert the values of dharma (righteousness), karma (action), and seva (service to humanity). Moreover, social organizations use the Mela as a platform to address critical issues such as sanitation, education, and healthcare, raising awareness and advocating for change. The gathering stands as a reminder that spiritual and social progress are intertwined, evolving together for the betterment of society.

The Role of Guru and Shishya

A central aspect of the Mela is the Guru-Shishya (master-disciple) relationship. Many seek divine teachings from revered Gurus who impart wisdom that transcends written texts. For seekers, the Kumbh Mela becomes an opportunity to receive teachings directly from enlightened masters, guiding them toward spiritual awakening.

Preserving Vedic Culture

The Mela also plays a vital role in preserving and reviving Vedic culture. Through rituals, discussions, and spiritual practices, the teachings of the Vedas and Upanishads remain alive, ensuring their continuity for future generations. The divine wisdom of Sanatana Dharma continues to illuminate the path toward liberation.

Insights for Reflection: Building a Greater India

As we reflect upon the Kumbh Mela's spiritual, social, and scientific confluence, it becomes clear that **a greater India** lies in the **unity of purpose**. India's ancient wisdom gives us timeless teachings on humility, simplicity, and self-realization, and the Kumbh Mela invites us to reawaken these ideals in our daily lives.

- **Unity in Diversity:** Just as millions of individuals from different walks of life come together at the Mela, we must, too, foster a spirit of inclusivity, where diversity is celebrated and our differences become a source of strength.
- **Sacred Duty to Society:** The Kumbh Mela also teaches us that spirituality and social responsibility go hand-in-hand. A greater India will emerge when everyone takes responsibility for **serving society, uplifting others**, and making collective progress.
- **Purification of the Mind and Soul:** The Mela reminds us of the importance of inner purification. A greater India requires

individuals who strive for **personal growth, self-awareness, and peace**. When the soul is at peace, its society reflects the same tranquillity.

- **Commitment to Sustainability:** The sacred waters of the Kumbh Mela symbolize India's **natural resources**, which must be preserved and protected for future generations. A greater India is one where **sustainability, environmental conservation, and wise stewardship** become a collective mission.

Inspiring Conclusion: Awakening to a Divine Vision

The Maha Kumbh Mela is not merely a spiritual event but a profound expression of humanity's potential to rise beyond worldly confines and awaken to higher states of consciousness. This sacred gathering offers a unique opportunity to reconnect with the divine within us and in the world around us. By blending spiritual wisdom, scientific exploration, and social consciousness, the Mela reminds us that true transformation is a shared effort. Every individual, community, and nation have an integral role in cultivating a more enlightened and harmonious world.

At its heart, the Mela teaches the values of selfless service, unity in diversity, and the pursuit of collective good. When embraced, these principles lay the groundwork for a future rooted in compassion and understanding—one that transcends borders and uplifts all of humanity.

तस्मात् भारत जन्म प्राप्य स्वर्गोऽपि गरियसि

"To be born in Bharat is itself a great blessing, surpassing even heaven."

As we honour the blessings of our heritage, let us commit ourselves to building a greater India—one that embodies spirituality, wisdom, and compassion for the world. The teachings of the Maha Kumbh Mela urge us to seek the ultimate truth and divine grace that dwell within each of us, guiding us to contribute to this noble vision.

Beyond spiritual awakening, the Kumbh Mela exemplifies the power of collective human endeavours. It showcases the potential for global collaboration to address urgent environmental, social, and economic challenges. This gathering stands as a living example of how the confluence of spiritual and scientific knowledge can foster meaningful societal change.

In essence, the Maha Kumbh Mela is not just a momentary event but a manifestation of the eternal connection between humanity and the divine. May this sacred convergence inspire us to realize our highest potential and rekindle our bond with the divine essence that unites all creation.

CHAPTER-52

THE ILLUSION OF POWER AND THE ETERNAL SHELTER OF GOVINDA

A Discourse by His Holiness Sri Vidya Narayana Theertha

What Gives a Person True Power?

Is it wealth, influence, or intelligence? Or is there a greater force beyond these? In the grand stage of life, society revolves around politics, money, power, and influence. These forces shape human interactions, dictating who rises and who falls. People assume that intelligence, status, and body language will carry them forward, but His Holiness Sri Vidya Narayana Theertha reminds us that these are fleeting illusions.

The true currency of power is influence—secured through connections with priests, temple authorities, scholars, and political leaders. If one possesses influence, the world appears to bow at one's feet. But what happens when the veil lifts and one realizes the hollowness of these pursuits? What happens when power and wealth, which once seemed invincible, crumble into insignificance?

The Awakening: Beyond Material Strength

At some point, life forces every individual to confront an undeniable truth: neither wealth nor status follows us beyond this existence. When this realization dawns, people often experience a profound shift. Those who once clung to power with desperation now open their hearts to generosity, giving freely without hesitation. But why wait until the twilight of life to discover this wisdom?

Sri Swamiji explains that our journey in this world is like a festival, and one of the most symbolic celebrations is **Garuda Vahanam (Garuda Seva).** The mighty Garuda, carrying Lord Srihari, represents the ultimate moment of surrender.

Garuda is not just the divine vehicle of Lord Vishnu—he symbolizes **speed, clarity, and unwavering devotion.** He moves toward the Lord effortlessly, just as surrender allows the soul to transcend worldly struggles. When individuals face insurmountable challenges, when they stand at the crossroads of despair, they instinctively raise their hands to the sky and cry out:

"Hey Govinda! Hey Govinda! Hey Govinda!"

This is the moment of true realization—the moment when the ego dissolves and the soul seeks refuge in the divine. Just as Garuda soars above obstacles, the one who surrenders is lifted beyond suffering.

The Story of Gajendra: The Cry of the Soul

The essence of this wisdom is beautifully illustrated in **Gajendra Moksham.**

Like Gajendra, we struggle in the waters of life—caught by attachments, fears, and suffering. We exhaust all our strength, seeking solutions from the world, but in the end, only one cry brings salvation: **"Hey Govinda!"**

When Gajendra, the mighty elephant, was caught by a relentless crocodile in the river, he fought with all his strength. But no matter how powerful he was, he could not free himself. His herd abandoned him. His might was of no use. At the peak of his suffering, he raised his trunk and called out to Lord Vishnu. And in that moment of absolute surrender, the Lord came running to his aid, cutting the chains of suffering and granting him liberation.

Swamiji reminds us that in life's most critical moments, **no relative, no friend, no wealth, and no influence can save us.** But Govinda—the eternal protector—rushes to our side the moment we surrender to Him.

The Path to Divine Upliftment

Swamiji himself has walked this path. Once, he too was a man of great wealth, believing in the security of material success. But then life brought him to a moment where nothing—neither wealth nor status—could rescue him. And in that moment of surrender, the divine voice whispered:

"Hey boy, surrender to me, and I will save and uplift you spiritually."

From that point onward, Swamiji dedicated his life to guiding others toward this realization. The Lord does not abandon His devotees. When called with a pure heart, He:

- **Protects** in times of fear
- **Guides** through the darkness
- **Supports** in all aspects of life

The Call of Govinda

What does it mean to call upon **Govinda**? The name **Govinda** carries profound significance. It is derived from the Sanskrit:

- **Go (गौ)** means *Earth, Vedas, Cows,* or *Senses.*
- **Vinda (विन्द)** means *Protector, Knower,* or *One who rescues.*

Thus, **Govinda** is "the protector of the Earth," "the knower of the Vedas," and "the one who rescues His devotees from suffering." He is the eternal saviour, the divine refuge for all beings.

Today, Swamiji extends this wisdom to all. He urges us not to wait until despair strikes but to embrace **Govinda Namam** now, in every breath, in every step of life.

Right now, wherever you are, take a deep breath. Close your eyes. Whisper His name:

"Govinda, Govinda, Govinda."

Feel His presence. Know that He is already guiding you.

Key Takeaways: Insights for Life

- **Material wealth, power, and influence are temporary.** They may appear strong, but they are fragile in the face of life's ultimate truths.
- **Surrender is not weakness; it is the greatest strength.** The moment we surrender to the divine, we rise above suffering.
- **Garuda Vahanam symbolizes surrender and upliftment.** Just as Garuda carries Lord Vishnu, surrender to the Lord lifts us beyond worldly struggles.
- **Gajendra Moksham teaches us the power of divine intervention.** When all else fails, the Lord alone is our true saviour.
- **Govinda is the eternal protector.** Calling upon Him with devotion brings guidance, support, and ultimate liberation.

Conclusion: The Eternal Refuge

Life's journey is uncertain. No one knows when a crisis will strike, stripping away our worldly securities. But one thing remains constant—the divine presence of Govinda, the eternal refuge.

Swamiji's message is a call to awaken, to break free from the illusions of power, and to embrace the true strength that lies in **faith and surrender.** We do not need to wait for suffering to remember Govinda. We can make Him a part of our lives now, in every breath, in every thought.

Let the call of Govinda resonate within you. Let His name be the bridge that carries you beyond sorrow into eternal peace.

Govinda! Govinda! Govinda!

CHAPTER-53

BRIDGING WISDOM AND LEADERSHIP: INTEGRATING THE PAST WITH THE PRESENT

Introduction

The following is a message from **His Holiness Sri Vidyanarayana Theertha**, offering guidance to young administrators undergoing training at the **Lal Bahadur Shastri National Academy of Administration (LBSNAA)**.

As future **Collectors and leaders of India,** you are entrusted with not just governance but also with **upholding Dharma through righteous action, integrity, and selfless service.** While this academy equips you with the skills of administration, **true leadership begins with character**, shaped by timeless wisdom and ethical responsibility.

His Holiness emphasizes that **blending ancient insights with modern duties** is the key to effective governance. The challenges you will face in service require not only **intellect and efficiency** but also **wisdom, detachment, and moral clarity.** This message serves as a guiding light on your journey—helping you integrate the **past and present to shape a just and righteous future.**

1. The Foundation of True Leadership

The **Lal Bahadur Shastri (LBS) Academy** trains individuals to become administrators of India, but the foundation of true leadership is laid much earlier—at home. It is within the family that one first learns the values of:

- **Integrity** – Standing by truth despite challenges.
- **Loyalty** – Staying committed to a just cause.
- **Honesty** – Ensuring transparency in actions.
- **Courage** – Facing adversity with determination.
- **Perseverance** – Never giving up on the righteous path.
- **Seva (Service)** – Serving others selflessly.
- **Duty** – Fulfilling responsibilities with sincerity.

While formal education imparts knowledge, it is **character that shapes true leaders**. Ancient scriptures emphasize that it is not intellect but **character** that enables a person to walk the path of **Dharma**.

Rebirth Theory: Responsibility Over Fate

The **Rebirth Theory** teaches two fundamental lessons:

- **Acceptance of the Present** – Acknowledging the reality of one's circumstances.
- **Responsibility for the Future** – Understanding that today's actions shape tomorrow's destiny.

♦ **Message:** The **LBS Academy** refines leadership skills, but true leadership begins at home with strong values. **Character, not just intellect, determines one's ability to uphold Dharma.**

2. Knowledge and Dharma: Overcoming Misinformation

Modern education often discourages the study of scriptures by promoting the misconception that **varna (caste) is determined by birth**. This is false. Ancient wisdom clearly states that **varna is based on one's karma (actions), not birthright**. You are not defined by where you are born, but by **what you do**.

India's scriptures and epics contain profound knowledge in:

- Economics
- Geography

- Mathematics
- Grammar
- Astronomy
- Medicine
- Logic
- Civics & Administration

This ancient wisdom remains relevant even today. It offers valuable insights for **decision-making and governance**. As administrators, you will face changing circumstances that may require you to adjust your stance—this is not a failure but a sign of **wisdom**.

Attachment vs. Devotion: A Lesson from the Mahabharata

- **Attachment is to a thing, while devotion is to the Whole.**
- **Dhrithrashtra's** blind attachment to his son, **Duryodhana**, led him away from Dharma, ultimately resulting in a devastating war.
- As leaders, always act with **detachment and wisdom**, ensuring decisions are based on truth and righteousness rather than personal biases.

◆ **Message:** Knowledge from scriptures remains relevant today. **Detach from personal biases and make decisions based on Dharma.**

3. Patience, Wisdom, and the Power of Spirituality

As leaders, you may not always get the desired results. However, the best approach is to:

- **Wait** – Do not rush into impulsive decisions.
- **Watch** – Observe the situation carefully.
- **Win** – With patience and wisdom, the right path will emerge.

There will be moments when difficult choices distort your reasoning. It is then that the 'Amrit' of spirituality will guide you to do the **right**

Karma. The scriptures urge each individual to reflect deeply on the eternal question:

⬤ **"Why do we do what we do?"**

Seeking this answer is your **Purusharth (personal duty)**. It is the **Seva (service)** that must be performed using wisdom and logical reasoning from the **Manual of Life—our scriptures**.

◈ **Message:** In times of uncertainty, **patience and spiritual wisdom** will help you make righteous decisions.

4. Faith and Responsibility: The Mark of a True Sevak

More than **130 crore Indians** place their faith in you to act in their best interests. **Faith does not mean passively hoping for good outcomes—it means actively doing the right thing, regardless of the results.**

- When **Viveka (discernment)** helps you identify the correct **Karma (action)** according to **Dharma (righteousness)**, you become a **true Sevak (servant-leader)**.
- A **Sevak** is not merely an administrator but a **superior, dependable, and honourable leader.**

◈ **Message:** True faith is not just belief—it is action. A leader must always strive to do the right thing, regardless of the outcome.

Key Takeaways

- ✓ **Leadership begins at home** – Strong moral values are the foundation of true leadership.
- ✓ **Knowledge is useful only when rooted in Dharma** – Make ethical decisions without attachment.
- ✓ **Patience and wisdom** – The best leaders know when to wait, watch, and act.
- ✓ **Faith is action** – Do what is right without fear of the outcome.

Conclusion

As administrators, you are not just policy-makers but also **guardians of Dharma**. Your duty is not limited to governance alone but extends to **upholding righteousness, ensuring justice, and serving the people selflessly.**

The **past and present must be integrated wisely**—learn from scriptures, stay rooted in spiritual values, and apply that wisdom in modern governance. Let your actions be guided by **truth, duty, and unwavering faith.**

With blessings and good wishes from **His Holiness Sri Vidyanarayana Theertha**, may you always walk the path of Dharma.

CHAPTER-54

LIFE: A JOURNEY BEYOND ATTACHMENTS THE SPIRITUAL INSIGHTS OF HIS HOLINESS SRI VIDYANARAYANA THEERTHA

Introduction

The Illusion of Ownership

Life is often seen as a pursuit of success, comfort, and fulfilment. Yet, in this journey, we forget a fundamental truth—nothing truly belongs to us. The material world is transient, and our attachment to possessions, relationships, and achievements only binds us to cycles of karma. His Holiness Sri Vidyanarayana Theertha reminds us that true wisdom lies in understanding this impermanence and embracing detachment.

As the Bhagavad Gita states:

"na tv evāhaṁ jātu nāsaṁ na tvaṁ neme janādhipāḥ
na caiva na bhaviṣyāmaḥ sarve vayam ataḥ param"

(There was never a time when I did not exist, nor you, nor all these kings; nor in the future shall any of us cease to be.)

Understanding life as a temporary lease rather than permanent ownership allows us to focus on spiritual growth rather than worldly accumulation.

Key Insights

- **Life is a Lease, Not Ownership** – Luxury and possessions are temporary; true wealth lies in spiritual wisdom.

- **Brahmacharya and Gruhastha Ashram** – The renunciate gives selflessly, while the householder must serve with detachment.
- **The Illusion of Control** – Attachment, even to family, creates karmic bondage. Letting go leads to liberation.
- **Mind Shapes Reality** – Thoughts dictate our desires and actions; detachment frees us from suffering.
- **Spiritual Hierarchy of Avadhootas** – Realized beings evolve through different stages, guided by divine energy.

Luxury: A Lease to the Body

Many believe that wealth and luxury bring happiness, but Swamiji teaches that they are mere illusions. Life in luxury is like a lease—temporary and dependent on external circumstances.

- **Bachelors (Brahmacharis) live on lease** – They renounce personal desires and dedicate themselves to selfless service.
- **Householders (Gruhasthas) live on rent** – They fulfill worldly responsibilities but should remain detached.

Adi Shankaracharya wisely reminds us:
"Maa kuru dhana jana yauvana garvam, Harati nimeshāt kālah sarvam"
(*Do not be proud of wealth, people, and youth; time takes everything in an instant.*)

True fulfilment comes not from material gain but from transcending worldly attachments.

The Path of Brahmacharya and Gruhastha Ashram

Swamiji explains that a Brahmachari (celibate seeker) and a Sannyasi (renunciate) are fundamentally the same—both dedicate their lives to spiritual growth. A Brahmachari's mind is trained to give, serve, and remain free from worldly distractions.

A householder (Gruhastha), on the other hand, must gain wisdom through responsibilities and service. However, if attachment persists after fulfilling one's duties, it binds them to karma.

A perfect example is King Janaka, father of Sita. He ruled a vast kingdom, fulfilled his duties, yet remained completely detached—earning the title of *Raja Rishi* (King-Sage).

Swamiji's wisdom teaches that true detachment is not negligence; rather, it is fulfilling duties with devotion while remaining unattached to their outcomes.

The Power of Thoughts and Detachment

"Your thoughts dictate everything," Swamiji declares. If one constantly dwells on desires, those desires gain control. Conversely, a mind rooted in detachment and self-awareness is liberated.

He gives the example of **Amma of Tiruvannamalai**—a spiritually realized soul who cared little for bodily needs yet maintained it for the benefit of society. Such beings live beyond material needs, deeply immersed in divine consciousness.

The journey of an Avadhoota (realized being) unfolds through different stages of awakening:

- Level 1: Awakening into a super-conscious state
- Level 2: Experiencing profound realization
- Levels 3 & 4: Gradual transcendence toward absolute enlightenment

Swamiji humbly positions himself between Levels 2 and 3, recognizing that spiritual evolution is neither linear nor self-driven but unfolds through divine energy. True saints do not claim attainment; rather, they surrender to the mystical force that guides their journey.

"Spiritual growth is not something we achieve by effort; it happens through divine energy. Awakening, realization, and enlightenment unfold naturally when we surrender to that higher force."

– Swamy Vidyanarayana Theertha.

As the Upanishads proclaim:

"Tat Tvam Asi" (*Thou art that*), meaning that the Divine is within us, and spiritual realization comes when we detach from the external and look inward.

Conclusion: The Path to Liberation

True freedom lies in recognizing that nothing belongs to us. Whether as Brahmacharis, householders, or renunciates, detachment and selfless service determine our spiritual progress. Swamiji urges us to let go of attachments, embrace wisdom, and chant the divine name with surrender:

Hare Krishna, Hare Krishna!

Ultimately, life is not about ownership but awakening to the higher truth. By shedding illusions and realizing our eternal connection with the Divine, we truly embark on the path of liberation.

As the Bhagavad Gita reminds us:

"Karmanye vadhikaraste, ma phaleshu kadachana"

(*You have the right to perform your duty, but not to the fruits of your actions.*)

By following this path of selflessness and wisdom, we inch closer to divine realization, walking in the footsteps of enlightened beings who have shown us the way.

CHAPTER-55

BEYOND MAYA: WISDOM FOR A FULFILLING LIFE

Introduction

Once, a wise sage gathered his disciples and placed two chains before them—one made of iron, the other of gold. He asked, *"Which of these chains is more dangerous?"*

The disciples laughed. *"Guruji, both are chains! What difference does it make?"*

The sage chuckled and said, *"Exactly! Whether made of iron or gold, a chain is a chain—it still binds you. The same is true for Maya. Whether you are attached to wealth or worries, praise or pain, luxury or struggle—attachment is what truly enslaves you."*

His Holiness Sri Vidyanarayana Theertha echoes this eternal truth, reminding us that the world is an illusion—*Maya*—that traps us in material pursuits, fleeting emotions, and false identities. But Swamy stated, *"Maya must not be feared or blindly rejected—it should be understood and reduced, little by little, with awareness and wisdom."*

In today's world, where people chase wealth but struggle with contentment, seek relationships but battle loneliness, and pursue knowledge but remain spiritually empty, His Holiness provides a guiding light. This discourse brings forth his profound wisdom, helping spiritual seekers and young minds navigate life with clarity, purpose, and inner peace.

Beyond Illusion: Recognizing Maya and Seeking Truth

Swamy stated, "Society is Maya—an illusion that entangles individuals in fleeting desires and false perceptions." While Maya is inherently negative, rejecting it outright is not the path. Instead, one must recognize and navigate it with awareness, gradually detaching from its hold while seeking the divine within.

Swamy stated, "Luxury weakens the soul, but hard work strengthens it." True realization begins when one understands that "I alone exist; I am in all." This self-awareness shifts the focus from external validation to inner fulfilment, from illusion to truth. The Supreme Mystery can only be known by those who choose to surrender and immerse themselves in the divine presence.

The Sacred Power of Relationships

Swamy stated one of the devotees, "Your wife is Jagadjanani. Your mother is the foundation." A family is not merely a social institution but a reflection of divine creation. Love and reverence for these relationships help a seeker grow and evolve.

The great epics illuminate the strength found in relationships. Sita's unwavering devotion in the face of trials, and Draupadi's fearless challenge to injustice, show that righteousness transcends gender. Their stories remind us that spiritual wisdom and courage are not confined by societal roles but arise from a deep connection to dharma.

Yet, one must be cautious. Swamy stated, "Be alert, awake, and live in peace." While relationships can be uplifting, they can also bind one to illusion. The wise navigate this balance, staying rooted in spiritual awareness without being consumed by worldly ties.

The Need for Harmonious Relationships

In the present society, women continue to face discrimination and injustice, which is contrary to the principles of righteousness. Despite advancements, many still struggle for respect, equality, and dignity. This is not the way of dharma. Swamy emphasized that true harmony arises when relationships are based on mutual respect and understanding. Just as revered women in the epics embodied both strength and devotion, today's society must acknowledge and honour their role in shaping a just world. A balanced society is one where men and women support and uplift each other, walking together on the path of righteousness and spiritual growth.

Living in Simplicity and Surrender

Swamy stated, **"Live a normal, natural, neutral life."** True contentment arises from seeking sufficiency rather than excess. *Samthripthi, Samanam Shanti*—contentment is the path to peace. When we stop chasing more and embrace what is enough, we find inner stability. A mind free from endless desires experiences true joy, and in that joy, peace naturally blossoms.

Spiritual realization does not require renouncing responsibilities but understanding their transient nature. Material wealth fades, but grace, divine blessings, and the awareness of the Supreme endure. Swamy stated, "Hard-earned money must be preserved wisely, while attachment to material possessions must be relinquished." This is the essence of a fulfilled life.

Conclusion

Swamy stated, "Shock is to wake you to awareness; shivering is to wake you to alertness." Every challenge is a divine nudge toward awakening. Life's trials are opportunities for spiritual growth. Surrender is not submission but an intimate relationship with the Divine.

To live in realization is to live with joy, clarity, and unwavering purpose. Swamy stated, "Chant the name of God, let go of unnecessary material distractions, and embrace the peace within." As His Holiness proclaims, *Hare Krishna, Hare Sai, Hare Ram*—the divine is eternal, always guiding us beyond illusion into the ultimate truth.

CHAPTER-56

NAVIGATING LIFE WITH SPIRITUAL BALANCE

Introduction

Life is a symphony of contradictions—motion and stillness, solitude and engagement, holding on and letting go. True wisdom does not lie in blind renunciation nor in relentless attachment, but in mastering the  delicate art of balance. **Sri Vidyanarayana Theertha** reminds us that **"Spirituality is not about escaping the world, nor is it about drowning in it. It is about knowing when to withdraw and when to engage—when to bolt, and when to open."**

A bird cannot soar with one wing; a spiritual seeker, too, must learn when to retreat into silence and when to extend outward in service. The one who remains immersed in the world without inner reflection is lost in chaos, and the one who withdraws completely misses the very purpose of existence. **Spirituality is not about choosing between silence and action, but about knowing when to embrace each.**

This profound truth is encapsulated in Swamiji's words:

"Bolt inside, open outside; bolt outside, open inside."

At first glance, this may seem paradoxical, yet it holds the key to self-mastery. **Are we mindlessly caught in the external, or deeply attuned to our inner sanctum? Are we shielding ourselves from distractions yet remaining open to divine wisdom?**

This delicate balance was embodied by **Sri Ramakrishna Paramahamsa**, who withdrew into deep sadhana, shutting out the world to attain divine realization. Yet, once the divine truth dawned upon him, he opened his heart to seekers, illuminating their paths with boundless love and wisdom. His very life was a testimony to Swamiji's words—guarding the inner sanctity while radiating divine wisdom outward.

As seekers in the modern world—where distractions are endless and the mind is constantly pulled in multiple directions—how do we cultivate this balance? **How do we stand firm in wisdom while remaining fluid in action? Sri Vidyanarayana Theertha's insight compels us to reflect, question, and ultimately, transform.**

The Dual Path of a Seeker

Swamiji's words serve as a spiritual roadmap for every aspirant:

- **"Bolt inside, open outside"** – Protect your inner self by shielding your mind from distractions, desires, and ego, yet remain open to serving and interacting with the world with love and compassion.
- **"Bolt outside, open inside"** – At times, detach from external influences like praise, criticism, and worldly noise to allow deep inner reflection and spiritual realization.

This wisdom finds expression in the lives of great masters. **Sri Ramakrishna Paramahamsa**, for instance, spent years in intense meditation, closing himself off from worldly distractions. Yet, once he realized the divine truth, he became completely accessible to seekers, guiding them in simple yet profound ways.

One of his most famous teachings is that of the **musk deer**, which tirelessly searches for an elusive fragrance, unaware that the scent originates within itself. Likewise, he taught that divine presence is not something to be sought in the external world—it resides within us. His openness to all faiths and his deep devotion to Mother Kali made him an embodiment of "bolt outside, open inside" in his spiritual practices and "bolt inside, open outside" in his role as a teacher.

This principle also shaped the destiny of **Swami Vivekananda**, whom Ramakrishna recognized as a world-changing force. Though deeply immersed in divine ecstasy, Ramakrishna remained present for his disciples, nurturing them with unwavering compassion and wisdom.

Balancing Detachment and Engagement

A spiritual seeker must develop discernment:

- **Detach from negativity while embracing divine wisdom.** Just as a lotus blooms untouched by the muddy waters around it, a seeker must remain untainted by external turmoil while radiating purity and grace.
- **Protect your inner sanctity while actively serving the world.** Saints like Swami Vivekananda exemplified this by immersing themselves in deep meditation yet tirelessly working for the upliftment of humanity.
- **Renounce not the world, but ignorance.** True renunciation is not physical withdrawal but attaining clarity and emotional discipline to navigate life with wisdom.

The Subtle Art of Protection and Surrender

A bolt serves as a safeguard. It signifies the need to protect what is sacred, either within or outside. In a seeker's journey:

- The mind should be shielded from restlessness and distractions, just as a fortress protects its treasures.
- The heart should be open to grace, devotion, and wisdom, like a temple welcoming the divine presence.
- One must lock away disturbances but remain receptive to higher consciousness, balancing inner peace with outward expression.

As **Swami Sivananda** said, "Detach from the world, attach to the divine." Knowing when to withdraw and when to open is key to spiritual evolution.

A Call for Inner Awareness in Today's World

In an era dominated by social media, instant gratification, and endless distractions, Swamiji's insight is more relevant than ever. **Today's youth, caught in a whirlwind of digital noise, often struggle to find inner silence. The mind, constantly engaged in external validation, loses its ability to reflect, to pause, to truly understand.**

How does one apply Swamiji's wisdom to this modern chaos?

- **Bolt inside:** Take conscious breaks from the digital world. Detach from social media's endless chatter and turn inward for self-reflection.
- **Open outside:** Use the same technology wisely to spread knowledge, connect with wisdom, and uplift others.
- **Bolt outside:** Guard your inner sanctity from toxic influences, peer pressure, and superficial distractions.
- **Open inside:** Be receptive to inner growth, authentic relationships, and deep contemplation.

Swamiji's words remind us that **inner peace is not found in running away from the world, nor in indulging in it blindly, but in striking the right balance between retreat and engagement.**

Key Takeaways

1. **Balance is essential** – Spirituality is not about extreme withdrawal or total involvement but about knowing when to close and when to open.
2. **Protect your inner peace** – Guard yourself from distractions but remain open to meaningful engagement.

3. **Detach with awareness** – Renounce ignorance, not responsibilities; engage without attachment.
4. **Spiritual wisdom is dynamic** – Just as a river carves its path while remaining connected to its source, a seeker must flow with life while staying rooted in truth.
5. **Live consciously** – Observe your actions and choices, ensuring they align with your higher purpose.

Conclusion

Swamiji's words are a beacon of wisdom, urging us to cultivate a life of balance—where solitude nurtures the soul and engagement uplifts the world. The art of spiritual evolution lies not in forsaking one for the other but in knowing **when to bolt and when to open.**

Like a turtle that withdraws its limbs when threatened but moves forward when the path is clear, a seeker must wisely discern when to retreat into inner stillness and when to engage with the world. This delicate balance, mastered with awareness, leads one toward a life of peace, wisdom, and divine realization.

Let us reflect: Are we consciously choosing what to bolt and what to open in our journey toward spiritual evolution?

CHAPTER-57

EGO: FROM EDGE TO ECHO

<u>Introduction</u>

<u>From Illusion to Illumination</u>

Ego—three letters, a million interpretations.

Some call it pride; others see it as identity. For many, it is both the mask we wear and the mirror we look into.

But what happens when ego is no longer the edge of self-importance, but becomes the echo of divine presence?

This piece is not a sermon—it is a soul-sharing. It arises from late-night calls, maternal glances, a brother's wisdom, and moments of silent grace. It is an exploration, not to destroy the ego, but to transform it. Not to battle it, but to tune it.

Let ego move from Edge to Echo—

The echo of divine presence in our human shell.

From Edge to Echo

Let ego move from edge to echo:

- **Edge** is where ego cuts—sharp, reactive, self-centred.
- **Echo** is where ego reflects—soft, divine, harmonious.

"Let ego become the echo of divine presence in our human shell."

Not eliminated—but tuned.

Not denied—but refined.

Like a flute that surrenders itself to the breath of God.

A Mystic's Midnight Question

It was an unusual hour—10:30 PM. Swamy rarely called at that time. Curiosity met reverence as I picked up the phone. His voice, calm and radiant, carried a question that stirred my being:

Emappa, Hari... Namaskaram! How are you doing, ra?
Tell me one thing—this ego, what is it really? Is it friend or foe?
Do we all carry it unknowingly, like the shadow that moves even when we're still?
Is it stitched into our minds by default, like breath, like heartbeat?
Should we hold it? Should we fight it? Or just witness it? I wasn't prepared. But something deeper responded:
I answered, Swamy... if we truly, heartfully grasp that life is a divine drama—not ours to write, but ours to live—and if we remember that God is the ultimate playwright,
then even if ego lingers, it won't erupt.
It might still be there, quietly sitting in a corner, not causing harm, not demanding attention. But the real problem begins when the mind takes over and says—
'I'm the one doing everything. I'm the one creating. I'm the one in charge.'
That's when things go off track. The ego starts believing it's running the show. But if we remember we're just actors in His play, and do our part with sincerity and trust,
even ego learns to stay in its place—calm, silent, and harmless.

That's like a son criticizing his mother,
forgetting he was shaped in her womb, fed by her hand,
and protected by her heart through storms he never even saw.
He may now look sharp—even heroic—in the eyes of the world,
but before God? He is a big ZERO.
Swamy listened in sacred silence—
not to reply, not to correct—
but to receive.
For in that stillness, the truth settles deeper.
No applause, no argument—just awareness.
That the moment I claim credit,
I've already stepped away from Grace."**

Wisdom of Balance: A Brother's Gentle Truth

Later that night, I recalled something my younger brother Ganesh had once said—words that lingered like a gentle echo in my mind:

"Anna, you can't just eliminate the ego. You can't throw out the night and keep only the day. You must learn to live with both."

He offered a vivid and memorable metaphor to bring his point alive:

"Imagine someone in the scorching heat of Anantapur's peak summer, wearing tight black pants, gloves, shoes, and a mask—he'll bake like a potato! Now, picture that same man standing in the bitter winter of Srinagar, dressed in nothing but cotton—he becomes an ice cube! Ego must be seasonally dressed—not suppressed, not exaggerated—but tuned to the climate of the soul."

He then turned to nature for further wisdom:

"The rose blooms and spreads its fragrance, but never begs for applause. The bee builds tirelessly, yet without banners. Even snakes are given shelter by humble termites. Harmony exists all around us.

It's only man who separates himself from it—and that, Anna, is where ego begins to diverge from divinity."

Ganesh paused and added something that stayed with me:

"If you have awareness that you're operating through ego for a higher purpose, it no longer corrupts—it serves. Take a mother, for instance. She may appear to be egoistic when scolding or controlling her children who are mischievous beyond control. But that firmness arises not from self-interest, but from love and responsibility."

He concluded with a powerful example:

"Even Swami Vivekananda was seen by some as egoistic—but only by the impure, who couldn't see the fire of divine will behind his words. His ego was not for himself—it was the roar of a lion awakened by purpose."

My Mother, Karunamayi Amma – The Sculptor of Silent Strength

My mother, Karunamayi Amma, was married before the age of ten. Before any of us were born, she endured the unimaginable loss of five children. We, the remaining four, were all she had. Now, only two of us remain—just my younger brother and me. And yet, through all this, she carried herself with unmatched tolerance. People say the Bhagavad Gita teaches patience, detachment, and strength—but for us, she was a living Gita, a woman with the rarest of rare virtues. We are proud to call her our mother.

Even when she was bedridden, I would make her strong coffee—her favourite. She'd simply say, "Thanks, Appa." That quiet gratitude pierced my heart. How many times had I truly thanked her for my life, my breath, my being?

She never gave speeches. She shaped us by simply being who she was. She called me "Hari Priya." I once asked her why. She replied, "You are both son and daughter to me. I lost many children—you are all in one. 'Hari' is your name. 'Priya' means dear."

To her, love was beyond roles and rituals. She used to say, "Boys must do all kinds of work, just like girls. There is no division in love." She raised us with responsibility, not entitlement. She didn't entertain ego, pride, or division.

She often told us not to be obsessed with rituals. We never had a thread ceremony (upanayanam) due to various factors, but she'd say, "You followed Brahmacharya truthfully. That is enough. Keeping your mind clean and your heart pure is more important than any ritual."

Her wisdom was simple but profound: "Never hurt anyone. Don't hurt yourself either. Everyone will realize the purpose of their life in the course of their journey."

Once, when I asked her about the children she lost, she looked at me and said calmly, "They were precious salagramas from the Gandaki River. You are stones—still being shaped into salagramas. Each has its own journey." There was so much meaning in her words, I didn't fully grasp them then—but I do now.

I used to cry whenever I saw tears in her eyes—though they were rare. She bore her pains silently, smiling through suffering so that we could live joyfully. Her strength wasn't loud, but it was steady. She never needed recognition. Her presence was her offering. And now, in her absence, I see just how much of her lives in us.

She nurtured me not just with food or care, but with attention to my inner growth. She never directly confronted my ego—but slowly, silently, she softened it. When I was angry, she stayed calm. When I was arrogant, she remained kind. She didn't preach humility—she practiced it. Her life became the mirror in which I saw my own excesses. Over time, without realizing it, I began to change. She didn't push me toward transformation—she simply stood there, unwavering, and allowed me to evolve in her light.

<u>My Father – The Unseen Avadootha and the Cosmic Mirror</u>

My father once said,
"Why do you say you're bored? Isn't life a string of repeated acts?
Washing clothes, drying them, ironing, watering plants, plucking
flowers for pooja—
these are not chores, son; they are quiet rituals.
Find creativity in repetition. Find wonder in the routine."
He didn't just say it—he lived it.
With every breath, every act, he wove mindfulness into the ordinary.
During prayer, I'd sometimes hurry him:
"Appa, come quickly, let's eat."
And he would gently scold me—without anger, without ego:
"Don't rush me. I take my time—I travel inward.
This is not a formality. It's my meeting with the Divine."
If I insisted, he would smile and say,
"If you're hungry, go ahead. I'll eat later.
I don't want to swallow food—I want to receive it."
Back then, I didn't understand.
I thought he was slow, old-fashioned—out of sync with the world I
admired.
Now, when I pause and look back,
I am touched by a quiet sorrow.
I had mistaken his depth for delay,
his calm for passivity,
his devotion for habit.
He was an avadootha in disguise—
simple in clothing, sovereign in spirit.
Whether watching cricket, praying in stillness,
tending to plants, cutting vegetables, or speaking with a stranger,
he moved with the same ease, the same poise.
His outer actions may have shifted with the day,
but his inner anchor never moved.
He was the same—gentle, grounded, complete.

And when I look at my own restlessness—
my hunger for speed, achievement, and noise—
I see how far I am from that quiet strength.
He taught me, without teaching:
Stillness is not weakness. It is wisdom resting in silence.
Now I understand:
Parents are not just caretakers of our childhood—
they are cosmic mirrors.
When we see them not through the eyes of expectation,
but through the lens of awareness,
we begin to see ourselves—
our ego, in its subtle and loud forms, becomes visible.
In their presence, our shadows are reflected—
not to shame us,
but to shape us.
Let us learn to bow not only before gods in temples,
but before the divine who served us silently at home.
Let us not wait for absence to begin our reverence.
Let us not wait for loss to start listening.

My Sister – The Silent Teacher of Endurance and Grace

My sister, Sai Niveditha, was more than a sibling.
She was grace in motion, an unseen sage clothed in simplicity.
Highly qualified, she held a doctoral degree—
but wore only humility.
Always draped in traditional attire,
always grounded, always ready to serve—
she played a role on par with our mother,
toiling for her brothers with selfless joy.
Her eyes brimmed with compassion,
her voice was soft,

her spirit, unshakable.
She once had a vision—of Lord Hanuma standing in our garden land.
It wasn't fantasy. It was revelation.
She nurtured the dream of installing His idol there.
That moment revealed her essence—
not just a devotee,
but an avatar of devotion itself.
What she bore in her body was beyond pain—
a slow, invisible crucifixion.
And yet, she never begged for sympathy.
She educated me.
"There are people who suffer more than I do," she'd say.
"Don't raise your voice to silence my pain.
I must live with it. Smile with it. Bear with it."
She taught me that strength is not in suppressing suffering—
but in embracing it without complaint.
Once, when I asked how she kept going, she said:
"If I fall into depression, who will take care of me?
I must manage myself. Or rather—
the God in me will take care of me."
Her faith wasn't poetic.
It was practical. Lived. Embodied.
She never raised her voice.
Never claimed to know better.
Never let ego flare—not even in flickers.
Some teachers hold a stick.
She held her pain.
Some teach by instruction.
She taught by being.
Her presence was a mirror—
not to shame, but to awaken.
In her reflection, I saw my own noise,
my impatience, my invisible ego.

Even now, she doesn't return to me in sorrow.
She returns as a sacred whisper:
to slow down,
to serve more,
to surrender.
She wasn't just my sister.
She was a crystallized soul—
a divine presence who walked beside me,
quietly sculpting my heart.

<u>My Brother, Dr. Naga Yogi Raj – The Silent Slayer of Ego</u>

My brother, Dr. Naga Yogi Raj, was a quiet giant—
A master of medicine, Telugu, and English—
Yet always a learner, never a showman.
To the world, he looked ordinary—
simple clothes, soft-spoken, unassuming.
But within? He was a spiritually awakened soul.
A sage in disguise.
He often said,
"Those who humble themselves will be exalted by God."
At night, he would quietly sit near my bed,
sometimes meditating in silence.
His curly hair would brush against my face—
like a silent blessing from the Divine.
He had a profound way of seeing the world.
I remember him saying:
"When you travel farther—deeper—
you'll realize that what you know
isn't even a drop in the ocean.
God alone is intelligent.
Draw from that inspiration, and move on in life."

His presence didn't need explanations.

It evoked transformation.

If, on some hurried day, he had spoken a harsh word,

he would come back quietly and say,

"I'm sorry, brother.

My words weren't perfect."

That humility wasn't weakness.

It was spiritual strength.

He didn't try to chisel my ego with sharp truths—

He melted it... with love, with silence, with grace.

He didn't preach. He lived.

He didn't shine for the world.

He glowed from within.

To this day, I carry his words,

his glances, his gestures—

like sacred mantras etched into memory.

Insights: From Conflict to Clarity

Not conclusions—just contemplations:

- **Ego is not the enemy**: Like fire, it can either cook or burn.
- **Ego is not to be erased**, but embraced with awareness. Tamed ego becomes divine echo.
- **Humility is the highest intelligence.** True masters never shout—their presence teaches.
- **Love transcends identity.** Whether maternal, fraternal, or divine—love silences the self.
- **Ego tuned becomes ego stilled**—like a wave realizing it is part of the ocean.

<u>Ego at the Edge – The Fault Line of Separation</u>

At its edge, ego divides:

It isolates us from others, truth, and grace.

It speaks in absolutes: "I did this," "I deserve that," "I am better."

It mistakes identity for essence: "I am the body, the title, the achievement."

But stripped of all that—what are you?

Edge-ego is brittle. Like a glass sword—it dazzles, then breaks.

🦋 <u>Ego as Echo – The Sacred Sound of Surrender</u>

Now, imagine ego transformed into an echo.

What is an echo?

- A sound that returns to its source.
- It doesn't initiate—it responds.
- It doesn't claim—it reflects.

Ego as echo means we no longer shout from separateness, but sing from Source.

We become the flute, not the player.
We stop asking, "What will I gain?"
Instead, we wonder, "What will God express through me?"

From Edge to Echo: The Transformation Process

EDGE	ECHO
Claims ownership	Returns authorship to God
Self-centered	Soul-centered
Seeks recognition	Seeks realization
Competes and compares	Collaborates and contributes
Reacts loudly	Responds softly
Is conditional	Is compassionate
Fears surrender	Finds freedom in surrender

When I spoke from ego—I shouted.

When I softened into echo—I listened.

Now my words are not mine.

They rise from silence—and return to it.

Conclusion: Echo of the Divine

The final truth?

When ego erupts—we stand at the edge.
When it echoes—we stand at the centre.
Before the Divine, we are not empty—we are ready.
From ZERO, we become vessels of the WHOLE.

Let ego be not the wall, but the window—
Where the Divine shines through our actions, humility, and grace.

Let us not destroy ego—let us transmute it.
Let ego move from edge to echo.

Not the echo of self-glory—but the echo of divine presence in our human shell.

That echo does not shout—it sings.

It doesn't dominate—it dissolves.

It doesn't say, "I am everything."

It whispers:

"I am nothing... yet held by Everything."

Let this be our journey—

From ego to echo.

From noise to knowing.

From illusion to illumination.

CHAPTER-58

BEYOND THE MIRROR: THE JOURNEY FROM KNOWING TO BEING THE COSMIC MIRROR: REFLECTIONS OF THE DIVINE

Throughout history, there have been souls who transcend worldly identities, not by renouncing life, but by illuminating its deeper truths. His Holiness Sri Vidyanarayana Theertha is one such enlightened master—one who journeyed from a distinguished physician to a spiritual luminary, uniting science, wisdom, and divine realization. He does not seek to escape the world, nor to reject it, but to reveal the sacred harmony between knowledge and self-awareness.

In the vast expanse of existence, humanity has sought the essence of the divine, looking beyond the transient world to understand the eternal truth. Whether we call upon Ishwara, Allah, Jehovah, Waheguru, the Supreme Consciousness, or the Universal Spirit, all faiths ultimately lead seekers toward enlightenment and realization. The divine does not confine itself to a single tradition, temple, church, or mosque; rather, it pervades the universe, residing within and beyond the known dimensions of existence.

Great spiritual masters have walked the earth, reflecting the infinite wisdom of the cosmos. Sri Ramakrishna Paramahamsa, the embodiment of divine experience, embraced all paths, teaching that every religion is a river flowing toward the same ocean of truth. He emphasized that direct experience of the Divine is the highest truth, beyond intellectual speculation or dogma. The revered Kanchi Paramacharya, a guiding Wbeacon of Sanatana Dharma, reminded us that humility, self-discipline, and devotion lead to the realization of the Supreme.

Adi Shankaracharya expounded Advaita, declaring the oneness of existence, where the self and the Absolute are but reflections of the same undivided reality. Sri Ramanujacharya, with his philosophy of Vishishtadvaita, emphasized devotion and personal connection with the Divine, guiding seekers to experience the divine presence in the world. Sri Madhvacharya, the proponent of Dvaita, revealed the eternal distinction between the soul and the Supreme, advocating unwavering devotion and surrender. Similarly, Sri Raghavendra Swamy embodied divine grace, teaching that faith, surrender, and righteous action open the doors to spiritual wisdom. Across traditions, these enlightened beings have illuminated the path for seekers, urging them to transcend material limitations and recognize the inner light.

The Physician's Awakening In this journey of self-discovery, the human body is an intricate temple, a vessel through which we can explore the mysteries of existence. Science dissects the body into cells, organs, and systems, but true wisdom asks: Who are we beyond this form? If we do not understand the essence of our being, how can we claim to know the world? His Holiness Sri Vidyanarayana Theertha posed this very question: "In one cell, how many parts? Brain, nervous system, kidney, lungs, pancreas, blood, heart. We do not understand who we are."

As a doctor, he understood the pulse of life running through each cell, the silent intelligence governing the heart, lungs, and nervous system. Yet, amidst the precision of medical science, he witnessed suffering—not just of the body, but of the soul. Medicine could mend wounds, but could it heal the sorrow of separation, the pain of longing, or the unrest of the spirit? His quest was not one of doubt but of deeper understanding. It was in this contemplation that his purpose expanded beyond the stethoscope, beyond the clinic, and beyond the limits of human reasoning.

Swamy's Message to Doctors Swamy reminds doctors that their role is not merely to treat diseases but to guide patients towards holistic well-being. He emphasizes that healing extends beyond the physical body and into the realms of the mind and spirit. "Doctors should patiently speak to every patient, understanding their pain beyond symptoms. True healing begins when a patient is comforted, heard, and guided toward inner peace."

A Dialogue with Swamy Seeker: Swamy, in the modern world, people are lost in endless distractions. How can one truly embark on the spiritual path? Swamy: "Silence your mind and listen. The world outside will always be noisy, but the truth speaks in stillness. Do not seek outside for what is within you. Hold onto Amma; seek Amma. She sees, she knows, she accepts."

Seeker: Many say that spirituality and material success cannot coexist. Is renunciation necessary? Swamy: "Renunciation is not of the world, but of ignorance. You may be a doctor, an engineer, a laborer—it does not matter. If you perform your duty with truth, love, and righteousness, you are already on the path."

Seeker: But Swamy, what of suffering? Why does the world experience such turmoil? Swamy: "The world is your mirror. What you see in it is the reflection of your own mind. If you sow violence, greed, and ego, the world will appear full of suffering. But if you cultivate peace, compassion, and wisdom, the same world will become divine."

Seeker: How does the cosmic mirror reveal the truth to us? Swamy: "The cosmic mirror does not distort; it only reflects what is. If you approach it with fear, it will show fear. If you approach it with devotion, it will show divinity. Understand yourself, and the mirror will reveal your true nature."

Swamy's Message in the Context of Global Unrest The world stands at a crossroads, divided by conflicts, greed, and illusions of power. His Holiness Sri Vidyanarayana Theertha calls upon humanity to awaken:

"The wars you see outside are the wars within you. The divisions among people are the divisions within the self. If the mind is fragmented by fear and ego, how can peace exist in the world? Do not look to governments, armies, or leaders to create peace. Look within. Wait, watch, and win."

The modern seeker faces dilemmas—caught between ambition and inner peace, between technology and tradition, between material pursuits and spiritual calling. Swamy urges: "Do not reject one for the other. Hold the balance. Use intelligence to analyze yourself; that is wisdom. Walk the path with awareness, and the cosmic mirror will reveal who you truly are."

Conclusion: The Final Reflection As we stand before the cosmic mirror, let us see not just our reflection but the reflection of the entire universe within us. His Holiness Sri Vidyanarayana Theertha stands as a cosmic mirror, reflecting to each seeker not what they want to see, but what they need to see. The world conditions us to look outward—to seek validation, to measure success by status, to define truth by external authority. But he challenges this illusion, urging us to turn the gaze inward.

"Open Swamy, daring Swamy, Andhra Tiger Swamy antaaru," he proclaims, not as a title of pride but as an invitation to courageously dismantle falsehoods and stand unwavering in truth.

The true seeker does not look outside for salvation. The true seeker waits, watches, and wins—not against others, but against the illusions of the self. And in that stillness, in that silent knowing, one beholds the

Cosmic Mirror and recognizes the divine not as separate, but as one's very own essence.

This is the path. This is the realization. This is the message for all who seek beyond the seen.

Wait. Watch. Win. – The Final Realization

These three words—Wait, Watch, Win—carry profound spiritual significance, forming the essence of Swamy Sri Vidyanarayana Theertha's message to seekers. This is not a call for passive waiting or blind watching, but a directive for deep inner contemplation, self-discipline, and ultimate realization.

1. Wait – The Power of Patience

In an era driven by instant gratification, we have forgotten the power of waiting. But true spiritual awakening requires patience—patience to understand, to grow, and to let the deeper truths unfold naturally. Swamy reminds us that waiting is not about inaction; it is about preparing the self, cultivating wisdom, and allowing divine grace to work through time. Just as a seed does not become a tree overnight, self-realization is a gradual process that demands unwavering faith.

Waiting means resisting impulsive reactions, stepping back from distractions, and allowing the cosmic rhythm to reveal itself. It is in waiting that we begin to recognize the subtle movements of the divine within us.

2. Watch – The Art of Awareness

Once we cultivate patience, we must develop awareness. To watch is to observe life without judgment, to see beyond the illusions of the material world. Swamy's message here aligns with the teachings of great sages: the world is a reflection of our own mind. If we do not observe ourselves clearly, we remain trapped in ignorance.

Watching means:

- Observing the mind—its restlessness, desires, and attachments.
- Recognizing patterns—how we respond to situations, how our emotions fluctuate, and what truly governs our actions.
- Being vigilant—understanding that every thought, word, and deed shapes our reality.

Swamy emphasizes that spiritual realization is not about rejecting the world, but about perceiving it correctly. When we watch with clarity, we realize that suffering, conflict, and division arise from within. With this awareness, transformation becomes possible.

3. Win – The Triumph Over Illusion

Winning, in Swamy's teaching, is not about conquering others, acquiring wealth, or achieving status. True victory is the triumph over falsehood, fear, and ignorance. It is realizing the self beyond the self, transcending ego, and awakening to the divine essence within.

To win is to:

- Overcome doubts and distractions that hinder spiritual progress.
- Attain inner peace despite external chaos.
- Realize that divinity is not separate, but one's very own essence.

The victory Swamy speaks of is not external but internal—the moment when a seeker truly sees through the cosmic mirror and understands that God is not somewhere else, but within.

The Cosmic Mirror and the Ultimate Realization

Swamy Sri Vidyanarayana Theertha does not ask seekers to blindly believe in doctrines. Instead, he invites them to look into the cosmic mirror—to reflect deeply, to recognize their true self, and to see beyond illusions.

In the end, the journey of the seeker is encapsulated in these three words:

- Wait for wisdom to unfold.
- Watch with awareness and clarity.
- Win by realizing your divine nature.

This is not a process that happens overnight, nor is it a destination that can be reached through mere rituals. It is a state of being—a way of living with truth, love, and righteousness.